Darling fron
I met ya i   nal
felt a soul comection.
I feel so blessed
to know a beautiful

THIRTEEN AND UNDERWATER

Soul such as yourself.
Jo much Love

One mum's heart-warming journey

MICHELLE WEITERING

National Library of Australia catalogue-in-publication data:

1. Non-fiction: Memoir. 2. Non-fiction: Health & wellbeing. 3 Non-fiction: Anxiety.

Design by Karen Mc Dermott

Printed in Australia

Karen Mc Dermott Publishing, Perth, WA.

Thirteen and Underwater/ Michelle Weitering.

ISBN: 978-0-6485123-4-9 (sc)

ISBN: 978-0-6485123-1-8 (e)

DEDICATION

Dedicated with much love and a forever grateful heart to the most amazing woman I was blessed enough in this life to call Mine.

Lynette Martin

8.2.1952 – 26.12.2016

-Mum, it was you who taught me the love of reading, of escaping our reality with a gripping book. The absolute delight I felt as a child, slipping into the world of the 'Folk of the Faraway Tree' and the many magical tales created by Enid Blyton. That's where it all began, and my love of books was the gift that you gave me Mum.

To feel the joy of laughing along with the characters those witty writers had placed upon their pages, to crying our hearts out to Jodi Picoult, Anna Barrie, La Vyrie Spencer, and oh so many talented authors that could make you feel their characters pain!

To being thoroughly terrified with a classic Stephen King, Sandra Brown, Nora Roberts and Tami Hoag, to being totally enthralled in a delightful Vampire world created by Anne Rice and Stephanie Meyer.

You were Jesse's biggest fan Mum, and you loved the idea of 'Thirteen and Underwater'. It was so much fun ringing you as I wrote it, to read out the funny bits, and we'd laugh together. And when I read out some of the harder parts of our journey, you would say, with tears mingling with your words, "That's enough for today Mickey!"

You always just got it Mum, even when you felt helpless in not knowing how to help me, or Jesse, you just got it......and you are so much a part of these pages Mum.

So, here's to you, Lynette Martin- Lover of good books: Epic tales of tragedy, Sappy love stories, Suspenseful 'who-dunnit's', Thought provoking thrillers, Mystery, Murder and Mythology, and even the Bible for Christs Sakes! 😵

Forever in our Hearts. Always by my side.

ACKNOWLEDGEMENTS

I find writing as gratifying as I do reading a riveting novel you can't put down at night, even though you're exhausted and you feel your eyes slipping out of your head as the words seem to slide off the pages as you blink rapidly to force them back into focus, and you can already hear yourself cursing as the alarm goes off in the morning and everything you'll look at will be coated in a red haze of tiredness!

But, it's worth it; being taken away to fascinating, fictional worlds full of intricate relationships where siblings and friends support each other when darkness falls, where lovers embrace and connect, forming an unbeatable force. Where parents bleed from every crevice when they find their child in unknown torment and family and communities come together to fight the good cause.

Writing Thirteen and Underwater may very well be non-fiction, but like the above characters, I have been so blessed to be surrounded by awesome souls, that have made the sad and heartbreaking events bearable, the funny moments, funnier. I am so grateful to so many that have helped me stay on track in the harder moments of completing this book, and believing in it, and myself again in the months after mums passing.

Jade, without your love, patience, support and friendship the past 25 years, I certainly wouldn't be the person I am today. Thank you for always believing in me and my, at times, boundless enthusiasm for all things great and small!

To my special girl who has seen as many highs as she has lows in this life: You are my everything. My other half. Without you I wouldn't make sense and I know we don't make sense to a lot of people! Lol! Leah Martin, I hope this is one of my books you can enjoy!

Sister of my heart: Louise Josephine Manna, your support, encouragement and belief in me is such a glorious gift! Please don't give up teaching me how to speak Italian! Here's to another 26 years of smashing it!

To the Taylor Clan: Thank you for being the most marvellous of friends to our family. Emily and Caitlyn, thank you for always having Jesse and Zane's backs! And of course, to you Sally, for being my own cheerleader with not only Thirteen, but all that I endeavour in this colourful world! Thank you also for being my own private perm culturalist!

A very big heartfelt thanks to my gorgeous Publisher, the talented Karen Mc Dermott, and the team at MMH Press. It was pure magic finally connecting with you. Having you by my side with your guidance, passion and belief in me, and equal enthusiasm for Thirteen, has meant everything on this journey! The way the cover evolved still gives me goose bumps when I think about it! I won't be able to thank you enough! But thank you anyway!

To all the organisations that help so many of us at times where we doubt ourselves and struggle with the unknown, and sometimes just need to hear that we are doing okay: Thank you. And for all those individuals that work tirelessly for those of us in desperate need, despite being exhausted yourselves: Thank you.

For anyone that needs help in Australia, please type in Mental Health Australia – 20 organisations with phone numbers, along with a web address, will be there for you.

At the beginning of Jesse's journey with anxiety, we felt so vulnerable and alone. It was those dedicated individuals that took their roles to the next level, that made an impact on Jesse, and Jade and I as parents. I'd like to thank, Steve Reid, Carol Mc Nair, Kelly Cooper and Stephen Brackenridge. You all shed light on the days that were dark. Thank you.

I'd also like to thank all those members of the online F.B group, Children with Anxiety/Anxiety Disorders. Sharing your stories and supporting ours meant the absolute world. Thank you all.

I dearly must thank my gorgeous girls from the Peninsula Writers' Club! Susan Wakefield and Coreena Le Gallienne! You have given me a safe harbour of sisterhood and I feel so very blessed to have you creative geniuses in my life! I'm looking forward to what's to come!

Last, but certainly not least, my two treasured souls. My beautiful boys, Jesse and Zane: My life. My Loves, thank you for loving me the way you do! And believe me when I say, as Bryan Adams once did, (Everything I Do) I Do It For You!

CONTENTS

PRAISE FOR
Thirteen and Underwater

"*Thirteen and Underwater* is the incredible story of one boy's harrowing journey through the paralysing forces of anxiety and mental illness that wreaks havoc on a suburban family. Lovingly told through the eyes of his mother, Weitering takes us into her family, exposing the good, the bad and the ugly of this increasingly prevalent disease and shines an all-important light on mental illness in all its debilitating forms. Deftly written, Weitering whispers to the emotional soul of motherhood and the unbreakable bond between mother and child, the fragility of the self and the resilience of the human spirit that lies deep within us all to never, ever give up - no matter what life throws at you."

Susan Wakefield ~ The New York Times

Memoirs are incredibly personal accounts, probing into the deepest corners of real life. Michelle Weitering writes her heartbreaking family story with blunt honesty, sharing the impact of her son Jesse's struggle with anxiety, stemming largely from being bullied in his earliest childhood years. This is a moving and honest account of the devastating effects of declining mental health on a family's day to day life, yet it also demonstrates the power of love and its ability to glue together a family in the face of adversity. The ability of Jesse, standing tall despite what life has thrown at him, shows a strength far greater than any bully who tried to verbally and physically push him around. He is a hero in every sense of the word, as is his brother and parents who stood by his side during this emotional rollercoaster. Reading Thirteen and Underwater is a reminder of what humanity is all about.

Kelly Van Nelson
Author of Graffiti Lane

"In writing 'Thirteen and Underwater' Weitering brings to light many of the previously taboo social issues, that in the past have often remained silently hidden behind closed doors.

She has crafted a heartfelt 'warts and all' narrative, that openly and honestly describes her own family's journey throughout the emotional turmoil and impact of childhood bullying and the resulting mental health issues that often follow.

'Thirteen and Underwater' speaks to the reader of the power of resilience and the unquestioning love of a Mother for her son.

Danielle Aitken
Author of 'Sarah's Story: Life after IVF'

Having anxiety is like being tired and
scared at the same time
It's the fear of failure but no urge to be productive
It's wanting friends but hating socialising
It's wanting to be alone but
not wanting to be lonely
It's caring about everything but
caring about nothing
It's feeling everything at once then
feeling paralyzingly numb
- Beyond Blue

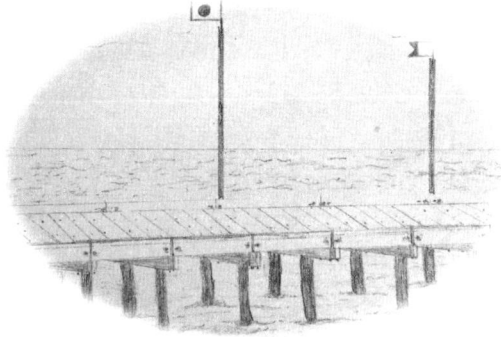

SIX WEEKS INTO DESPAIR

He opens his eyes slowly and frowns at the ceiling, slowly releasing his breath as a wave of ever-present sadness washes over him. *'Here we go again, another day,'* he thinks to himself as he squeezes his eyes shut. He feels his palms tingle and brings his hands up to look at them before rubbing them together. A feeling of dread begins to spread in his stomach. He knows she'll come in soon – it's almost time to get up for school. The thought of school sets a sense of panic within him, and he finds it difficult to catch his breath, as the seemingly constant throbbing in his head gets stronger. He covers his face with his hands, trying not to panic as pain spreads throughout his body. He curls into a tight ball, confused as to why he feels so overwhelmed. He tries to control his tears. *'Every morning. Every day. Why, why is this happening? I don't understand. No-one does. No-one cares. I feel so alone. She's going to yell again when I say I have a headache. She won't believe me. She never does! I can't handle this for one more second! I just can't! It would be better if I were dead!'* He squeezes his eyes shut as he rolls over and screams silently into his pillow - feeling like his racing heart is going to explode from his chest as he hears her footsteps approach his room.

2014 Jesse Weitering 13 years of age.

Anxiety: *noun apprehension, concern, dismay, disquiet, dread, foreboding, fear, misgiving, nervousness, stress, tension trepidation, uneasiness, worry*

The Australian Integrated File, the Future of Australian English Oxford Dictionary and Thesaurus

Sounds simple enough, doesn't it? When you divide it into separate little words and remove all feelings. How hard can it really be? To understand and overcome such a little word?

For all of us living with someone who suffers so cruelly at the clutching hands of anxiety, especially a beloved child, it is never simple. The blame game becomes more exhausting as each stage of the mission to conquer the mystery of *'what is happening?'* depletes us as individuals and as a family unit. Watching their world, and then yours being turned upside-down on a wicked roller-coaster of— *'What's going on? I don't understand! What's happening now? How can we fix this? Why? Why? Why? What have I missed? What have I done wrong?* can be such a debilitating, lonely, heart-breaking phase for all. Following this is the overwhelming, often crippling guilt of not seeing and understanding the situation for what it is, earlier on.

This is our story, like so many others out there. Families on the never-ending quest to help their loved ones to a place of, *'we can survive this.'* This is for all of you— all of us. So please, pour a cup of tea, coffee or icy beverage, snuggle on a couch with a toasty warm blanket or sit in a garden full of scented blooms and join me and know you are not alone, and we can all survive this, seemingly endless voyage, together.

Warmly,
Mickey.

BEFORE THE BEGINNING

15th September 1999

Hello Darling Being!

At this stage, you are not even conceived yet, but I've kept journals since I was a teenager, and as boringly uneventful as most of them are, I thought if I didn't write about this stage in my life, I wouldn't be keeping things real. The thought of creating and having you, is one of the most exciting things I could possibly imagine! So, I most definitely need to start a journal about your life.

I am 27 years old as I write this. (Your mummy!) I think family members' opinions matter the most when describing a fellow relative. Brutally honest. I get a lot of, *'Oh Mickey, you're a dag, don't ever change!'* Considering this is something that hangs off the arse-end of a sheep, I'm not sure if it's such a good thing. But it's how my family sees me, so I'll take it and wear it with pride. (Thanks mother and Aunts!)

If I had to describe myself, I'd say: A hard working go getter, who will make every opportunity arise to celebrate life. Unfortunately, at times I wear my heart on my sleeve and can't speak properly to save myself and could write my own dictionary! For example, I said to my good friend the other day, I often feel, 'in*subconsequential'*. Yep, that's what I'm dealing with! I am not alone in the world, with this often-embarrassing speech pattern. The correct terminology is 'idiolect', which is a person's specific, individual way of speaking. Like your fingerprint, your idiolect is unique. Dad calls them Mickey-isms that make up part of my '*quirky*' personality. I'd rather be known for something amazingly clever or remarkable, but I have years ahead where I can surely improve! Please let it be so.

I believe we all should have a theme song to survive and enjoy every occasion. The good and the bad. Reflecting on my difficult childhood I'll say thanks to Kelly Clarkson for her wonderful song - *'What Doesn't Kill You Makes You Stronger!'* I rebelled against the wrong-doings done to me and turned my own world in the direction I believed it deserved to go. But I won't go on.

Who hasn't had a difficult childhood right? You certainly will not!

My mum, who I call Mummy-Bear, is also one of my very best friends. You will call her Nana Lyn, and will love visiting her, as she still lives in my hometown where I grew up, Glenormiston South. Beautiful countryside full of horses and hay stacks! Nana is an amazing woman and still works full-time at the May Noonan Hostel as Head Cook and Food Safety Supervisor. Nearly thirty years full-time. They don't make them like Nana anymore.

I was blessed enough in this life to be given a twin sister, Leah. She will simply be 'Aunty' to you. A complex and colourful creature. She certainly makes life interesting and at times, ball-breaking. She is adventurous, courageous and can be slightly unstable in an adorable, pulling-your-hair-out, wanting-to-punch-yourself-in-the-face-at-times kind of way; and it has only been the rare occasion where I have wanted to high five her in the face, with a plank! She wants people to believe she doesn't give a toss what they think about her or her opinion; what she does, decisions she makes or things she says. But deep down, she does care what people think. We all do. We are human. At the end of the day, she is my best friend and has a generous, big, soft heart, wrapped up in a go fuck yourself attitude. Life contributes to shaping us all.

We are very close and are as different as the sun and the moon.

Her son is one-and-a-half-year-old Thomas. He is my little Tommy Tucker and an adorable little boy.

My cousins are like my sisters and will be like aunts to you. Nadine, Kylie, and Rachael. A small, close family we have always had great times together making Christmas and Easter celebrations, along with birthday and family re-unions so much more, due to our closeness and commitment to make every catch up more epic than the time before, creating memories of mischief and adventure. Cousins can certainly become your best friends in life, as you head into adulthood.

Once I finished Year Twelve at Terang College, *(which I failed, due to reading Nana's Mills and Boon's books, instead of studying for the three hours every night, when I was closed in my step fathers bedroom,)* I left home and moved from Melbourne to Bendigo and back to Melbourne, where I worked many jobs and finished a Nanny course through Krisala Nanny School in Prahran. I was sensational with kids and their families. Educated, patient, creative, dedicated and loyal. All the signs that led me to believe I would be the most sensational, epic, energised, mother ever! Seriously, how hard can it be?

How did I meet your Dad? Well apart from a brief high school sweetheart, I did not have a serious boyfriend. Through Aunty Leah's boyfriend at the time, a martial arts instructor, I was blessed enough to not only meet an Italian girl who became more like a sister to me than a friend, Louise, I met your Dad. I was training as a martial arts student, and met another brilliant instructor, Wing Chun, martial artist, and oh-so-talented Cameron Douglas. He was a lively, enigmatic man. Women fell over themselves to get near him. *(I confess, I adored him too!)*

Please! And then he introduced me to one of his students. DAD! Thank you! He was appealing in so many ways. Intelligent, handsome, witty with a good heart and in the end, he fell for me too! I won't question my good luck and ask why. I mean, honestly, this guy was a spunk. The physique of a gymnast, the stealth of a martial artist; that cool, confident, laid-back streak of a surfer. Dad is certainly one of the good guys and I love him to bits.

Thanks to Grammy, Dad and his older brother Grant, had a very sport-orientated childhood. Dad was Australia's Under 13 Judo champion back in the day, was an excellent gymnast, and taught gymnastics to the younger classes. He studied Human Physiology when he finished high school, and surfed in-between finding himself, which he did at Melbourne's stunt agency, New Generation Stunts. Here he met a dear friend to this day, Stuart, and they worked alongside the best in the industry.

Poppy, Grammy's second husband, is a rock star and both Dad and I adore him like a father. It takes a special man to love another's family like they are his own. Both he and Grammy will be amazing grandparents. I know this for sure as they are patient, thoughtful, creative, and so very young in their outlook in life.

Uncle Grant is an awesome bloke and as he and Dad are only two years apart; very good friends also. Ex-army, and a free spirit, who is overseas and travelling the world as I write this, he will be such a positive influence in your life. To love you and guide you. Support and believe in you.

They are *your 'Family of the blood'*, then, there are all the other people we are blessed to have in our lives that will love you and be here for you. Our *'Family of the Heart'*. Aunty Louise, Uncle Cameron, and Uncle Stuart. I think I have the major players covered.

2nd September 2000
Hello Baby,

Well, it's an eventful weekend. Dad and I are up in Heathcote at Grammy and Poppy's. It's the 2000 AFL Grand Final. Essendon versus Melbourne. I have barracked for Essendon since I was eight (loyal to Nana Lyn's team), although I wouldn't really call it barracking, just a team to follow. Dad barracks for Carlton. And yes, I would severely call it barracking! I always think back to my primary school days, to a young boy named Leon Cameron when I think of Carlton. He was an athletic, passionate young boy who loved Carlton from an early age and dreamed of playing for them. *(At least that's how I recall it from a young girl under eleven)* He gave me some good pointers on how to get over the high jump bar. (*They were good pointers, but nevertheless, I ran into the bar and went under it more times than over. You will definitely have Dad's athletic traits! Please, not mine!*) Anyway, Dad has convinced himself no matter what, you will be Carlton all the way too! Uncle Grant is coming home from England in two months' time and Dad and I will be getting married at Brighton Beach in three months which leaves us two months to buy our first home! So much to do, and with the blessings from the angels, we will find out if we are pregnant with you!

24th September 2000

Dearest Baby!

Today, sunny Sunday morning, we did a pregnancy test and found out we were pregnant with you! I could not stop crying and jumping up and down like a loon! Dad was also over the moon with awe and happiness, just with more finesse. This is such a wonderful day. To think in ten months' time Dad and I can hold you in our arms. You are actually inside of me, growing into a perfect little human. I Cannot fathom it, or wait! We bought our house off Uncle Cameron. It's in Frankston, off Whistlestop Reserve; a beautiful area to raise a family —and not far from Langwarrin where Dad grew up. You can even see the Frankston beach from the top of Skye Road. So, two months of the year left. 22 days to move into our new home, get married, celebrate Christmas, and prepare for the most wonderful year of all. The year you'll arrive in my arms!

Love, Mummy. Xxx

The Unexpected Part of Expecting.

Hello Darling Heart!

Dad and I found out what sex you are today! I can't write it down as others who write in your journal will see! And almost everybody wants it to be a surprise! But Dad and I are extremely excited. Well, we would have been either way, but now we can really concentrate on names and imagine what you'll be like! We have set up your bedroom in our new home. It is sensational. Dad, being a painter now, has selected bright colours with feature walls throughout, to create a feeling of space and warmth. It's a lovely, modest three-bedroom house, with open plan lounge, kitchen and dining. Big open windows to let the sun and light in, and a large yard with lots of space to create colourful gardens for all to relax in after a day's work. That's my therapy for sure, plunging my hands into the soil and connecting with mother-nature. Although I absolutely loathe weeding!

Now that I've finished work, I've had lots of time to plan so many things for your arrival. My pregnancy has been pretty awesome. I am healthy, strong, and have not had one ounce of morning sickness. I am in such a great headspace. Dad has been reading every book he can get his hands on regarding fatherhood. He wants to be the best dad possible. I know he doesn't really need these books; in his heart, he already knows what he needs to do.

So, between visits to Aunty and Thomas in Essendon, spending time with Aunty Louise in Bentleigh, a trip down to Warrnambool with Nana Lyn, who bought you a gorgeous Winnie the Pooh pram, and having Grammy and Poppy visit and gift us with the sweetest cot for you, all is flowing as it should be. Uncle Grant came for a visit for the wedding and has headed back overseas once more. He will not be here for your birth, nor will Aunty Nadine who will be in Scotland.

Off I go, to get organised and prepared, my Darling Heart to be the best mum to you I possibly can. How hard can it be?

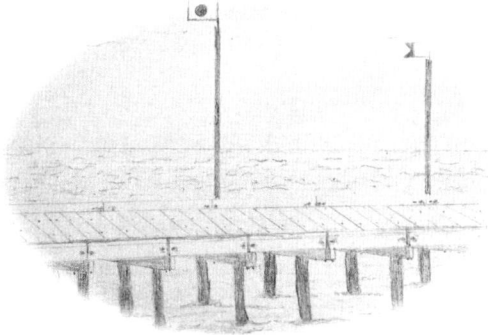

AND SO, IT BEGINS: JOY

The day I held you, my first-born, in my arms, was beyond anything I could have ever imagined. Pure magic! A breathtaking moment in any happily expectant mother's eyes to be sure.

You, my child. My son. It was love at first sight. An overpowering feeling of protectiveness surged through me as your little lips pulled the warm milk from my breast into your mouth. How did you get to be so clever and just know what to do? I did the laugh/cry thing as joy spread throughout my entire body. It was unlike any joy I had experienced in my twenty-odd years. I looked up into the eyes of my love, your Dad and saw equal happiness reflected at me.

It was one of those moments in life that you'll never forget. Unless of course dementia kicks in. You were loved, and you were wanted. You were celebrated like your Aunty Louise said no child had ever been celebrated. (Which of course wasn't true as her children, Rylan and

Taylah were just as loved and adored when they entered this crazy, beautiful world of ours). But I loved that she said it all the same.

Journal entry No. 1 Dad 28th May 2001

Hello, my beautiful baby boy. Welcome to your new world! You are the most special little person in our lives. Your mum is THE MOST amazing mother already and can't get enough of you. You are being breast-fed now and you take very well to the breast. (*As I knew you would, ha ha!*) Mummy is going to dictate to me now as she is a little busy…

Dear Jesse Liam Weitering. You are a gift from the angels above! In the 36 hours, you have been in our lives the sun has shone brighter than ever before. After a natural, 24-hour labour, you arrived at 12.44 am on the 27th May 2001. From Rosebud Hospital, to Frankston via ambulance and back to Rosebud, we are settled in a beautiful room full of flowers and the happy ambience of visitors gone. So, here you are. Finally, in my arms. This is it. Motherhood! I am in love like no-one would believe unless they are in the same position. I feel like Super girl and Thor combined. Exhausted and sore sure, but a super hero all the same. It's true what they say. It really is love at first sight. I am so happy your journey of life has begun. What fun we are going to have! Xx

YEAR ONE

Those first few weeks flowed quickly into months. I could not get enough of you. I absorbed every breath you took, every move you made. Sting was correct, and so was Queen, it was a kind of magic. I had never done drugs of any kind in my life, but I equated the fierce love I felt for you, on top of the lack of essential sleep to be on equal par. It was like you had been with us forever. You belonged.

I remember your first dream. You were snuggled on a pillow across my lap after falling asleep being breast-fed. I was sitting on the window-seat, overlooking the garden, in a semi-coma/day-dream of my own as you had been feeding off and on again throughout the night. (They don't explain the real exhaustion of sleep-deprivation in the parenting books!) You started making little squeaky sounds, screwing up your eyes and mouth, your little fists grabbing the front of your one-piece jump suit. I stroked your baby hair, so soft and whispered words of endearment to settle you. Like most mothers, I'm sure, the complete surge of love I felt for you whether you were sleeping, eating, smiling, or soiling in your nappy, constantly overwhelmed me. I wanted to protect you and make you happy forever. To see you smile and grow into a confident little person with the world at your feet. It broke me more than I like to admit in the end, when the darkness came, that I couldn't. Because for me, every day that you drew breath, the sun shone brighter than ever before.

*****

Okay, milestones. As far as I could see your first year of life was a success. All your health nurse visits were up to date and you were doing everything you were supposed to be doing, according to the East Karingal Maternal and Child Health Centre.

The only time you screamed and cried was in the car. It was my absolute nightmare. You made such a fuss in the end, that I hated the thought of driving anywhere. It was as simple as you not being able to see me. (I mean seriously, I was gorgeous! Let me dream!) You could not handle it. I know I performed *'Incy-Wincy Spider'* at a professional level over, and over again, and any other nursery rhyme I could think of. I would sing at the top of my lungs till I was hoarse on trips to Essendon or Bentleigh. Often when you were breast-feeding, you would pull my long hair through your fingers, so Dad brought you a hair-scrunchy that you could hold in the car hoping that would help you. It did not. You would push it into your face and scream blue murder. As soon as I was able, I would pull the car over and reach into the back seat, kiss, and stroke your tears away and reassure you all would be well until you calmed. I'm sure I am not the only mother that made road trips lengthen due to my desire to make my baby happy. I'll admit, some days if I had not had enough sleep the night before, I'd cry myself. How relieved I felt when we made it to our destination and I could pull your warm, sweaty little body out of the car seat and hold you against me.

Your little arms would wind around my neck and your ragged little sobs would calm and turn to hiccups. We were both happy in that moment. It was beyond a blessing when you got old enough that we could turn your car seat to face the front and I would put the mirror in a position where you could see me singing or talking to you.

*****

Your very first three steps towards me were in fact three days before your first birthday. Dad and I were clapping and cheering! (Show me a parent who wouldn't!) The day you turned one you were walking and could walk especially fast behind your little push trolley full of blocks. Your first birthday cake was shaped into the number one, (strange isn't it!) and covered in smarties. Grammy always made perfect cakes for you, although Aunty always commented to me that they were too dry!

You were a splendid one year old. Dad described you as a loving, sweet, and clever little person. You were so affectionate and emotional for such a tiny being. It amazed me daily how expressive you could be. You and Dad were the best of mates. You had a very loving relation-ship, the kind of relationship all mothers desire their sons to have with their fathers. That's something that made my heart smile every day. The look on your little face when Dad came home from work and we would tell him about all the activities we had gotten up to. Shopping, playing in the garden, singing songs in between housework and a million other tedious things that only other stay-at-home mums, dads and carers can fully comprehend, how exhausting it can all be, day in day out. (Yes, of course rewarding, but bloody exhausting too!) You ate like a champion: fruits, vegetables, pastas, breads, yoghurts, cheese, and baked beans. Aunty Louise introduced you to the lamb chop. Yes, your diet was sen-sational.

Dad often said to me that the more time he spent with you, watching you, he learned something about himself. I thought that was such a beautiful thing for him to say. The love I felt for him magnified more so when he was such a loving, giving father to you. He was my Henry Cavil when fatherhood shone so lovingly from him to you.

We had relaxing weekends away up in Heathcote and enjoyed our time together. You would feed the chooks with Grammy, collecting eggs, and watching the wildlife and birds around the property. You enjoyed helping Poppy bring in the firewood with your little wheelbarrow and you loved going off on adventures with Dad, looking for old sheep skeletons and throwing rocks in the dam where the turtles and ducks swam. It was such a peaceful place to be and being there put a smile on your face.

Nana Lyn came to visit on your birthday every year and we would visit her and see her at our family's annual Christmas party up in Inglewood. Aunty Rachael and Uncle Darren had their baby girl, Kiralee, three months before you arrived, so you had a little playmate, plus Thomas at family gatherings where you socialised like a champ. So, between all your Grandparents, Cousins, and Family of the Heart, love surrounded you. Aunty Louise, Rylan and Taylah moved to Mildura when you turned two, and I missed her every other day I couldn't speak to her. She was definitely one of our bigger supporters on the journey that is Motherhood.

For your second birthday, *'Little Mama'*,(who is now 98 as I write this) Grammy's mother, bought you your first kitchen. And did you love it! You cooked and created with play doh and grass, leaves and the plastic food that came with the kitchen. Your imagination was huge. You weren't too impressed the day Thomas sprinkled the sand from the sand pit onto a choc chip cookie and told you it was cinnamon sugar. Dad and I were not too impressed when an insecure, male relative of ours mentioned that you, playing with a kitchen would make you gay. Ignorant idiot! Hadn't he heard of Jamie Oliver, Gordon Ramsay, or Pete Evans? Besides, straight, or gay, you'd be ours and we'd be proud. Society wonders why some kids are arseholes. It's because they're being raised by one. There are a two things I am particularly passionate about: cruelty to children and animals. Discrimination of any kind makes my blood boil. As a mother, if I can pour all my goodness and love into you, well, fingers crossed, you will definitely be a good-hearted human with our guidance.

*****

Cousin Thomas was a good little cousin to you when you were younger. And we made the most of your time together before Aunty moved to the country. There was an incident in our backyard whilst you were playing on the monkey-bars. You were two, he was five. You raced inside, cross and crying. When I asked you what was wrong you folded your arms and huffed out, '*Tommy said my make-believe friend isn't real!*'

You were so adorable in your little two-year-old huff. Aunty rolled her eyes as I assured you Thomas only said that because he couldn't see your make-believe friend. That appeased you and off you went to play on the trampoline; informing Thomas there wasn't room for him as you and your 'friend' were jumping. What a healthy imagination you had! I loved that about you.

All-in-all, you got along well over the years, although Thomas had a way in which he would always find the negative in anything you did. It was so disheartening to see as you got older. I could see it in your face when he spoke a certain, careless way, or got physical. If only I had seen the signs back then. Would it have made a difference? That's the thing with not just being a first-time parent, but a parent in general. You question absolutely everything you do. (Well, if you are a caring parent that actually gives a shit about the life you created and put on this earth.) Even when things go well, and everyone is smiling at the end of the day there are so many questions —. '*Did I say the right thing? Discipline the correct way? Did I cuddle you enough? Tell you, 'I love you' enough?*' It was so easy to doubt myself some days. Although, for the first two years at least, I could pat myself on the back and give myself the '*Mother of the Year*' award.

Our poor, darling Thomas had his own demons to fight and as much as he was loved and spoilt, it wasn't always smooth sailing. Life's not always easy, that's for damn sure. And we are only human. None of us are perfect, although we try. We really do try. I wish I could say that all those around us tried to be as positive and loving. But we are not all designed that way. We had one relative who couldn't keep his opinions to himself. If you sighed too much, you were depressed. If you cried, you were a handful. When Dad and I attempted the positive parenting approach and tried to use an alternative word to 'no' you were a brat and we were stupid. One day, you will understand the deep love you can have for someone, whilst wanting to punch them in the face at the same time. No, I do not condone violence. But to imagine it and imagine it only, at times is extremely therapeutic. Okay, Dad and I will definitely get you a punching bag when you are older.

What can I say, parenthood and age opens your world up to quite a few facts in life, one of them being that everybody has an opinion, and secondly, not all of them are correct. It's like that saying about arse-holes. True story. And that's okay. You can choose to take the advice given to you and use it, or not. You can choose to react, or not to react. I'll go back to saying, we are only human and we all handle things the best way we can.

PERSONALITY PLUS

You were so much like me. We loved the outdoors, gardening or playing in the sandpit, collecting leaves, and going for walks. At 17 months, you said 'shubel' in place of shovel, 'sish' for fish. You said 'cat', 'dog', 'duck', 'Daddy' and tried very hard to say, 'shoes and socks'. You were so clever. I was very proud. You loved story-time anytime, as I had read to you since you were a week old. We put you to bed in your own room, but you would toddle on down in the middle of the night to get in between Dad and me. What child wouldn't want to sleep in between the safety and warmth of their parents? And honestly once you were there I slept better anyway. It was such a gift to wake up to your little arms around our necks with kisses and your sweet toddler's voice saying, *'I wuv you.'*

We had started mothers' group when you were four months old and after a couple of months, the mothers and I volunteered once a week whose house we would have our next get-together at, so mums and little people could socialise. My relatives and close friends all lived hours away, and although Dad grew up in Langwarrin, I knew no-one around our area. So, I entered mothers' group with a positive, happy attitude of, *'Here we go, a chance to make some new friends!'*

The first group, of course, was new mums sizing up new mums. I don't mean that in a bad way. Just in the — *'Who are you?'* way. *'What's your story?'* kind of way. *'Are these our kind of people?'* way. It was like a war-zone; excited women who had the chance to share, compare and discuss without embarrassment, their recent journey into motherhood. New mums trying to prove a point. Who laboured the longest, with the most pain unlike anyone else's that changed history as we know it!

For the most part, it was fun. A great way to get out of the house and meet new people with the common denominator of a new baby in the family. Like most women, I didn't fully have the *'Me'* factor in my mid-twenties. I truly believe that once you hit 35 you really discover who you are as a woman. You love, believe, and like the person you have become, and at the end of the day, don't give so much of a fat rat's arse crack *(A phrase you so elegantly taught me when you were thirteen - charming right?!*) if you are liked or not, because you are keeping it real, being the best human you can be and are appreciated by the good people you have selected to have in your life. The beauty of options. So, although a confident gal now, back then in our mother's group, I was that shy girl, wanting to be liked and accepted by my new group. To overcome any shyness and that awkward, getting-to-know-you phase, unfortunately, I babbled. I thought it was relevant babbling, to do with babies, sleep deprivation and joy. Perhaps not, after one of the mums decided to share with me, once she thought we were close enough to do so without hurting my feelings (she was wrong), that she had dis-cussed with her husband after our first mothers' group, that one of the mums was a complete annoying pain in the arse and no-one else could get a word in with her around! Yes, she was talking about me!

It actually made me sorry that I had, in that first group whilst we had a guest speaker, alerted her to the fact that after her son had finished breast-feeding, she had not covered her nipple completely, and it was poking out proudly for the group to see with a steady, continuous flow of milk pooling on the floor to the side of her. It would have made a Jersey cow proud with that thick, steady stream!

Despite the fact, that some weeks I questioned my role in our mothers group, you loved it. We were involved with Mini Maestros, community arts and took little trips here and there around our beautiful Mornington Peninsula to educate you little beings on all the wonders around us.

Dad and I were so proud watching you grow into such a sweet little person. You were quite clingy when we were out and about but certainly nothing to worry about. Some of the other toddlers were the same, it was normal according to your health nurse. You knew your ABC's perfectly and could count one to twenty. I stopped breast-feeding you when you were eighteen months, you were happy and ready to stop. You absolutely loved playing with your blocks, cars, and train set. You even made up little songs when you played. I noticed you were a little 'OCD' when you played; all the blocks had to be perfectly aligned around the cars — *Keeping them safe* — you said. You were a very neat child. I assumed that was because I was always neat and organised. (Perhaps not always the laundry and pantry, but there are only so many hours in the day, right?)

You were an excellent sharer when we had mothers' group over for morning tea. Handing out your toys with ease, playing nicely with the other toddlers. It was an interesting lesson for you and some of the others when we went to a certain mum's house. Her son did not like sharing whatsoever and you each experienced being pushed over, kicked, and bitten if you so much as touched one of his '*special*' toys. The mum wouldn't even have the decency to look embarrassed as she defended him. '*Oh, that's a special toy he got for his birthday,*' or, '*Oh, well they're all different, aren't they?*', or some such excuse. Like the rest of you didn't have special toys you had to share. You'd think as the months rolled on, she may have figured out the best thing to do, was put his special toys away before we all arrived, to save any justifiable scenes for her, and painful experiences for the rest of you. If the child learned to share, it would have made sense to leave his toys out. But he did not.

As the first few months flowed I became close to one of the mums, Jen. She was a free spirit and thinker who didn't conform to what was expected. She was a beautiful mother, full of love and creativity. Her son Kai and you were good mates and had play-dates throughout the years until you turned four and gradually lost contact as life got busier with pre-school and then primary school.

YEARS TWO AND THREE

A couple of wonderful things occurred when you were two. Uncle Grant came back home to Australia and you met for the very first time and became the best of friends. He was so delighted to meet the happy, clever, loveable little two-year-old that you were. Being an uncle certainly gave him something to smile about. He took you on little outings to the Frankston foreshore, where you played football and ran around in the park, and we did family trips up to Arthur's Seat. You loved visiting him in St. Kilda, especially in the summertime, where we would meet up with Aunty Nadine and stroll around the market and treat ourselves to sweets and ice-cream.

Your personality was huge. I just knew you would be a survivor when you were older. You were so independent, spirited and always, always loving. Despite our occasional test of wills, we had such a fantastic relationship. It was just so easy having one child to pour all our love, time, energy, and attention into. I think all first-time mothers with one child will agree with that. Your confidence was amazing and your trust in those you loved was brilliant. Dad could throw you high into the air and you had absolutely no fear, your trust that he would catch you was limitless. Interestingly, when we walked along hill-tops and piers or high stairs, you would become stressed. Worried that you, or we, would fall. We reassured you that we would not let that happen to you, that we always had your hand and would not let go. That fear stayed with you well into your early teens.

When you were two years and seven months old, Christmas day 2003, after a year of trying, Dad and I were thrilled to find out I was pregnant once more. Not only was the entire family excited, you were too! You made up songs as you thrashed around on your new drum set and rode your tricycle around that Aunty Nadine bought you. A certain relative made the comment that you would be a jealous boy once your sibling arrived and a real handful. Seriously! Count to ten, then one hundred. Yes, still want to punch said relative in face! It wasn't the first time and it would not be the last. I'm sure if everyone is truly honest with themselves, they will agree to the pure enjoyment of at least fantasising about taking one relative out to the mud-wrestling pit and knocking them the hell out. Or, it could just be me!

The months that passed were busy and full. We spent time buying baby things and talking about what a wonderful big brother you would be. I soaked up every single day we had alone together. We would go and feed the ducks at the George Pentland gardens, weekend trips to Flinders with Dad, and catch up with family and friends as often as we could. One hobby we loved to do was mosaics. You would help me smash up colourful tiles and select what colours we would use first and what patterns we would design. Decorating pot plants and a number plot for our house. It was a creative way to add some brightness around the home, whilst we spent quality time together. It was an activity we enjoyed with our new friends in the years to come.

Once we found out that our baby was a boy, we bought him little clothes and spent days getting his room ready, folding blankets, and sorting out where you thought the baby might like pillows and wind chimes. I tried not to make it all about the baby as the months rolled on. As excited as I was thinking about having two gorgeous boys, I still could not imagine not having you all to myself. You and I constantly did a lot of craft and activities together, mornings at Ballam Park and we had your little mate over for play-dates.

On the weekends that Dad wasn't away scuba diving, spear fishing or camping with Uncle Stuart, you and he spent a couple of weekends building a very cool rabbit and guinea-pig hutch with a decent run. Uncle Grant came with you and me to buy the furry little creatures from a lady in Cranbourne and when the time came we all loved handling their soft little bodies. You felt very important feeding them of a morning, picking fresh grass to go along with their grains and salads. It made Dad and me happy that you were so kind and gentle to your animals and you continued on that nurturing path for years to come.

As you grew, so did your personality. There was a day Dad wanted us to go for a walk. You sat on your bed and actually screamed that you did not want to put your shoes on. Of course, we had seen small fits of temper the past year, but you had never actually been a screamer. It shocked me. Dad and I had such an amazing relationship (24 years and going strong as I write this!) where we never raised our voices at each other and often would give each other the so called *'respectful'* silent treatment if we disagreed. (Was it respectful? I don't know but it always suited me best, as once negative words are said and put out there in the universe, the damage is done).

I wish I could honestly say I stuck to that belief as the years passed. Please someone; show me a mother that never lost her shit when the world turned into a void of the unknown and emotional exhaustion, of darkness and chaos mixed with a complete sense of, *'What do I do?'* or, *'How do I fix this situation?'* Yes, of course venting verbally is not the correct thing to do and as I said, for many years I was that perfect, sweet, soft, gentle mother that always said and did the correct thing, but as life went on, my perfection did not. I'll make no excuses. As an adult, you know immediately you have definitely said the wrong thing, when your first thought after you've carried on like a complete-out-of-control-lunatic is, *'Did the neighbours hear me?'*

And on this day watching you sit on your bed, your little cheeks going red with the effort it cost you to scream, I hardly recognised you, or the diverse emotions going through my own head. I was in shock. I don't know why. In hindsight, it was a picnic for what was to come, but for a young, loving mother, I could not believe my little boy was not only screaming at me that he did not want to put his shoes on, he also did not want to go for a bloody walk! There was no way we were going for a walk until you calmed down. That took about an hour. I could see the frustration on Dad's face as I yelled at you for the first time, not knowing how to deal with my furious toddler. He was as equally unimpressed with our new, volatile situation. We had both left childhood homes *(and I can only speak for myself here, as I did not grow up in Dad's house)*, where there was a father figure of arsehole proportion and we had promised ourselves a peaceful, positive, happy life for ourselves and our children, where there would be none of that negative bullshit.

I did not handle you screaming at me whatsoever. I left home at eighteen, had nine peaceful years with no-one screaming at me. And then, there you were, the love of my life, my tiny little human, unintentionally forcing me back to my childhood memories of all those insecure, unloved feelings. It was a moment where Dad and I did have a chuckle about it hours later. So, your sweet little temper started to develop, as did your stubbornness. That's a healthy sign, right? Like I said, you were not a brat, but if things didn't go the way you envisioned them in your head, you could not handle it at all well, which usually resulted in you storming down to your bedroom yelling out, *'Don't talk to me. I'm going to my room,'* sometimes slamming your door. Once you were calm, we would explain to you that it wasn't nice for you to yell at us and probably not great for the door hinges if you kept slamming it. You got it at the time, said sorry with kisses and cuddles and all was well. Until the next time of course! You were after all, a toddler. You were still clingy although you had days here and there where you would spend an hour or two with Aunty Nadine, Uncle Grant, Grammy, and Jen. At two and a half, you had never had a night away from Dad or me.

When I had morning sickness with your brother and was throwing up in the toilet, you would come in behind me and rub my back, asking, *'You sick, Mummy?'* Then when it was over you would ask, *'You happy now, Mummy?'* So, so caring. As my belly grew you would put your arms around me and say, you were cuddling your baby brother. I remember how you would press your face against my belly button with one eye shut, to see if you could see him inside, saying, *'I love you, Baby.'* You were just so cute. Everything about you was so adorable. Perhaps not your growing temper, but you were human. You sang about everything, from going to the toilet, to having Aunty visit. We even made up songs together for Dad to sing with you when I was in hospital. One song was for the car. Of course, you called it, *'The Car Song'.* The other song was your, *'Sleeping Song.'* We wrote it all down along with a four-page spread for Dad, of all the things you loved to do when I went off to have your brother. You were so outgoing and happy, toilet-trained, and completely out of nappies at two and a half. And you became the most loving, proud big brother.

*****

I had popped you into bed before my water broke (just good timing, not a premonition!) and as my labour commenced we rang Grammy to let her know, as she was going to stay with you while we were at the hospital. It was a little over a two-hour trip for Grammy to get to Frankston from Heathcote, so it was a big drive for her in the dark, trying not to hit Skippy on the way down, which was exhausting enough for Grammy, with the excitement of another grandchild on the way.

We also rang Aunty Leah as she was our support person. Yes, she was a great comfort as I was about to deliver your brother into the world and she decided to pass out. Not only did Dad rush down to help her, so did both the midwives in the middle of a mind-numbingly painful contraction (is there any other kind when you do it natural all the way?) When she came-to, she looked like the frightened squirrel from Ice Age, constantly chasing the acorn. Yes. Aunty may have not been supportive at all, but she was there alongside Dad, to witness the wonderful birth of your beautiful baby brother. As much as I would love to go on about how sensational it was to bring your sweet little brother into the world, at 3.53 am on the 23rd of August 2004, this story is about you my darling. And I feel as a parent, as a mum, that I have let you down enough. I won't do it here.

So, while we were having a bit of a celebratory time at the Frankston Hospital, poor Grammy and you were trapped in a bit of a nightmare. We left you sound asleep at 2 am with a gentle kiss to your face before leaving home. Unfortunately, when you did your usual 'bed-crawl', you could not understand why Dad and I were not where we were supposed to be and became very upset. Instead of making the house dark with perhaps the comfort of a small light on, poor Grammy lit the entire house up like Christmas, with basically every light on as you ran from room to room crying, searching for Dad and I. You did not settle until 6 am when you finally fell in an exhausted heap in Grammy's arms. Oh, I felt so sorry for you both when you came to visit us in the morning.

I was up, dressed, and ready to bath baby Zane (the midwives and nurses very impressed, as I had only given birth four hours ago) when you marched tiredly, happily, and proudly into my room that morning. Dressed in your jeans and favourite red t-shirt at the time, with a picture of a spider hanging from his web, swinging your arms with a smile on your face. I burst into tears when I saw you, hand-balled your brother to Dad and swooped you up, burying my nose into your little neck. It hadn't been too many hours, but it had been the longest stretch I had ever had away from you in three years. I was telling you how much I missed and loved you while you were struggling to get down to meet your new baby brother. You were so wonderful from the get-go. Stroking his baby fine hair in wonder. It reminded me of when I had stroked yours as a baby. Where does the time go? You kissed and gently cuddled him from Dad's arms and helped give him his first bath. God, you made us proud! Knowing in our hearts you would be such a sweetheart to your brother was one thing. To actually witness it, I don't even know if words can describe that feeling. Watching Grammy sit tiredly on the bed filled my heart with so much love for the mother-in-law I was blessed to have. Always so supportive and giving. It was lovely having her be as much a part of Zane's journey, as she was yours. We had fun snapping the usual first family pics of all holding the baby and you got to open a present for Zane, plus a colouring book for yourself to do once you got home. When it was time for you all to leave, I struggled not to cry. I was tired, obviously sore, and just wanted to go home with my family, after only six hours in hospital. I had been told by so many relatives, *'Don't rush to get home. Stay, relax and enjoy being waited on and spending time with your second baby.'* I think they were, in fact nuts. (Love them dearly though!)

Dad was so wonderful coaxing you gently from the room after we said our goodbyes. I think Grammy was close to breaking point, not only being so tired, but loving you so much also and hearing your little voice so pitifully crying out as Dad carried you from the room, *'I want to stay with Mummy, I just want to stay with Mummy.'* Over and over, from the room to the corridor, and even out to the car park. Hearing your cries, holding the body of my new little son, it was so easy in my exhausted, emotional state to let the tears flow once you were out of my line of vision. It worked out so very well that Zane and I were able to go home the very next morning.

I remember my first morning waking at home. Zane and I slept in the spare room, allowing you and Dad to get a decent night sleep.

Breast-feeding a new-born throughout the night was as exhausting as I remembered it, and as your cheerful little self-popped into the room first thing in the morning, I burst into tears thinking, *'Is it that time already? Time to actually get up?'* I felt like I had only just fallen asleep. The beauty with only one baby is, when they sleep, you do. But with a baby and a toddler that rule does not apply. Thankfully it was the weekend and Dad was home. You called out to Dad as you ran down the corridor to him, *'Daddy, Mummy's crying!'* Poor Dad, he ran in himself to see what was wrong with emotional little ole me, only to discover I was sleep deprived and simply needed some more zzz's. And I was guiltily grateful once Dad steered you in a direction that allowed me to get a bit more shut-eye.

*****

Our first full day at home, you were so excited and overwhelmed once the visitors started arriving to meet your new brother. Dad and I constantly reassured you what a fantastic job you were doing as a big brother and how much we loved and appreciated you. Unfortunately, when one relative arrived, you ran up to him as you usually did, expecting your usual tickle and tackle routine, but he gently moved you to the side and said, 'No, I'm not here to see you today, I'm here to see your brother.' The look on your face! Confused. Hurt. My immediate thought was, *'What a fool.'* (Actually, *'Silly dickhead' was what I thought*). What was so wonderful, as Dad's eyes met mine across the room was, he was in-sync with my thoughts as he swept you up and tickled you. Listening to your laughter as Dad swung you around with love, eased the pain in my heart for your confusion.

This was the first of many moments that I believe increased your belief, that we all loved your brother more than you. It was a split-second moment, a thoughtless comment from an adult, like so many others that were to come, that all add up to a toddler and make a change to their little personality. To this day, I cannot fathom how we let you down so badly, that you truly believe in your sweet, young heart, that you were worthless. Nothing. That we never listened to you. Heard you. That we let you sink down into such a cold, dark place. So many little things making such an impact on an impressionable young human.

*****

Dad had given us a project to do on our first day home alone without him as he went back to work. He called the project, 'Pic of the day.' He wanted us to capture a feeling of each day, to share with him, what we were up to whilst he was away. Our first pic was a peaceful one, of you on the swing singing a song. And it captured the feeling of the entire day to a 'T.' It all just seemed so easy breezy. We spent time playing outside on the swings after we had done the housework and put Zane down for a morning nap. We played puzzles and you set up a bookstore for a while before your friend Kai came over to play. It was a calm day where I thought, *'How easy is this? How good am I? Two kids and a playmate and all is flowing without a hiccup.'* Those were good days, the happy, smooth-sailing days. The days where I did feel accomplished as a mother, perfectly juggling a happy active toddler and a gorgeous baby.

Our weekends were either very busy or very relaxed. We'd take day trips along the beautiful Mornington Peninsula, visit the Melbourne Zoo and Aquarium, or catch up with family. When Dad took off on weekend or day trips with Uncle Stuart and Uncle Cameron, it would give your brother, you and I some extra 'us' time. You especially loved to go for bike rides around our block. It was such a pretty area; proud neighbours with landscaped gardens full of colourful blooms, amongst some renters that couldn't be bothered, with their overgrown lawns. Our circuit backs onto the gorgeous Flora and Fauna Reserve, and the scents of gum leaves and peppercorn trees in the warmer months after a summer's rain, take me back to happy times as a child at our Inglewood Christmas parties, where we kids would gorge ourselves on Aunty Mollie's ginger fluff, (sounds ominous I know!) and any other tasty morsel we could get our hands on.

I loved to walk with you, whilst pushing Zane in the pram, it was a relaxing time for me; breathing the fresh air, listening to your little three-year-old chatter about things we would see along the way, as Zane would either sleep or take in his surroundings. Most of our walks were peaceful, and on few occasions, they were not. On this days walk, as we were approaching the hillside of our return journey (which was hard enough dragging you on your bike with one hand and pushing the pram up the incline), you totally lost it over a dead bird in the gutter, covered in ants. You wanted me to get the ants off the bird, so it could get up and fly away. I tried to explain to you, that the poor bird didn't have any hope of flying away, with or without the ants. You got off your little bike and tried to push it over. As it was balanced well with its training wheels, it stubbornly refused to be knocked over. You took that person-ally and yelled, giving it an extra hard push, which sent it to its side. By this stage my bladder was calling out for release and baby Zane was starting to get agitated not being able to see what the fuss was all about. I reached out a hand to stroke his little face as I rocked the pram back and forth and tried to reassure you, that the little bird was in a peaceful place. Your small fists were balled tight as you screamed out that the bird was not in a peaceful place at all and I was a liar. You stood there looking at me, tears welling in your eyes. I turned the pram around, so Zane could see what we were up to and asked if you wanted a cuddle. No, you did not. You simply wanted me to wake up the bird, so it could go home.

I totally got why you were upset. Seeing anything dead at an early age wasn't pleasant. Any age really (for most people anyway). I got down to your level and expressed what a kind-hearted boy you were to care about the little bird, but there was nothing we could do for it and Mummy was busting for the toilet and Zane was needing his milk. You started crying. Fat tears rolled down your chubby cheeks, your little safety helmet sat crookedly on your head. My sweet little boy! I stood your bike up and pulled you in for a cuddle, where your cries became inconsolable. After a few minutes, standing in the summer heat, your brother crying and my bladder shouting for surrender, I said to you, *'Let's go home.'*

You weren't walking anywhere. I shoved the front wheel of your bike into the bottom basket of the pram, sat your bottom on the prams handle bars and resumed up the hill and towards home, with you close to hyperventilating and poor Zane getting restless and hungry. Not one of our most relaxing walks. I had a few friends say, *'You should have waited him out and made him walk.'* Yeah sure, that would have been fine if say, I had a Depend on and Zane didn't need to be breast-fed. So, for that walk and a few others like it, I got a bit of extra exercise. Was I soft at times? Bloody Oath I was. If a mother can't be compassionate and sympathetic to the tiny humans she created, in times of their confusion and frustration, well, she shouldn't have become a mother in the first place. I like to think most of the time I deserve to be called Mum. I guess that's debatable at times for us all.

There was a day I wasn't so proud of myself. Standing in the queue at the busy Safeway deli. Another hot summer's day. I was wearing a knee length skirt, holding four-month-old Zane whilst you were dancing around my legs hugging them, singing, and chatting quietly away. You were so adorable. You really were. I don't know why you thought it would be a good idea to walk behind me and hold up my skirt for all the deli customers to see my backside. Trying to remember which knickers I had put on that morning, praying it was the pretty lace, not the practical, comfortable cotton, I turned in a circle, trying to grab your hands to make you let go. You cleverly turned with me, not in the least perturbed by my growing anger and embarrassment. There were of course, both sympathetic eyes, and snickers from unsympathetic on-lookers, which added to my growing embarrassment. No amount of, *'Please, mate, can you stop that?'* helped me whatsoever, which led to,

'If you don't drop Mummy's skirt right this minute, you are in big trouble!' So, you finally dropped it and then to my ongoing horror, lifted it up again and tried to hide under it! I wished I had known then how uncomfortable you were with all those people's eyes looking on at you. You were simply trying to hide. Hindsight!

But, my skirt was not long enough for that! Trying to grab hold of your arm and not drop your brother at the same time, with curious eyes watching to see what would happen, I grew frustrated enough to lash out my hand and whack you where I could reach without bending down and making my backside more of a show for the onlookers. Regrettably, I slapped you on the back. You dropped my skirt in an instant and stopped dead in your tracks. The shame I felt when I saw your little head drop, and your very young three-year-old eyes lose their sense of merriment. You didn't cry, despite the fact that the slap would have stung, you just wrung your little hands together for the remainder of the outing.

Doing up your seat-belt after you climbed into your car seat, I dropped a kiss on your head and said how sorry I was for hurting and embarrassing you and tried to explain, I simply wanted you to let go of my skirt so all the people wouldn't see my bottom. You said nothing, just looked at me, then out the window. Once we were home you took off your little red converse shoes and sat in your room quietly playing with your cars and train set. I felt like a criminal.

*****

Three-Year-Old Kindergarten Orientation was an exciting afternoon. There were eight of you in the rotation group for morning and afternoon; that way there wasn't the entire class of children to overwhelm you all at once. We arrived with Zane and my camera ready to capture the adventure of your day. As soon as you spotted the train set, you were off. I couldn't stop taking photos, the joy of seeing my little boy playing so happily in a new environment that would be the start of another chapter in our lives. One of the mums offered to hold your brother so I could click away baby-free. I smiled at her and said thank you. She was a lover of photography also and could understand me wanting to get as much footage of you at play to take home to show Dad. It was a short session and when it was time to pack the toys away you were the only boy left, who stayed behind and put every-last piece of the train set away. The pre-school teacher was very impressed, and I was so happy for you and all the fun times that were to come your way with all the activities and learning that came with the early pre-school days.

*****

Christmas, New Year, and the summer holidays rolled around. Days filled with stimulating and relaxing activities. The Frankston Water-front Festival was always something we looked forward to. The atmosphere had a chilled vibe of people on holidays, the air filled with scents of the sea and scrumptious foods. You loved the games, sand sculptures and especially going on the dodgem cars with Dad. Seeing you in Dad's arms as you whizzed by, a thrilled look on your little face made my heart so full. Times like that, seeing your child simply happy, those are the moments, the pictures in our memories that we bring forward, with tears choking us when things became so very dark and seemed so hopeless. They were the memories I would recall, when your eyes were bright with the carefree light of a three-year-old, when all was right in your world.

It was so lovely to sit on the sand under a shelter with Dad and Jen and watch you and Kai run in and out of the waves, build sandcastles and fling jellyfish eggs. Your childish laughter filled Dad and I with joy. Getting home from the festival, your brother chirped like a little bird in his jolly jumper whilst you ran around the house entertaining him, hitting yourself and everything in sight with your giant blow-up hammer Dad won for you at one of the games stalls. You were unstoppable, until 4pm came and, Praise the Lord, you finally fell in an exhausted heap.

Dad went back to work, and we took a week's trip to visit Grammy and Poppy in Heathcote, followed by a trip to Aunty Louise in Mildura and totally refreshed ourselves for the kindergarten year to begin. Once we were home again, we talked about kinder from time to time when we were out in the backyard on the swings or playing blocks and cars in your room. Certainly not wanting to over-saturate you with kinder talk but keeping it occasionally on your mind. You were thrilled when Grammy said she would drive down and do kinder duty and see what fun you would get up to. (Show me another Grandmother who would travel two hours to do kinder duty, then travel home afterwards to look after orphaned wildlife. Legend.)

Two weeks before your pre-school journey began, so too did small signs of the growing predator. Of course, I didn't see them as signs then whatsoever. I saw them as normal responses to a changing situation. They may well have been normal. I wasn't knowledgeable enough at the time about what was and wasn't 'normal', in regard to a toddler's mental state.

One night, Dad and I had put your brother to bed and did our usual routine with you after dinner. Bath, book, and cuddle time, then sleep time for you. On this night, you were shocked and appalled when we said it was in fact bedtime after cuddle time, it was like, all of a sudden, we had dropped a bomb on you and changed your routine. You were not ready for bed and had no intention of going any time soon. Thus, a slight pattern began — of you becoming extremely upset when your world wasn't as it should be, according to you.

We had visitors coming for the weekend and you were determined to finish painting their 'welcome' banner before dinner time. You were concentrating as you ran the brush here and there over the table sized paper, looking seriously proud of yourself. 'What a wonderful job, mate. That looks awesome.' I smiled down at you.

'It's not finished yet,' you said, dabbing your brush in a yellow gob of paint, before smearing it along the bright yellow circle of the sun you had just painted, 'I've got heaps more to do.'

'That's okay, you can finish it in the morning before everyone arrives,' I said to you, as I started collecting some of the other brushes to help you wash them out.

'No, I haven't finished yet, Mummy!' you said crossly, as you reached for the brushes in my hand. *'I have to finish this tonight!'*

'Look, let me wash out the brushes so they don't get yucky and hard and maybe you can do half an hour more after dinner with Dad.' That sounded more than reasonable to me.

Not to you. You threw the brush down on the table and said in a voice filled with urgency, *'You don't understand, I need to finish this now!'*

'It's alright, love, we have heaps of time for you to get it done, but we need to have dinner now so it's time to clean up the table.'

Well, the look you gave me as you started to cry, shaking your head your fists by your sides as you shouted, *'You're a naughty arsehole, Mummy!'* And with that, off you ran to your room shouting one more time before you slammed your door, *'A naughty arsehole!'*

And there you have it. A three-year-old expressing himself and his unhappiness to the best of his ability. There were many times when you would become cross with both Dad and I, and you would march down to your bedroom and slam your door, screaming out as you went, *'You naughty arseholes!'*

At Nana Lyn's one weekend, Thomas, Zane, and you were digging for worms as you helped her do some weeding, when you come across a very long earth worm. Placing it aside you informed Nana you were going to put him somewhere else in the garden to keep him safe. Thomas, being an eight-year-old boy thought the better idea would be to chop the worm in half with his little spade, so then there were two worms to give a new home to. He was also known as *a 'naughty arsehole'* after that incident.

At times if a situation upset you too much and you became extremely upset, we were also known as *'Naughty F-ing arseholes.'* Not bad considering Dad and I did not use that word often, and especially not in your hearing. Life was still filled with sunshine and lollipops then. But boy did I learn to swear like a trucker in the years to come. Not proud of course. But that's life. There are some things I'm not proud of. I am human. But, I always tried my very best once common sense kicked in, to take a deep breath and say it in my head. Sometimes it worked, but let's be honest here, there is truth in the fact, that swearing out loud, even to oneself, is very therapeutic! One thing I always thought was brilliant about you as a toddler to a teenager. You may have lost it in your place of safety, home; but you never carried on in public. I suppose we could say that that was due to the fact, that you wanted to fly under the radar, with no attention drawn to you whatsoever. That or you had fabulous self-control!

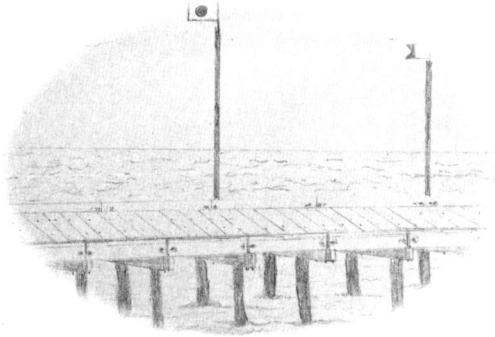

2005 - EAST KARINGAL PRE-SCHOOL: Three-Year-Old Kinder

The day came for you to go to kinder. As a mother, I felt excited and nervous for you at the same time. What fun you were about to have! Making your own special group of friends, experiencing all the wonderful things kinder had to offer a three-year-old turning four that year. I could not wait to see you in action. Yes of course like any mum whose first child starts a new stage in their life, I had a small bag of concerns and *'what-ifs'* in the back of my mind: *What if another child hurt you and you were afraid to talk to the teacher? What if you couldn't express yourself and became scared or sad and wondered when I'd be coming back for you?'* Of course, that's all part of the pre-school journey for your personal growth, to gain those social skills you'll need in life to communicate with many individuals.

Of course, I didn't voice my concerns out-loud. I knew all would be well and I had a large amount of respect for the wonderful pre-school teachers and trusted in their duty of care to you young ones. They were just little concerns I assumed a lot of first-time parents had. Unless they were the kind of parents that couldn't wait to dump and run and have a few hours to themselves! (No, I do not blame them.)

The short drive from home to kinder that morning, I noticed you were certainly quieter than usual. I put that down to the early start where we had to be dressed, eat breakfast and be out of the house a little earlier than normal. I chatted to you and your brother happily about all the fun times you were about to have. Looking in the rear-view mirror, I noticed your usually rosy cheeks were pale. Pulling into the small kindergarten car park and shutting off the engine, I stepped out of the car and opened your door, unbuckled your seat belt and before I could help you out of the car, you launched yourself out of your car seat and into the front passenger seat. You started fussing quietly saying, *'No, Mummy, I don't want to start kinder today, I'll start tomorrow.'*

I was fairly calm, thinking, *'I've got this'* as I unstrapped your brother. I said to you gently, *'It's alright, mate, look, Zane and I are coming in with you.'* As I closed Zane's door and came over to the side where you were sitting, I could see the sheer panic on your face. I had not seen that look before. I opened the door and shuffled your six-month-old brother from my arms to my hip, in the hope that I could easily pry you from the car. I was aware of the other mums and toddlers arriving around us, happily walking in with their excited, confident children looking forward to their new adventure. But not you! Your quiet fussing soon turned to tears and as I reached my hand in to pull you out, your crying turned to shouting as you stood on the seat and wrapped your arms around the head rest clinging on for dear life. I was keenly looking for another child that looked as terrified as you. Yes, I could see your panic as clear as the day, and it close to broke my heart. I was actually considering putting your brother back into his seat and driving us back to the warm, safe sanctuary of our home. But I knew I couldn't do that. It was time to start kindergarten, it's what good parents did. It is what society expected. Get your kids to three-year-old kinder and start setting up their social and learning skills. Right?

But watching you panic, cry and cling, I stood there with some of the other parents watching, wondering, how-the-hell I was supposed to do this? How, with my arms full of baby was I going to get you out of the car in a calm, positive way? I wanted to hear the voice of my husband, get his advice. I was about to panic. I could feel my throat tighten as tears threatened. Here I was, standing in public

on what was supposed to be an exciting new adventure in your life, and there you were, screaming and crying blue murder like I was about to throw you out of the car into a pit of hungry wolves.

This was certainly not how I envisioned the day. I felt confused and frustrated. They didn't talk about this step in the parenting books. Actually, there is so much they don't talk about! Probably just as well, or there may be a lot less couples willing to plunge into the world of loveable, heart-breaking chaos that is parenthood! This step was too hard, these emotions of knowing what I had to do compared to what I wanted to do was so conflicting. No amount of coaxing was going to get you out of this car. I felt so alone. (Embarrassed? Of course, I was a woman under 35 and hadn't discovered my strong sense of womanly confidence and self-awareness that I mentioned earlier. I'm sure if the lovely women under 35 who are reading this, think to themselves, *'Crap, I know and love myself now and am very confident, — wait till they hit 35 plus. They will feel empowered enough to run the world!*)

Zane was quietly doing his baby talk and I looked away from your tear stained face and glanced down the footpath, wondering what to do. I noticed another mother approaching me, marching with quiet purpose and an almost no-nonsense attitude, pushing a pram with a sweet baby girl inside and bouncing happily beside her, a pretty, blonde toddler looking very proud of herself indeed. Was she just going to walk on and say nothing like some of the others whilst you screamed the carpark down?

'*Hi,*' the mother said, '*I'm Sally and this is Caitlyn and Emily.*' She indicated first to the happy toddler then the infant who looked the same age as your brother.

'*Hello,*' I said, remembering her from orientation day last October. She had held your brother while I had taken photos of you. I tried to smile and look confident, but she saw right through my attempt to mask my uncomfortable situation, her eyes landing on you still clinging to the seat like a life raft, crying your heart out.

'What's happening here?' she asked.

'*I can't get him out of the car.*' I didn't intend my voice to break and I cleared my throat as if to make out a simple frog, not me on the verge of tears which may have embarrassed us both. She took quick note of the situation and unbuckled her infant from the pram. I was wondering what she planned as she set the tiny girl, not actually an infant, onto the footpath beside her bouncing toddler.

'*Pop your bubby in here,*' she indicated to the pram, '*that gives you two free hands to pull him out,*' she nodded towards you, still crying. I placed your little brother in the pram, strapping him in, grateful for my long, dark hair covering my face to give me a few moments to take a deep breath and regain my composure. I stood and thanked Sally as I walked over to you. Leaning down I began to stroke your back and kiss your hair, grateful to be able to put both my hands on you. To give you as much comfort as I could. Your little body felt hot as I wiped the tears from your face. '*It's okay darling; it's going to be okay. And look,*' I nodded over to the little girl, her blonde pony-tails bobbing up and down with her enthusiastic movement, '*there is your first friend at kinder. Say hello to Caitlyn.*' Your crying had softened as I continued to rub your back as you looked over at the little girl. Sally stood near the trio of little ones, guarding them as her eyes watched us. '*Come on now, mate, it's time to go in.*' I tried to pull your strong little arms away from the headrest as your crying became more persistent once again. I did not think you would be so determined. I wish I had understood how scared you must have been. *God, I must have been so dumb!* Looking back, reading over the journals I'd kept for years; it shocked and saddened me when I read them seeing all the signs. I felt like an actual failure. Yes, some were *'normal'* toddler reactions to your fears. Others were not.

I finally pulled your arms free from around the headrest and picked your resisting, wriggling body out of the car as you screamed out, *'No, Mummy! No!'* Once you were out and you saw everyone watching us, your crying ceased, and you buried your face against my neck, wrapping your arms around me, trying to hide from the onlookers. I was shaking, and took a deep breath, shutting the car door with my foot.

Sally smiled at us and said, *'Come on,'* to our group. She took Emily's tiny hand as her happy toddler trotted beside the pram as she pushed your brother inside the kinder gates. Well, at least we were out of the car. Going into the kinder doors, signing in the arrival and departure book, and taking in the atmosphere of excited toddlers and enthused parents, I got you interested in some puzzles at one of the toddler-sized tables. Squatting beside you, I talked to you quietly about how very exciting this all was. You kept your head down, your fingers sliding the correct pieces of the puzzle into place, your eyes remaining down. After a few minutes, I asked you if you were okay. You nodded, saying yes. I asked you if it was okay for me to take Zane home now to put him down for a nap. *'No,'* you replied, getting quickly out of your seat, and grabbing tightly onto my arm. I wasn't going anywhere anytime soon.

The pre-school teacher, Mrs Anderson, was so lovely and completely understanding of your situation. And mine! Thank goodness for wonderful, caring and understanding pre-school teachers who pave the way for parents of socially clingy children to make a clean, hasty, positive exit when the time arises. They keep them occupied with a happy song, a story, *a 'Let's go outside' or 'Look at this little chick…'* and not see Mum slink quickly off, full of guilt and a quick prayer of, *'Please let him be happy and have fun!'*

I could not leave you for that kinder session. Nor any session for weeks to come. In the tenth session, the fifth week, Mrs Anderson and I had a quiet chat about setting you up with an activity you enjoyed so I could leave you happily with her. When I could finally leave, unfortunately you weren't as happily occupied as we thought, and ran crying to the gate, as I slipped out and around to the front of the building. Crying myself, I could hear you calling my name over and over, with Mrs Anderson gently trying to encourage you elsewhere, I leaned against the brick wall and let my tears fall freely as I was out of sight. A woman I didn't know, rushed up to me and hugged me, actually kissed me on my cheek. I was taken aback. Not because I didn't appreciate her kind gesture, but because I needed it so much!

It was in those months, leading to well over a decade, I began to learn what friendship with another mother meant. Aunty Louise and I had formed a solid friendship over 25 years; meeting whilst we were single, friends supporting each other whilst falling in love, getting married and having kids and contemplating life in between all the ups-and-downs. We went back to the beginning of time where we always kept things real with respect and appreciation and being each other's soft place to fall. But we were hours apart and led different lives and as soothing and comforting as a phone call can be, nothing beats a good sit down over a cup of tea, allowing simple conversation to turn to deeper, more cleansing, verbal detox.

Building a relationship with another woman, cultivating the friendship if you like, getting to know them, their family, whilst growing in the same direction, as our children started their journey together of preschool, primary school, high school and all the milestones in between, it bonds women with a strength that can at times be stronger than family. That gorgeous saying, *'Friends are the family we choose for ourselves,'* Love it. Agree. There were days to come as the years flowed by, that I seriously don't know what I would have done without Sally.

She was in that first day, and so many days after, the sunshine and support to not only me, but our entire family.

There was a day when it was particularly hard to leave you. Squatting at one of the tables, Zane sitting on my lap watching you play, when Sally approached me. *'Do you know where Lucerne is?'*

I nodded yes.

'Well, I'll give you my address, so once you settle Jesse in, pop on over for a cup of tea.'

'Thank you that would be wonderful,' I smiled at her. I was so excited about the prospect of sitting with a cup of tea and getting to know her. Unfortunately, it took me awhile to settle you in that day; you were upset, clingy and crying when I tried to leave, and by the time I could walk out the kinder gate, put your brother into his car seat and drive in the direction of Sally's house, I had forgotten the name of her street and ended up taking Zane home. Sad that you may have been unhappy and yet here I was desperate for that cup of tea with Sally, wondering if she thought I couldn't be bothered turning up. Thankfully at pick up time, she was there with a smile as I explained the situation of not being able to firstly, get away and secondly, finding her house. She had laughed and said, *'No problem, follow me in your car.'* It was such a lovely afternoon, to be able to sit in her humble home and be made to feel so welcome, watching you play and explore your new friend's house, while we chatted away, sharing a little information about ourselves and our families. You were so excited to get home that afternoon to tell Dad not only about kinder, but your visit to Caitlyn's house.

Throughout three-year-old kinder, you seemed completely happy, making new friends, and enjoying all the activities and special days East Karingal Pre-School put on. It was such a wonderful, caring environment that catered to your emotional and developmental needs perfectly, which of course is what kinder is all about. You especially loved it when Grammy came down to do kinder duty with you, which she did at least twice a term. Her love in doing that gave me a few small breaks throughout the kinder year which I appreciated greatly.

Sally and I formed a friendship with a couple of the other kinder mums and became a solid, supportive little group that was not only a bonus to us mums, but an extra added security for you young ones to feel like you belonged. We each took in turns to do lunch once a week, usually in between the kinder days. It was so refreshing to sit and discuss all your similarities and differences, to share discipline tactics and laugh together at the pulling-hair-out moments of motherhood.

It was hard at times, to watch you suddenly become upset or sad after you had been playing so happily with your new little friends. You would find somewhere to hide and escape the group's eyes, usually behind a couch. It confused me then, as there you were, laughing and enjoying yourself, and suddenly snap, you would withdraw and hide. If I tried to approach you, you would get upset and tell me to go away, which of course I would as I didn't want to upset you further. You would allow one of the other mothers to sit behind the couch with you and she would talk to you about this and that, calming you down and trying to get to the root of your unhappiness. I appreciated the fact that she took the time in those moments, as others couldn't be bothered with your emotional ups-and-downs, and I noticed over time friends pull away, treating you as if there was something wrong with you. That hurt more than I'd like to admit at times. I had always, *always* been a supporter to anyone's child that needed extra love or attention, to feel as though all could be well in their world. Yeah, even adults suck at times too.

I struggled watching you become frustrated or angry whenever we got with the other kids. It was never at kinder. There, you just drifted into the background and went along with the flow of things around you. But with our group, it wouldn't take a great deal to set you off, where you felt the need to move yourself away from everyone. The thing was, you were never nasty, cruel, or hurt another child. It wasn't like that. You simply became jam-packed and full to the brim with overwhelming and confused emotions. I get it now. I did not get it then. Shame on me! A lot can be exposed in thirteen years.

The world of knowledge regarding any topic is so readily available in this day and age of 2018; with the touch of your fingertip on the keyboard, type in one word, and a flood of information is there to either reassure you or expose your mistakes as a mother. Yes, I did take a lot personally when the truth was revealed to me. It showed me the direction I was going in was the wrong one. And thank goodness for the angels on the other end of Beyond Blue's helpline, openly discussing our situation and sending me in the direction I needed to go for both our sakes.

But before the bigger, clearer picture was revealed, we experienced days where your 'personality crisis' would consume our lives. Social gatherings that I, on one hand so looked forward to and on the other hand, secretly prayed you would have a lovely time and simply be happy, that we would not be the focal point of any drama, and that the tight fist in my chest would go away. Days, weeks, months rolling into years, that the blackness shadowed us. Sounds dramatic I know, but in those times, I can honestly say I questioned what life was all about.

It was easy, watching you sleep, to answer that question. Life was about you and your beautiful brother. Life was about Dad and I, doing all we could in our power to show you how much we loved you. Offer you any opportunity that would help your emotional and physical growth; Auskick, martial arts, fishing, trampolining, swimming, snorkelling, gymnastics to name a few. How much we wanted to protect you and if we could, take any slither of pain away from you. We, like all loving parents, just wanted you to be happy, to feel how much we, as your family, loved you and hoped you would grow into a happy, confident little human.

Like all things, confidence needs to grow and fundamentally, it grows through positive experiences. Although I guess negative experiences can become positive if they are handled in the correct way.

Half way through the year, Aunty Leah and I took you shopping to buy a present for a party you had been invited to. Dad had Zane for the morning and Aunty was in such a happy mood; six months pregnant and excited to be buying baby girl things. We were having a lovely morning out and about as we had had a coffee at Starbucks first and since Thomas was with Aunty Nadine, it gave Aunty and I some quality one-on-one time with you and a chance to catch up on family gossip. You and I were looking at some clothes when Aunty said to you, *'Let's go look at some toys for Daniel's party.'* And off you went. When Aunty came to find me several minutes later without you, the look on both of our faces as we exclaimed together, *'Where's Jesse?!'* This would have been purely comical if it had been any other situation. Pure panic set in for me. Trying to be calm, I kept telling myself you were okay and simply in the toy section of Big W. Telling myself to be calm was one thing, but my nervous system and body had a mind of their own. I felt as if my heart was going to explode it was beating so fast, with thoughts of abducted children flashing through my mind. We dashed off to the toy section, calling out your name as we went, wondering how long it should be before I called out to store security. What was probably less than a minute, seemed like ten. I found you standing quietly near the Matchbox cars holding a special pack of twenty. *'Daniel likes cars, Mummy,'* you said.

I smiled as I gave you a quick hug, not wanting to act like you had in fact, been left behind by your pregnant Aunty. *'The perfect present, well done.'* Aunty Leah felt so guilty, you took home a couple of new Matchbox cars for yourself!

LITTLE MELTDOWN

Buzy Kidz was a place for kids to let off steam, run around and go totally nuts if they so desired. And once you and all your kinder-mates got inside the doors and we mums selected our tables, you were off in a flurry of excited squeals and energetic yells. You settled in quite quickly with so much to see and do, and after I had walked you around the area with a couple of your friends, you were quite happy for me to go and sit with a cup of tea, to relax and chat with the other mums. After I gave Zane a feed of milk, I took him across to the baby section and we played in the ball pit for a little while, had some stimulating play, then left to search for you and see what you were up to. After searching for a few minutes, with no luck finding you, I asked Sally and another mother to help me search. We finally found you minutes later, hiding underneath the giant blow-up slide, crying your little heart out. Your tears of fright stopped once you realised I was still in the play centre, your relief turning to anger. I got it. Apparently when I was in the ball pit with Zane, you couldn't find me and thought I had left. Sally took Zane so I could give you a cuddle and reassure you I would never leave without saying goodbye first. You looked up at me with dark, angry little eyes and screamed at me to *'Bloody GO AWAY!'* And so I did, giving you as much time as you needed to feel calmer about the situation until you were ready to talk. And that's how we rolled as the years flowed around us; 16 years and still counting. Still trying to figure out the perfect timing for the ever-changing roller-coaster of a typical boy that goes through life's turning cycles from all the emotions of a toddler to a young school boy, older school boy and high school, all the hormones, brain development and everything in-between.

Steve Biddulph, author of *Raising Boys* and many other life-saving books, was a complete legend in our eyes. That book was like a checklist of things to expect, the best way to handle certain situations and all the things we should and perhaps should not be doing. Done, check. A gold star for us. Or perhaps not, when reading on, quietly nodding our heads thinking; *'Right that makes sense, that's where we are going wrong'.*

Young boys are more prone to separation-anxiety than girls, *(according to many studies and Steve!)* and when you were three, I needed a dentist appointment. Sally was the first person ever to look after you and your brother outside of the family, and the first person to look after baby Zane at 6 months old, whilst you and I trundled off to my dentist appointment. I was keen to leave you with Sally as I knew you would have a great play with Caitlyn and little Emily, but there was no way you would let me go to the dentist without you. So, there you sat on the cold, sterile floor eating your biscuits and cheese in the corner of the dentist's room, whilst a strange man had his hands in my mouth. I was so proud of you just sitting there not making a fuss, as on the drive there you were quite upset about the *'strange man'* that was going to *'have his hands in Mummy's mouth',* even though I calmly explained to you that he was going to be helping me. Once your cheese and crackers were finished, I was expecting some sort of emotional outburst, but with much relief and pride, you simply sat quietly like an angel.

*****

It was the night before your fourth birthday. Standing over your bed watching you sleep, I felt such an overwhelming rush of love for you. While you lay there so peacefully unaware of the world around you, I thought back to the past year and all your accomplishments. How hard some days were for you and in between all the good, fun times, you were such an argumentative, disagreeable, frustrated little boy. No matter how stressed or unhappy you were with a situation, you would always vent and cry about it at home. As soon as we went to the shops, dentist, kinder, any place in public with other people really, you would close yourself off, like the storm cloud of epic-proportions had never affected you, moments earlier. I guess home was your place of safety where you could totally explode. You knew you would always be loved, no matter what you did or said when you were in *'the moment'* of frustration. In saying that, you always, always had a heart-of-gold, and you were so quick to say *'sorry'* and *'love you.'* I kissed you goodnight whilst you slept, whispering for the last time ever, *'Goodnight my three year old.'*

FOUR-YEAR-OLD
BIRTHDAY PARTY

Your fourth birthday party was pretty epic. The theme was dinosaurs and thanks to Dad's ingenuity, everyone received an invitation in the shape of a dinosaur foot. (Creative I know!) We had the Wiggles music playing, which was your favourite at the time. We hired Jen, who was amazing at running kids' themed parties and your party was no exception. It was so lovely for me to be able to enjoy the day without the craziness of doing the kids' activities; where I actually got to watch you and your friends be thoroughly entertained for hours by Jen, and had plenty of time to walk around and have a chat to Aunty Leah and have a cuddle with your new cousin, baby Ireland. It was so lovely to catch up with our relatives and the kinder mums; making sure everyone had a full cup of tea and something to eat. To watch your little face light up when Jen set your volcano cake alight, with the runny jelly lava flowing down the sides and around the edible dinosaur shapes below. A typical four-year old's party; kids happy and excited being entertained the entire time with games and activities. Music drifting, conversations flowing and a houseful of happy people commenting on how delicious the risotto was. I had a few requests for the recipe, which I smiled politely saying I would get it to them, feeling both guilt and hilarity; as earlier I had walked into the kitchen to find Aunty Leah at the risotto pot, a glass of wine in one hand, her breast in the other, squirting a healthy dose of breast milk into the risotto! Just another day's work for Aunty really! That's how she rolled!

Yes, it was a sensational day for you. And although we had a few hiccups in your first four years of life, they were flowing, loving, fairly peaceful years, years in which I felt Dad, myself and loyal friends and family had your back and poured their love into you, and we drank you up beautiful child.

2006 – FOUR-YEAR-OLD PRE-SCHOOL

You went into four-year-old kinder happy that you knew most of the children and as we had caught up with our group over the summer holidays, you were confident and as proud of yourself as we were of you. Personality-wise? Volcanic! Sweet as a pea one moment and then beyond feral. These moods usually transitioned when you were either misunderstood and couldn't get your point across or became frustrated when Dad or I didn't *'get IT'*. Dad was always so lovingly patient during these times and as frustrating as it was for me, I would mostly feel so sorry for you when you got into your screaming frenzy and worked yourself up into a ball of rage. There would be no trying to reason with you or possible way of calming you down. We would simply leave you in your room until you cried it all out of your system, always letting you know we were here for you. It didn't take too long for you to return to a calmer reality.

Looking back, this was definitely a wonderful year for us all. Especially you, where we could see your confidence shine and the happy manner in which you embraced all the wonderful things we did together. You loved our continued trips to Heathcote, Inglewood, Glenormiston South, and Mildura— having family and friends come visit. We had Thomas once a month and on those weekends, Dad would take you both exploring along the coastline, to the circus or the park, which gave Zane and I some time to catch up on things he liked to do. When we had Thomas for a fortnight over the school holidays, we would do farm visits, go to the movies and organise lots of activities to do in a calm, loving environment. Which wasn't always the case as, at times, you and Thomas would be so disagreeable together; you bickered and argued more like brothers than cousins. But I still tried to make the environment positive, after I screamed at you both *to 'Just bloody get along, or I'd bang your heads together!'*

Mrs Weber was your pre-school teacher. She was one in a million. An absolute diamond who shone brighter than any other teacher I have seen in many, many years. Her dedication and joy in teaching you little people, with so much enthusiasm, compassion and love earned her the Victorian Teacher of the Year Award a few years later. You adored her and had such a wonderful kinder year packed full of exciting, educational activities from hatching chicks, a variety of dress-up days with cooking special treats like pizza muffins or cupcakes. You certainly loved it when it was a special events day with Grammy, Uncle Grant and Dad coming in to be with you, and especially the rare times Nana Lyn got some time off work to come and see what you got up to on your kinder days.

Mothers' day morning tea was my favourite. It was such a pleasure to come to kinder and not be on duty. To simply sit and watch a special performance or song put on just for us mums. I loved watching you do the little actions to the songs. Sometimes you would join in with the singing, but mostly you would sit and watch the other children sing. There was another little girl, who was similar to you in this, where you both seemed happy to sit with your group and watch. You certainly sang the songs at home no problems, which was pure delight for me.

I loved watching you grow into such a caring sweet boy, playing so well alongside your special kinder friends, enjoying your little selves right through the year. Your last term especially was highlighted with primary school orientation, an exciting visit to the Rain Hayne and Shine farm, and then the final Christmas concert. I knew I would cry at your Christmas concert. I didn't even try to hold back. A flood of memories from the day you were born to now. All your accomplishments, your footprints in the sand that made you this unique, special little man. Thinking how happy you were, how proud I was and how your future couldn't be anything but shiny and bright.

2007 – PRIMARY SCHOOL: GREAT EXPECTATIONS

Like most parents, we wanted your primary school experience to be filled with carefree, happy days learning in a safe, positive environment. Especially in that first all-important year of prep. We thought we had chosen the perfect school for you, and for many others it was. Most of your kinder friends went off to other schools such as St. Johns, Ballam Park, and Karingal Heights. As parents, we select the schools that are either close to our homes or future high school and of course, base our choice not only the school's reputation, but also the feelings you get when you first step onto the grounds on that initial school tour.

You were okay, despite the fact that all your friends bar one, went to other schools. Luckily Jarrod was in your prep class, a familiar face, and someone you became closer friends with over the next two years, sharing play-dates and joining Auskick together. His parents were lovely and had strong family values like Dad and I.

That first morning popping on your little uniform, straightening your hat and taking that first-day-off-to-school photo was another one to file away into the memory banks. How did this day come so quickly? You looked too tiny for school and thinking about it, five years old going off to school? Crazy! You were all just babies in the grand scheme of things.

Thankfully Grammy and Aunty Nadine were with us for moral support and to celebrate your special day, which helped me keep my smile in place. And it stayed in place, whilst we drove you to school, walked inside the gates and into the classroom. We stayed as long as parents were able, settling you in and showing Grammy and Aunty Nadine your classroom and introducing your teacher, as you chatted to Zane and showed him the pet finches. When it was time to leave, I kissed and cuddled you, wished you a fantastic day then quickly walked from the classroom while you said your farewells to Grammy, Zane, and Aunty Nadine. I then allowed my smile to fall and the tears to flow. The beauty in this instance was I was not the only mother crying her eyes out. The gift of that day was that I left a happy you behind.

By the time Grammy, Aunty Nadine and I arrived home with Zane, to say I was desperate for a cup of tea would have been an understatement! My emotional nerves were screaming out for a shot of Earl Grey. But due to my little habit of always needing the kettle full and boiled, I believe I had over done it that morning, flicking the switch back on after it had already blown its head off, and as Aunty Nadine flicked the switch on for us all to calm with a cuppa, the fuse blew and tripped out the entire house. Nothing a saucepan and gas can't fix! That was my last electric kettle for some time.

You were so much braver than I that day and I will admit, I cried for the next two weeks as well! Very cleansing. Seeing you transition into a little school boy, coming home with stories those first three weeks of all the things you were learning, snuggling with Dad or I at the end of the day reading your reader. So, so proud. Your personality was still vibrant and happy and your energy levels kept you going right through the school day, to coming home in the afternoon, feeding your bunnies and guinea pigs, playing with Summer, our little butterscotch coloured English Staffordshire, and bouncing on the trampoline with Zane. So, for the first couple of months at least you seemed happy. Of course, there was always the minor niggles of school-yard antics like such-and-such called you a loser, and someone else said you couldn't play with them because you weren't cool. One fact in life. Kids are cruel and can be arseholes.

You had your first play-date at Jarrod's after school one afternoon. Zane and I came also; a nice way to catch up with Jarrod's mum and have a chat about how we were all settling into school-life. We had been there before, as Jarrod had had a jumping castle for his fifth birthday and you and all your kinder friends had been invited. Tania and I may have been on our second cup of tea when you approached me saying in a very firm five-year-old voice, *'Mummy, let's go home. I want to go home now.'* You had a certain look in your eyes that I did not want to argue with. I couldn't put my finger on it. Let's just say, my mothers' intuition has always been strong, (even if it's been off the mark, it has been strong!) and I knew I had to get you home. That happened constantly on play-dates. You were fine for a bit, but then you'd shut down and simply had to get home. The interesting thing was, you really enjoyed Jarrod's company and felt special that he considered you a friend, who allowed you to come to his house for a play. We did remain close with our kinder group, but for me, it was very important for you to bond and make new friends with your new school group.

And you did. You were invited to several parties and as you were such a gentle kind boy, became very popular and well thought of by the girls and their mothers. As the year progressed you became good mates with another little boy and seemed happy enough most days. It was the days in-between those days that I questioned you about what was making you sad or angry. When you would come home so tired and down and become easily frustrated and lose control; calling Dad or I idiots, telling us to shut up and not speak to you or simply losing it and falling to pieces over the tiniest thing. Speaking with our friends, a lot of their kids were tired also, testing the waters and seeing how far they could push the boundaries. It was very frustrating at times. Here you were, such a beautiful, sweet boy and then, well you just weren't. Okay, so it may have been normal, but when you are living in the moment, day after day, dealing with these repetitive trying times of a constantly frustrated five-year-old, the normality of it doesn't make it any easier. Although it was comforting to hear that other children were also testing their parents, it didn't lessen the moment-to-moment heartache, dealing with what feels like the demise of your child.

We felt we had a positive rapport with the school, participating in any fundraisers where Grammy would also put us to shame, ringing the office ladies and donating generously. I volunteered to do readers, cut up fruit, was invited to go on excursions and enjoyed the special activity days. I tried to be as much a part of the school community as I could, to help you feel like you belonged and honestly, it was interesting to watch from a distance, the children that particularly made your life extremely unpleasant. The children who made mine and Dad's life, heart-breakingly unbearable for a time to come.

I remember you coming home one day, silent during the car ride home. You were visibly getting more tired as the weeks rolled on. Walking into your room to hang up your bag as you pulled out your reader. Dropping it onto your bed, you kicked off your shoes, listening to me chatter about what Zane and I had been up to for the day. My chatter ceased as I pulled your school shirt over your head. A clearly defined, angry, red bite mark was on your upper back. Five years old. My stomach muscles tightened of their own accord and I felt a wild sense of wanting to slap whoever did that to you. Gently running my hand over your back as I gave you a cuddle, I asked, *'Who bit your back, my darling?'*

'It hurts, Mummy,' was all you replied hugging me back. I didn't push you for information as I set you and Zane up with afternoon tea. My blood was boiling! I waited a little while for you to eat and listened to you chat about your day before I asked you again, *'Who bit you, love?'*

'I don't know,' was your only reply. When I asked if you told the teacher, you shook your head.

'Do you remember if it happened at recess or lunchtime?'

'Lunchtime when I was going down the slide. I was on the top waiting for Holly to go down and then someone grabbed my shoulders, then my back stung and then I got pushed down the slide.' You were poking your pancakes and fruit around with your fork, watching your plate as you spoke.

'Who was behind you on the slide, mate?'

'I don't remember,' you answered quietly. I could sense your frustration brewing, so left it at that.

I waited for you and Zane to go outside to feed your pets and play on the swings and trampoline before I rang Sally.

After telling her about the situation and getting myself quite upset about it, she was just as upset as I was, and suggested I ring the school then and there and not wait till the morning. Unfortunately, by the time we finished our phone call and I rang the school, your teacher had already left for the day and the Vice Principal was in a meeting. So, arriving at the school a little earlier in the morning, I had a quick chat to your teacher, who was upset for you and wanted to know who bit you. *You told her you didn't remember.* She frowned and let me know she would get to the bottom of it.

We never did find out.

That was the beginning of the physical bullying and of course the emotional bullying was two steps behind. You turned six a few weeks after and as the prep year rolled along, so did Dad's and my bewilderment, of how quickly a young family can feel like it is falling apart.

*****

For weeks, you would come home, your lunch untouched saying you weren't hungry, which was cause for alarm for me, as you had also stopped wanting to eat breakfast in the mornings. You had always been such a good eater and although you may have made up for it after you were home from school, wolfing down bowls of cut up fruit, pancakes, sandwiches and the like for afternoon tea, it was missing all that important energy for growing and learning you needed throughout the day that worried me. How long was this stage of you not eating properly going to last?

A bit of cheer in the family was Aunty Nadine marrying Uncle Jarrod. They had a beautiful wedding at the Mount Macedon ranges and you had such a great time running around with Kiralee and Hannah and as Aunty Rachael and Uncle Darren had also had a baby boy, so little cousin Wyatt got to hang out with you all too, along with Thomas and Ireland. It was such a gorgeous wedding and a carefree day for Dad and I, to relax with all the family, and as the menu for the kids was chicken schnitzel, chips, and ice cream, with the comforting company of your cousins, you certainly ate well that day.

During the term two holidays, we had the chance to spend a week with Aunty Louise, Rylan and Taylah. She noticed two things in the first few hours. How emotionally drained I seemed to be and even though happy to be with our favourite people, how quiet you were. Of course, being with my dear friend immediately gave me a burst of energy, catching up on all the gossip of both of our families, what Dad had been up to and all the transformations of our kids' lives in the past few months. Even our heart-breaking conversations ended in fits of laughter, shaking our heads wondering at times what the hell life was all about. Talking about my fears with Aunty Louise, about how prep was transforming you into an angry, sad, frustrated little man, seemed almost ridiculous. Watching you run around laughing with your brother and adopted cousins, seemed to make all the unhappy incidents of the past two school terms disappear into a question of, *'Was it really that bad?'* It was a week of total relaxation and towards the end, as we were getting ready for the long drive home, you were the calmest and most peaceful I had seen you in the past couple of months. A happy and contented six-year-old, as a six year old should be.

Our last week of the holidays started off so well for you. Dad took you camping, along with Uncle Cameron and his daughter Jasmine, who was only a few weeks younger than you. You loved it so much; sleeping in the tent, sitting out by the campfire melting marshmallows and motor-bike riding with Dad.

For the end of the last week we had Aunty Leah, Thomas and Ireland spend a few days with us and had a few play-dates with Tania, Sally, and our other kinder friends. On our last catch up, three days before school started for term three, we went to a play centre to allow you all to run about and give us mums some much-needed chill time. I absolutely, always adored the time I got to spend with you when it was school holidays. It was time for us to re-connect, to breathe and just enjoy each other's company without the busyness that the school schedule delivered. In saying that, it was also such a busy time trying to fit in as much as possible in the two short weeks we had together— it was quite exhausting by the time we hit the end of it. So, enjoying some sit-down *'mum'* time whilst watching you and your mates enjoy each other's company in a safe, stimulating environment, was perfect.

On this outing you were excited to have your big cousin with us and as Thomas had met our friends over the years, was comfortable and quite popular with a couple of the other boys, who unfortunately thought it would be cooler to all hang out together without you. This of course, upset you and made you a little sad and grumpy. So, when it came time to order some snacks and it was your turn to say what you would like, you replied in a grumpy, (probably ungrateful sounding) tone. I got it. You were hurt.

Show me an adult, let alone a child, that can speak with perfect, proper manners when they've just been kicked in the teeth. Of course, between Dad, myself, Nana Lyn, Grammy, and Poppy, we all had help in teaching you respect, manners and all the etiquette a six-year-old requires to go into society a polite little being and also be pleasant to be around. There are times in this life, we can all react unpleasantly. Not an excuse. Reality! Yes, it does take a village to raise a child and Dad and I have always been very grateful for any support we received in regard to you and your brother. One thing we both did not appreciate was other people stepping in, right in front of our faces, to discipline you. To me, it was outrageous that any other mum (especially those not related) would think they had the right to say what was on their mind to another person's child. Disgusting and rude also when it is said in a condescending way in which one should never speak to another's child.

I guess I was always passionate about this topic simply because, as someone that worked with other peoples' children for years, helped raise my nephew and look after my friends' children whenever I could help them out, I always did so with love and fun, and only gentle firmness when it was required, out of respect to the child's feelings and to their parents. I may have had a firmer approach with Thomas, but it was no different to the way I treated you, and only because I had him so often in those early years. (And I was never really that hard when you were all little, although, your interpretation on that score will be different to mine!)

A simple fact. Mothers know their own child better than any living soul. What makes them tick. What you say and how you say it to them, will either close them off and shut them down to any possible positive outcome and make the situation worse. Or, when it's best to let the little things slide by for the moment, until there is a calmer more suitable time to explain and discuss any incident that will make sense to a six year old, and what is expected of them. (I'm still perfecting this 16 years into motherhood!)

Seeing you sit there this day, after knowing how difficult school had been for you, after a brilliant trip to Aunty Louise's and now being surrounded by our friends that were supposed to be our greatest allies, it cut me to the core and gobsmacked me at the same time, when, after you grumpily responded to the snack order, one of the mothers leant across the table looking you dead in the eye with a snarly curl to her lip I would have loved to slap off, snapped out, *'You won't be getting anything if you speak like that!'* Then, glanced across at Aunty and rolled her eyes. I didn't need to hear that she thought you were a little shit. It was all over her face. I didn't think your dark little eyes could grow sadder. They did. Could she not find it in her heart to be a little sympathetic? She knew what you had been going through at school and had just seen her boys and Thomas exclude you the past hour. Some people just don't care enough about what another child may be feeling, or what they are going through, as long as their own children are happy. It's very sad.

Luckily there are other kind-hearted, understanding mothers out there, that do actually like other people's kids. Sally and Tania bustled around setting up snacks, giving you and the other kids something to eat and drink and made the uncomfortable situation, of me trying to compose myself and hold back from telling this friend to mind her own business, where to go and how quickly she could get there. It wasn't the last time another adult thought they had the right to *'parent'* you, and it didn't take me too long to grow the balls (yes, confidence is a nicer word, but doesn't quite have the same effect!) necessary to tell them not to worry about me and mine, but to concentrate on their own family, or perhaps get a job as a counsellor if they enjoyed giving advice so much. Like all of us, we appreciate good advice when it is intended with respect and love. We receive it openly with an appreciative ear. When it's not, you feel it. You don't want it. Interestingly enough, advice was never given in front of Dad. What a shame, that would have been entertaining indeed.

Once we were home and Dad had finished work and been informed quietly about our day, he pulled you into his arms, along with Zane and you settled down together to watch a DVD, chatting happily throughout it. It was in those moments, seeing you talk to Dad so carefree and happy like there was nothing wrong in your universe, that made it so easy for me to breathe. It was all too soon after that moment that the world seemed to run out of air and every breath I took was painful.

DESPAIR

The second day back at school you received a punch in the stomach. And throughout the following weeks we had regular feedback from you regarding all the stressful moments you endured throughout recess and lunchtime. Being teased constantly by the same group of boys, left out of games, and feeling like you were not worthy, on top of the physical abuse, left you feeling degraded and unworthy. As pleasantly boisterous and confident as you were at home, you did not let that assertiveness shine through at school. Of course, I rang the school office, sometimes daily, to make an appointment to see either your teacher or have a chat to the Vice Principal. The Vice Principal was sympathetic and did try to sort out the bullying. Your teacher, who was great with all the children, strangely regarded the parents as if they themselves, had some kind of learning disability. (It could have just been the way she spoke to me, but thankfully as I communicated with some of the other mums they felt the same way). It was difficult some days, trying to keep composed and relay your daily encounters without getting too emotional and coming across like an overprotective, irrational parent. Mind you I was probably within my rights to act that way, but I just didn't feel like that was the way to go, to get a productive response to our situation.

The absolute game changer, began two months after you turned six. Our usual calm nights of dinner, bath, movie, book, and bed, became a repetitive nightmare, trying to cope, and survive the battle of bedtime.

That first night started off as usual. We had dinner and chatted around the table about our day. Dad ran your bath as you and Zane selected what essential oils you wanted in it, (a great way to relax and calm any savage or not so savage beast!) You selected Tarzan as the movie. We got through quarter of it when you started to become restless. This was unusual for you as you were a movie buff and loved the chance to sit and lose yourself in the story-line. We called it quits for the night, popped on our relaxing music, and started story-time. You were not into it whatsoever. It was the first time in six years you walked out of the bedroom, in the middle of Dad or myself reading to you.

'Okay, mate, you must be tired and ready for bed then.' Dad put the book away as I was settling Zane into bed with a kiss and a cuddle, watching his tired little eyes flutter close, only to pop open in fright as a blood-curdling cry erupted from the dining area.

'It's okay, darling, you go to sleep.' I kissed his smooth forehead before I rushed out of his room and towards you, hearing you crying uncontrollably, thinking, *'What the?'* There was Dad standing in the hallway, the expression on his face was also one of, *'What the?'* And there you were. Our little boy, sitting in your red flannel pyjamas, clinging to the thick wooden leg of the table crying out at the top of your lungs, over and over, *'I'm not ready for bed! I don't want to go to bed! I don't want to go to bed!'*

Yes, over the years, we had seen you have the typical temper tantrums, they were after all a normal part of childhood. Although unpleasant, (and yes at times ball-breaking!) nothing to worry about and they were never the kind where you threw yourself down and pounded or kicked the floor. They were the ones where you simply became so frustrated and being the age you were, not knowing how to cope, you basically closed yourself in your room and cried. It generally didn't take you that long to calm down.

But this? This was something entirely different! You were not just having a simple hissy-fit because it was bedtime. You were having an absolute six-year-old nervous breakdown. I would never have said it then, but years later, looking back, that's exactly what it was. Of course, I am no expert and that is a broad statement but it's the way I feel. It's the way it felt—*encompassing a huge variety of suffering and feeling overwhelmed. And suffering and overwhelmed you certainly were. That fact was as clear as I wish the coming years to be.*

Watching you sit and cry as Dad tried to remove your arms with comforting words and a gentle back rub, I reached down to scoop up Zane who had come out to see what was going on. Rubbing his back as he tucked his head under my chin, my love for Dad grew as he finally, gently, pried you from under the table and mirror-imaged your brother and I, with you. Our eye contact said it all — *'Whatever's happening, we've got this! Positive parenting, right?'* To at least believe all will be well, and strive to do whatever it takes to make it so!

Your little sobs grew quiet after a while and we all settled into Dad's and my bed with the relaxing music finally putting you and your brother to sleep. I was glad when that night was over. Retelling the episode to Sally the next day, when you were off at school, made me feel so sad for you. We both decided then and there to make a point of getting all your close kinder friends, and any other good mate you had made the past few months, and do a weekly activity after school.

And so, began a routine we all looked forward to once a week after school. Rotating from Ballam Park, to the Frankston Foreshore and our Whistlestop reserve, we'd do a BBQ afternoon tea, play football, and watch you run around together. When the weather was wet, we would meet at the Red Fire Lounge, Stacks Pancake Bar, and Hogs Breath.

They were the afternoons that I look back on and still feel so good about; remembering seeing you so happy and thinking, *'There's no way he'll get upset tonight.'*

But you did. Every night! For weeks on end! A repetitive nightmare we could not change. Dinner, bath, movie, book and then screaming and crying under the dining table. You would get as far under as you could so Dad and I couldn't get to you as easily or quickly, crying, screaming. On and on and on and painfully, on again. Some nights we simply waited you out. That was agonising. We talked about changing schools but that upset you, as you didn't want to leave the friends you had made. We certainly didn't want to make things any worse for you, so at this time, you would remain where you wished. We changed the routine up, hoping that would help, cancelling the movie to playing a quiet card game, reading, a massage and music. Anything we could think of to make bedtime more appealing for you. I knew I was getting into a dark place, feeling almost numb, when one night as you were screaming your head off, clinging to the table leg for dear life, all I could think about, looking at your filthy little feet was, *'The floor must need a mop.'*

We fought against the dismal feeling bedtime brought to the household and there were nights when you were finally in bed asleep, I would search for your Dad, to find him sitting, head in hands, crying in despair. To love a man as much as I loved your father. A man who was loyal and loving. Everything he felt at times, his own father was not. To see how dearly he adored his sons and did everything possible to provide them with a loving, peaceful, secure sanctuary; seeing him sit there in despair not knowing how to help you and stop this situation, broke me too. Walking in, putting my arms around his shoulders and hearing his voice full of torment, *'I don't know what's going on; I don't know how to help him.'*

'It's going to be okay,' I'd say, hoping that was true.

Of course, it didn't take us more than a handful of nights to realise what the problem was. Bedtime equalled the coming school day. It was just figuring out where to go for help for a six-year-old with these issues. Bullying, low self-esteem, frustration and easy to anger.

Talking to Aunty Leah and breaking down on the phone one day got us in a direction we needed to go. She contacted a counselling service close to us and got the details required to get the ball rolling in a helpful, positive direction. After making a doctor's appointment and explaining all the happenings from school and your bedtime terror, up and down mood swings, along with your changing appetite, we got the referral needed for you to see a counsellor at the Mirrool Counselling Centre on Skye Road.

THE HAPPY LADY

Our first session with the lovely Alison, was very much appreciated and daunting at the same time. Sally offered to have you and Zane which was a blessing and allowed Dad and I to talk openly and freely. Sitting in the waiting room waiting for our names to be called, I kept thinking, *'This is really happening. We are about to start counselling for our six-year-old son.'* It just seemed so surreal. I was nervous, thinking we were about to be judged on our parenting — *I mean what other parents need to start counselling for their six year old?* (Yes, I know now, a lot!) Those thoughts didn't stay with me for too long as I knew deep down in my heart we were doing the right thing and tried hard to shrug off any self-doubt and blame and think positively. We were here because we cared about and loved you and wanted you to be truly happy right through to your good, sweet little core.

I was relieved when we were finally called in as it stopped all my light and dark thoughts from flowing into a tidal wave of highs and lows. Once Alison took us into her room and closed the door, Dad and I sat, and I took in the comfortable area. The walls were a soothing colour of green, a small desk where Alison sat with a little chair and table, adorned in colouring pencils and paper, and some toys in the far corner of the room.

After our introductions and quiet small talk about the weather, Alison finally asked us how she could help us today. Dad and I exchanged a glance wondering who should go first. Dad smiled at me and gave a quick background story of how old you were, your personality and what essentially, a good boy you were. I then spoke of why we were here, how low your self-esteem was getting, your loss of appetite and how easy you were to anger; some of the incidents at school the past few months and finally your episodes at night under the dining table and how it was affecting our family. She sat there kindly, when my voice broke. Retelling parts of the story, especially of you being bitten, brought back all the feelings of helplessness and sorrow of how much my little boy had been through and how he was not coping. I simply wanted all your pain to *stop*. Dad reached across and held my hand when I got a bit emotional as I apologised to Alison who, of course, said it was fine. She asked quite a few questions about our background, how the school was dealing with your bullying and what we were doing for you at home when you became extremely upset. She wrote in her notebook quickly as we answered her questions, gave us some advice and encouragement, and said she was looking forward to meeting you in a couple of days. The session ended, leaving me feeling calm and in control and we left to collect you from Sally's.

Sitting on your bed that night Dad and I chatted to you about Alison, letting you know how lovely we thought she was.

'Why do we have to see her Daddy?' you asked, pulling at the edge of your blanket.

'We need to see her to make our family happy again,' Dad answered.

'As simple as that', I thought to myself, kissing you goodnight.

I felt such a sense of a new beginning the following morning as Zane and I took you into your classroom. We were in control and taking steps in the right direction to make your path clear for happy days ahead.

As I had been communicating as much with your teacher, as I had with the Vice Principal, I thought I'd best let her know that you were starting counselling this week and to just be aware if you were having any emotional moments, it would probably be due to that.

'Good morning.' I smiled as I approached her.

She smiled at you as you hung up your bag before you walked over to the reading corner where Jarrod was sitting. She turned to face me. *'Good morning. How's everyone today?'* She asked, nodding at a few other parents and children as they started coming in.

'We're all good thanks.' I glanced around, grateful to be out of others' hearing range. *'I just thought I'd let you know Jesse is starting counselling tomorrow after school.'* I didn't feel the need to go into the whys, then and there. We had had plenty of talks the past few months on how the bullying had been affecting you.

'Is it really that serious?' she asked me, looking at me in a peculiar way, with one eyebrow raised.

'Well, considering his mood-swings and all his emotional outbursts at bedtime, we believe so.' Her eyebrow remained raised, and I thought back to all our conversations. Whenever I had told her about how upset you were with the group of boys bullying you almost daily and how down on yourself, and frustrated you would become, she would always say. *'I don't see that behaviour here, he gets along so well with everyone. He is one of the loveliest students I have had in years and is such a pleasure to have in the classroom. He always just seems so happy here.'*

As the classroom began to fill, I scooped Zane up saying, *'I just wanted to let you know.'* After all, she and I were a part of a team in your life. As I turned to go and kiss you goodbye, she said, almost as an afterthought, *'There must definitely be something going on at home because he's always just so happy here.'*

I froze, a deer in the headlight kind of moment. Did she really just say that? Out loud? To a mother that had been coming to her for advice, help, and at times was emotionally just hanging on by a thread?

Yes. Yes, she did!

Looking back on that moment even now, I still feel disbelief. That a teacher, or anyone really, would have the balls to basically state, that we as parents must have been the cause for your unease and unhappiness. I mean, what an insult to any mother who goes to the ends of the earth to find some sort of resolution for their child's unhappiness.

I was, unusually gobsmacked and had no reply. I didn't even glance around to see if any of the lingering parents had heard us. I quickly kissed you goodbye and with Zane, left the school with more thoughts flooding my mind. As I popped Zane into the car, did the shopping, unpacked, set Zane up with some craft activities at the table before preparing his morning tea snack, along with dinner, and getting household chores done for the day, I continued thinking about the statement she had made. And of course, I'm sure like any parent that has been questioned, I kept thinking of all the times I had over-reacted to you either being a typical six-year-old, back answering or being rude, or to times where I had been exhausted and probably had not been as patient as I should have.

By the time I had put Zane down for a nap, I was doing my own head in. As much as I wanted to talk to Dad, I thought I'd leave him in peace whilst he was at work and decided to run the morning's conversation over with Aunty Louise. Never short of a strong opinion, she was mortified and outraged at such a flippant comment and basically lectured me on all the self-doubts I was having.

'Mickey, are you insane?' she said this in a quiet voice, which let me know I was in trouble. *'What mother is as cool as a fucking cucumber every second of the God-damn day? Show me any decent, loving parent at one stage or another that doesn't regret something they said*

or did to their child? It does not mean you are responsible for his emotional downfall! Seriously how dare this teacher suggest otherwise!'

I sighed, grateful for the verbal back-up that was always there. *'Yeah, I know. It's just so easy to doubt yourself in this situation and everything I've ever said that wasn't Mum-of-the-Year-award standard has come back to haunt me since she said it. I guess I can sort of understand her saying it to a degree; he is always so quiet once we hit the school grounds. He is that perfect student that does what he is asked, when and how and is agreeable to everything everyone says. It's like, he waits till he gets home and he can finally breathe and be himself again. I really don't know.'*

'Simple fact is we'd all prefer our kids to be polite and respectful in public and go off their nut at home. As much as what she said would shock any parent, try to forget about it. She doesn't really know you and Jade; she just needs to make sense of it all from a teacher's point of view. Of course, they are judgemental, they have to be, but they should also be bloody diplomatic.'

'I can't believe the way she looked at me. The fact that she said what she said was bad enough, but that simple look with that raised eyebrow. I wanted to rip it off!' I shook my head grateful as our conversation turned to lighter topics and our phone call ended on a happy note. The beauty of friends is, they help us see things in a different light, always have our back, and at the end of the day simply make everything better.

*****

Aunty Nadine came to play with Zane when we had our second appointment with Alison. (*Exciting news— she was pregnant!)* You weren't too nervous at all. You sat with Dad and I in the waiting area, watching Thomas the Tank Engine on the little telly they had propped in the corner, turned nice and low. I was watching your face as you followed the story-line, something about the Fat Controller helping Gordon take a lion somewhere. You had seen it all before and were telling Dad what was going to happen. It was comforting for me, to see his arm around your little shoulders. Hearing your voice chirp away like you didn't have a care in the world. Precious moments.

When Alison came into the room and called your name, you swivelled around and reached for Dad's hand. He took it in an instant and we followed Alison into her small, comforting room. Once we were seated Alison introduced herself to you and asked you how you were doing today. You replied, *'Good.'* She got you to sit on the little table and chair by her, and gave you some paper and pencils. After saying a quick hello to Dad and I, she started off the session by asking you *some 'Getting to know you questions,'* that were to put you at ease and hopefully make you comfortable. You chatted away as you drew her a drawing of your pets, followed by a drawing of your family. It was when she started asking you questions about school that you went a little quiet. She asked you to draw you when you were at school. You drew two little stick figures watching a group of stick figures play a ball game.

'Who are these two, Jesse?' she asked pointing to the two figures looking on at the others playing.

'That's me and my friend.' You rubbed your ear.

'What are you doing?'

'Watching all the others play a game.'

'Why aren't you joining in?' she asked kindly.

'I'm not cool enough to play with the others, so my friend won't play with them either. He plays with me.' You clutched the pencil in your lap with both hands.

'He is a good friend then, isn't he?' she smiled.

'Yes, he is the best.'

She prompted you about friends, your favourite subjects and lunchtime activities. Your answers were short and sweet as you coloured away. She changed the subject and moved on to all the things you loved to do at home and you were more than happy to chatter the session away with her.

The third session, Dad and I were to drop you off, and leave you alone with Alison. You came home and announced that you had a new name for Alison and you were going to call her the '*Happy Lady*'; your two reasons being she was helping our family be happy again and she was always so happy and made you feel happy when you were with her. Your time spent with her was definitely predominant in your behaviour when you became upset. You seemed so much more relaxed and when you became angry it didn't take you as long to calm down once more. So very proud of you and relieved for us all to have this helping hand.

The fourth session we were all to attend, including Zane so she could watch you interact with him and see how we all rolled as a family unit. The fifth session was you and Alison once again and our sixth and final visit was Dad and I alone. Alison let us know we were doing a great job in supporting you emotionally with your difficult days at school. She informed us that yes, your self-esteem was low, but we have dealt with it in time, before it got out of hand and formed into something more serious like Depression. And yes, you displayed signs of anxiety before bedtime as you were so stressed anticipating the coming school day. We were on the flip-side, getting tips to deal with your anger, self-esteem and forming anxiety. Also, the question of changing schools was brought up. She had mentioned it to you and you stated firmly, as you had done with Dad and I, you did not want to change schools as you had some good friends you did not want to leave behind. An important factor we kept coming back to as the situation became so dire.

Finishing term three and rolling into the final term of prep for me was a mixture of, thank god, we're nearly at the end, and oh my god, I can't believe we are nearly at the end. I was wanting it to be over, as much as I wasn't ready for it to be. You had such a big year of not only starting primary school but all the hurdles in between. I just wanted you to have such a wonderful first year and in a lot of ways you did. And in so many unpleasant ways, you did not. The last week you met your new teacher for Grade One, and she was a star.

2008 – GRADE ONE

The beginning of Grade One for you was also the beginning of something new for your little brother. Zane was starting three-year-old kinder and luckily, we had one week to settle you into Grade One before kinder began. You were such a sweet big brother wanting Zane to be safe and cared for at kinder. You commented more than once that you were worried for him. We assured you he would be fine, reminding you of the fun times you had at kinder and the good friends you made.

Week one started off so well for you. Your teacher was amazing and being new to the school, had a lot of enthusiasm and good intentions, getting to know the parents and those that put their hands up to help when they could, to spend any extra time with their children. I of course, was wanting your school year to be everything your first year of primary school was not, and obviously being a bit protective of you regarding your past year, wanted to be a presence in the classroom for you, so would put my hand up whenever I was needed.

In the second week of school, on the Tuesday, Zane began his first day of kinder. Unfortunately, the night before you had an episode where you came home from school in a terribly sad mood. You wouldn't speak to Dad or I about it, and of course it wasn't until bedtime where you cried for over an hour, that the story of your day came out. And it was *horrific* for a six-year-old to face at the beginning of a shiny, brand new year. There seemed to be a constant army of disgruntled butterflies attacking my stomach with the overwhelming feeling of, *'When is this all going to end?'* You had been pinched, pushed over, and teased. Yes, there was a bruise on your arm where a boy had pinched you. A boy who had been part of the same group that had tormented you last year. (*Tormented, is it too strong of a word? I don't think so*). I was beyond frustrated.

What should have been an exciting day for me, sending my youngest off to kinder, was anything but! I walked you into your classroom that morning, as you hugged Zane goodbye and told him to have fun on his first day. I had fifteen minutes to get him to kinder on time, kissed you and left.

East Karingal Pre-School was in eye-sight to Karingal Heights Primary School where Sally sent her girls, and bless her, she met us at kinder, to wish Zane a great first day. She had recently given birth to her son, Adam, who was the apple of her and her husband, Rob's eyes.

She approached me with a smile as she hugged your brother hello, asking how everything was going. It was just like that first time I met her, here on the same strip of footpath, four years earlier when you had started your kindergarten journey. I was so emotional, and when her eyes finally met mine, I burst into tears, explaining to her that I had to drop Zane off and go into your school to speak to the Vice Principal, as I needed the bullying to simply stop. I just wanted you to be okay, to be happy, to simply enjoy your days at school. Hell, you were going to be there most of your childhood; of course, I wanted you to enjoy it.

Explaining what had happened, Sally was so upset. *'I'm going with you.'* She wasn't asking.

There I was, the beginning of your little brothers' kinder journey and I was crying my eyes out for all the wrong reasons. It certainly wasn't how I envisioned this day. And the guilt I felt, explaining to your little brother that I couldn't stay, that I had to get to your school and help you. His little serious face! Always understanding and mature beyond his years. His kinder teacher Melanie, was so lovely after I had explained what had been happening to you, she assured me she would be there for your brother and wished me luck sorting it out.

Leaving to meet Sally in the car park, I saw another mother watching me. When my eyes met hers, she looked quickly away, as if embarrassed to be caught staring at me. *'I wouldn't want to look at me either'*, I thought. Red eyes and a runny nose! Her son, Liam, became your brother's mate for a few years to come, and she became a close friends.

Sally and I went back home to have a much-needed cup of tea as I rang the Vice Principal to make an appointment. Luckily, we could go in within the hour. Sitting opposite her in her office that morning I felt a sense of déjà vu. I explained what had happened to you the day before, as calmly as I could, not wanting to appear as if I were over reacting. Funnily enough, Sally lost it. Diplomatically of course! It was so refreshing looking back, seeing such a good friend step in and protect you. She expressed her outrage through her tears of frustration, not wanting to see you once again, fall into a bad place because of bullies. We left after we had discussed a plan of having you walk around the yard at recess and lunchtime with the yard duty teacher. It was a start.

But, of course, lunchtime was an hour and that was time you looked forward to playing on the play equipment and being with Jarrod and a new friend you had made, Max. So that plan did not last too long.

The weeks rolled into months. Aunty Nadine gave birth to Ava May and we took a day trip over to Pascoe Vale to welcome the newest addition to the family. You have always been such a wonderful older cousin to the young ones that came along. Caring, sweet, and gentle. It was so lovely to see— *a little human who felt so down about himself due to the way others treated him, treat others so kindly.* A testament of what a unique, special person you are.

For your seventh birthday you wanted to have some friends over after school, along with your old kinder-mates. You were happy and made to feel special and of course on the weekend we had all your favourite people over. Grammy and Poppy, Uncle Grant, Uncle Stuart, Aunty Leah, Thomas, and Ireland. Unfortunately, poor Thomas was hitting a bit of a ten-year-old rut himself and his attitude towards you wasn't very pleasant whatsoever. It was a relief when he left and we could cocoon you in happy, positive vibes once more before the school week began and the impending worry of, *'Will they leave you alone this week?'* started all over again. Interestingly enough, Aunty Leah gave you a spectacular book, called, *Go Away Mr. Worrythoughts.* It was a children's book, illustrated and written by Nicky Johnston, to help and encourage children to manage and overcome their anxiety.

(And what was so phenomenal for me as a mother with a little boy who worried about so many things, eight years later, I got to meet the lovely Nicky at a Beyond Blue Bash! What an amazing, small world).

Your teacher was beyond amazing, patient and understanding towards me as a mother who was often in, almost daily with another complaint, story, detailed saga whatever you want to call it. She was a treasure who often said, *'I remember when my children were little, Michelle, I was exactly the same. If we don't look out for them, no-one will. It's our job.'* Those words, every time I apologised to her for taking up her time. I appreciated her greatly. The school were blessed to have her and indeed a major factor in why we remained there firmly that year, plus the fact you were still determined to stay. You gradually became withdrawn and your appetite dissipated once more. You became sullen at home and quite rude to me. If there was even a slight argument between your brother and yourself you would become outraged before I even had a chance to speak a word, and you would yell,

'You always take his side!' Or, *'You never listen to me!'*

This of course was simply not true! But the way you felt was the way you felt! What saddened me to no end was when you felt I had let you down, any photo that I had put in your bedroom, whether it was a family photo or one of you and I, you would pull it out of its frame and scratch our faces off, or rip the photo in half. The day Grammy presented me with a laminator was the day I felt relief in the sense I could put our family back in your room and help you know you belonged and were loved, without you being able to destroy 'us' so easily.

We were spending an afternoon at Sally's, celebrating Caitlyn's birthday. There were ten of you children, all having a great time. Somehow, Emily got her finger jammed in the door when you were all running around playing 'hide and seek'. When I came upstairs to comfort Emily and see what was going on, I thought I would explain to the entire group of you children to be careful with the each other. Before Caitlyn could explain that her girlfriend had jammed Emily's fingers in the door, you had gone off in a fit to hide in Adam's room. It took Sally ten minutes to calm you, and realise you were freaking out because you thought we were going to blame you for the incident. That happened so often. It became sadly, so frustrating to me, I would have to prime myself to speak a particular way and in a light tone so I wouldn't set you off, for you to think I was angry or blaming you for anything. And in the end, I could fly in the room like Tinker Bell, blowing fairy-floss out of my backside singing the Sounds of Music and you would still freak out. *(Actually, I'd freak out at that image too!)* But seriously, it was like I was an abused wife tip-toeing around my drunken husband, afraid to set him off. And the seriousness of that statement, reflecting my feelings towards my seven-year-old son does not escape me.

Term 1, 2 and 3 had you reporting incidents of this group of boys throwing chip bark into your face whilst you were hanging onto the monkey-bars. Grabbing your legs and pulling you whilst you were on the monkey-bars, which had you face planting into the chip mulch. Kicked, punched, and bitten again. Of course, this all went along with the daily emotional bullying. I never doubted your encounter of your days. Your mood-swings over the past 18 months said it all, but to hear your friends tell me their version of the same story, filled me with dread. There was no exaggeration to the horrendous degrees of your days.

Talking to Dad about what else we could do, we were both in agreement to writing a friendly letter to the principal to express our concerns and see what we could all come up with to make your school days more enjoyable.

THE LETTER

TO WHOM IT MAY CONCERN

"I am writing this letter to voice my concerns regarding my son's wellbeing and happiness whilst he is at school.

For the past 18 months, Jesse has enjoyed his classes and has developed a good rapport with his teachers. My husband and I are happy with what the school has to offer Jesse and chose to send him to your school because of the curriculum and the surrounding school grounds, which we believed provided a comfortable environment for the children to play in. What concerns us at the moment has been ongoing and we believe it is affecting Jesse's confidence and health. The incidents that we know of to date are as follows:

2007 – Bitten on shoulder / punched in stomach / constant emotional bullying.

2008 – Pinched / pushed over / kicked / sand and mulch thrown into his face / pulled off monkey-bars / bitten (twice) / being teased, called a loser, and excluded from a number of games. To name a few!

These briefly outline some of the uncomfortable situations our son deals with almost daily. He is happy in the classroom and adores his teacher, whom I know to be a wonderful educator. But the fact is this: *he does not feel comfortable or safe in the lunchtime break. It is much too long, and Jesse feels vulnerable and is an easy target for certain children to bully.*

When he is coming home from school sad and down on himself, saying he isn't *'cool'* enough for anyone to want to play with, is heart-breaking. He has completely lost his appetite of a school morning and barely eats at lunchtime, as he is *'worried what someone might do to him today.'*

This is unacceptable. A child of seven *(any age really)* should look forward to their school day, to want to play with friends and feel safe. In his own words Jesse has said he doesn't feel good at playtime as there is, *'No-one to look after me.'* I understand the school's situation with one teacher on yard duty, but with the lunch-break being so long, and the school's grounds quite large, it certainly leaves children with a lot of time on their hands, and not always someone looking over their shoulder.

Jesse is not an assertive boy within uncomfortable circumstances and we feel the treatment he is receiving in the playground is making him become withdrawn. I'd just like to end this letter in regard to past chats with the Vice Principal. Thank you for listening and making the time to discuss any issues I have had with Jesse being bullied. It is hard trying to communicate a sensible plan of action to protect your son, when you are feeling so emotional and helpless to stop the bullying then and there.

I do have a list of the boys' names and their offences against Jesse. If you need them, please let me know. We simply want Jesse to look forward to school and enjoy his days with you, not just for his education but as equally important, his social growth.

Sincerely MW

Now, I thought that was a nice letter to your school, let's face it, it could have gone a whole other way, but no, it was polite and calm. No form of abuse or accusations. But unfortunately, what I did not realise was, that addressing a letter in such a way was frowned upon by said Principal, as it was now a formal complaint. Was it really so different from any other complaint I had been making? Yes, apparently it was.

Going into the office the following morning, the Principal walked past me without a glance, or polite hello. Nothing! The Vice Principal who had always been sympathetic, supportive, and approachable ushered me into her office followed by, *'The Principal is furious, Michelle'* in a not-so-friendly tone.

As unhappy, or to be more accurate, uncomfortable as this made me, it was neither relevant, or my problem. After 18 months of not only your unhappiness but the affect it had on our entire family, it really had to be dealt with once and for all. And Dad and I were hoping this was the answer. It certainly seemed to be for a while, and the last term of 2008 went a lot more smoothly. Yes, there were still incidents along the way, but you were gaining more confidence and didn't seem as deeply affected by the boys that were a thorn in all of our sides.

It was, essentially a wonderful school, and was appreciated by so many others and like every other school before the beginning of time, there are, unfortunately troubled kids that come from troubled families in every suburb, state, and country, that sadly can affect the lives of others. Simple fact of life! The good and the bad. Like politicians! In time, after getting to know some of the families' backgrounds, I explained to you, in an appropriate way for a seven-year-old to comprehend, these poor boys may not have had what you have, may not be lucky enough to get three meals a day, a bath, or a cuddle before bed.

In saying that, arsehole kids also come from loving, happy homes too. (*Is that harsh? Should I call them challenging, or troubled?*) No, I'm sorry if it offends, but I will keep it real. And of course, if I need to clarify, I am definitely not talking about our special children with special needs, or mental health issues. I am simply talking about down and out, nasty children that as yet have not discovered how to behave the correct way, in treating others with respect. Although we all know some adults don't we, who never grow out of that nasty phase! That's humans for you.

Another mother had pulled her son out of the school due to not getting anywhere with the same group of bullies harassing her son. He was happy to go and did not put up any resistance, whereas you were firm in your stance not wanting to go anywhere else. It was such a difficult battle. Knowing you needed to go elsewhere, but whilst you were slowly beginning to gain your happy personality back, there was no way Dad and I wanted to take the chance of backward steps or disrupting the harmony that was slowly coming back into our home.

Looking back I wish we had. I wish we had grabbed you out by your little arms, perhaps kicking and screaming and plonked you down somewhere else where surely, eventually you would have happily settled. Another mark against me, as a mother, for not making a firm decision sooner. Maybe I'm an arsehole too? Why was I so scared to go against your wishes and make the decision to do the right thing for my son? Yes, you may have been unbearable to live with for a time while your worry dissipated, but it's not like living with you up until this point had been all peaches and cream.

The answer is so obviously clear. Living with a void of darkness for 18 months, watching the little human you created with the love of your life, simply not cope, not be his happy self, to watch him become something other than feeling he is loved or worthy, for me as a mum, I was too afraid to do anything else that may set you back further than where you were.

2009 - GRADE TWO

One day in the middle of term two, I was pulled into your classroom after school, to be informed that you retaliated and stood firm to one of your bullies. You had been playing a ball game with one of your friends, when the group of boys approached you, demanding you give them the ball. You and your friend exchanged a glance and you said no. One of the smaller bullies had a large stick and lunged forward poking you in the stomach, of course making you drop the ball. Your little friend was quick to grab the ball before the bully boys could, which unfortunately caused him to get a whack with the stick also. This resulted in him crying, which set you off. Apparently, you screamed at the boys and as they ran off, you chased them. Someone yelled for the teacher; they dropped the ball and the leader of the group dashed into the out-of-bounds building during lunchtime. You had grabbed the ball and followed him in, where you threw the ball as hard as you could into his face once he turned around to tell you to rack off!

The entire group of you had been pulled into a room for a full report on what had gone down and as the six of you retold basically the same story to the teacher, I received a pretty clear version from your teacher that afternoon.

She stood there, chest puffed out looking like a proud rooster. She was actually letting me know this was such a wonderful thing, that at seven years of age you had started to learn to defend yourself. We both agreed that it was watching your little friend get hit with the stick that set you off, but this was also a good thing. You were loyal and defending a mate. Unfortunately, the following day your little friend was sick which left you alone and an easy target to get chased and hit with a stick during lunchtime. Apparently, you were told, *'Pay-back's a bitch.'* And this at Grade Two! Charming!

Sadly, you weren't just feeling a target at school, but also with Cousin Thomas as time went on. There were times we would make the trip down to see Aunty when Thomas had his weekends with his father, but I still loved seeing my nephew and having all the cousins together, so we would also plan to go down when he was home for the weekend.

On this particular day, after travelling two hours to get to Drysdale, you were excited to see that Thomas had one of his mates over. You had met him on previous visits. He was a rough and tumble boy, as he had three brothers to contend with, but had always been nice to you and your brother. Thomas and he were about to take off down to the creek to see if they could find some tadpoles. It was shallow enough and you had been down there before. I was not worried in the slightest and was thinking, *'Yes, my boy is about to go and have some decent, relaxing time with his older cousin and mate!'*

Aunty and I were relaxing with a cup of tea and some catch up chat, whilst Ireland and Zane played out in the sandpit. It was one of my favourite places to go. I loved Drysdale. Aunty and I said if she were to go to her beach, and I to the Frankston pier, looking over the waters of

Port Phillip Bay, we could see each other. It was a nice thought. I loved her dearly. As much as she was my twin she was one of my best friends too. No matter what the world threw at us, we always stood firm together. But our relationship hit the occasional rocky road once I had you and your brother. And the best thing about that, speaking to so many other sisters, their relationships were the same. Peaches and cream, and then once the kids started coming, rocky roads. I had one mother tell me, how much she absolutely adored her sister and her nieces. Once her own children hit a certain age, she said her sister found it difficult not to step in and parent them or offer her unwanted opinion, along with always blaming her kids when the cousins had a to-do, which drove her crazy, and having a very strong personality would step in and they would have their own World War.

I think that's global. We become parents and, after giving birth, as mothers we develop our inner animal. Tigers go to any length to protect their cubs. I have seen the most elegant, educated mother, turn into a snarling, feral animal when she thought her child was endangered or being threatened in even the slightest way.

So, the moment of enjoying a relaxing cup of tea with my sister, did not last more than twenty minutes. Seven-year-old Jesse, came in the front door, wet, covered in mud with a frown on your face. Thomas and his mate twenty steps behind shouting, *'He was trying to hit us with a stick.'*

And rightly so after the little angels (NOT) began by teasing you and threatened to throw you in the creek. The stick was your self-defence that did not protect you against two boys, three years older and much bigger than you. And yes, sadly you ended up in the creek.

So, you were unhappy, and Thomas and friend got a talking to, with Aunty ending the sentence with, *'Well, it's their rite-of-passage, isn't it, being older.'* I don't know how many times I heard that over the following years. *Rite-of-passage for this and rite-of-passage for that!* I wanted to roll my eyes every time she said it. Maybe it should have been my rite-of-passage to slap Thomas's backside all the times he was a horrid cousin to you?

And even though, as the years flowed by, you were such a wonderful big cousin to Ireland, there were occasional times I would be so protective of her and disappointed in you, if I saw or heard you treat her in a similar, although never as horrific way, as Thomas had treated you. But you were always sorry afterwards and especially if you made her cry, you would do or give her anything to make her smile again. Cousins can end up being best friends for life if they are steered positively in the right direction.

After you were given a nice bath, and clean clothes, you ended up doing something for Thomas, which kept you busy and made him happy for a while. You cleaned his room. And over the years, hearing Aunty mention what a mess Thomas' room was, you were always the first to get in and clean it. You were a doer, and a pleaser. And as unpleasant as Thomas could be to you at times, you always loved a trip away to your cousin's house. You actually loved car trips and travelling in general. You seemed to go into a bit of a coma, very quiet and deep in thought, relaxed and calm. Dad and I found it amusing over the years when we would pack the car together, everyone putting in their own pillows, or favourite blankets etc. Then we would go back in the house, have a cup of tea whilst making sure everything was locked up tight. We'd call out *'toilet time'* before we all got in the car, only to realise you were missing. And there you were already. Sitting in the car with your seat belt on and ready to go. And you were the same on the trip home. We'd be packing the car up and getting ready to say goodbye to whoever it was we were visiting at the time and there you were, sitting in the car, buckled in and ready to go without so much as a goodbye to our loved ones. I could understand your enjoyment of travelling, being taken away somewhere to escape it all. I know for Dad as a child, one of his favourite places to holiday away to was Wedderburn, which is crazy as that's half an hour down the road from Inglewood where my family spent Christmas and Easter holidays. *(Small world)*.

As a young girl, I had two favourite places I loved to go to. One was cousin Kylie and Nadine's, *who appeared to live-the-dream* of two young girls in a lavish double-storey house in Coburg, in-ground pool with side spa; anything their hearts' desired was theirs. Their mum, my darling Aunt Dorothy, was the most sophisticated, elegant woman. She was one-of-a-kind and made an enormous impact on all who met her. She spoilt two country girls whenever she had the chance. Aunty Leah and I were living the dream when we holidayed there! And on the opposite side of the tracks, my other favourite place to get away, was in Warrnambool with very special people — Peter, Kerrie, and Rory Fletcher. *(Poor Rory, Aunty made him pee on the electric fence around the stallion's paddock in Glenormiston once. Poor kid didn't know what hit him!)*

The time we spent with them was both healing and therapeutic, where we were allowed to simply be, two young girls enjoying time away, taking long walks with Rory along the quiet back roads to get to the Warrnambool beach and watching the Karate Kid over and over again. Whenever I hear, *Cruel Summer* by Bananarama, I think of those wonderful days with a family that loved us unconditionally and were so generous with the time they had with us and treated us like we were their own. They were the holidays I wanted for you too. To get away, feel loved and like you belonged to more than just one place.

You had had a few sleep-overs with Aunty, Thomas and Ireland by yourself and at Grammy and Poppy's, but that stopped when you were in Grade One. Poor Grammy drove an hour to Doncaster, we met her half-way and she took you off for what was supposed to be a four-night holiday, which unfortunately ended the next day as you wanted to come back home. And being the love she was, not wanting to make you unhappy (or herself!) as you had been having such a hard time of it, drove two hours from Heathcote to Frankston, to get you back where you wanted to go. Now that is a dedicated, loving grandmother.

*****

As the school year progressed and coming close to the end of term two, you were getting more tired and down. We were reaching the point where soon something had to give.

And then the family received some devastatingly sad news that Aunt Dorothy had passed away. It was a painful time for Nana Lyn, as she had lost not only her sister, but best friend and of course for poor Aunty Nadine and Kylie losing their mum. I made the decision with Dad, not to take you to the funeral in Inglewood. I believed at the time, it was something you did not need to be part of and wanted to save you from the overwhelmingly sad atmosphere in general. It's not that I don't believe in taking children to funerals, not at all. We all need to learn about death and celebrate the passing of a loved one. But there was no way whilst you were in the headspace you were in, I wanted you to be a part of it. I simply wanted Dad and Sally to get you to and from school and for you to enjoy the fun activities Sally had planned for you all in the afternoons before Dad collected you after he finished work. Was it so wrong to want to protect you from thinking about anything sad for the time being? The worry of wondering how you would react during this time? For some family members, yes it was. They couldn't understand why your Dad did not come and pay his respects. That was simple. Dad stayed behind to be the rock and routine for you, which you needed so much at this stage in your life. I believe me being there was enough to represent the Aunt I loved so dearly, but that's family for you. You cannot make every bastard happy, and we'd be crazy to try.

BREAKTHROUGH, FOR A MOMENT

Whenever we received a phone call from your teacher with another event of you being bullied, we would ask, *'Are you ready to move to a different school yet, mate?'* You would reply, *'No, my friends are here.'* Your replies would become less enthusiastic, so without your knowledge I had been head hunting other schools.

Amongst those, I rang Karingal Heights and had a chat to one of the lovely office ladies Pam, stating that you had been bullied for a number of years and we weren't making any progress sorting the situation out and felt it was time to make a move. Pam informed me, in these situations it was best to sort it out with our school and probably be in your best interest to leave you were you were. Of course, not knowing the entire story, I'm sure that's what they have to say. I felt frustrated and was down for about five seconds, before I rang the school back, slightly disguising my voice. (I was an extra on T.V for commercials and some brilliant Melbourne shows when Dad was a stuntman, so could easily play the part!) I basically asked for a tour as my four-year-old kinder boy was starting prep next year. Worked like a charm, I had a tour booked with the very charming Principal the following day. I didn't discuss my plans with anyone. I felt it was something I had to do on my own, go through on my own and make a firm decision if this was the best place for you. The Principal was of course, very informative and enjoyed promoting the school in its best light, chatting away about all the new buildings that were taking place, the programs it offered the preps and extra activities. I knew immediately it was the right place for both my sons. As we passed by the library, there was Sally, stacking books, always volunteering to do something for anyone who needed a hand. When she spotted me with the Principal she was as shocked to see me there, as I was at the tears that lodged in my throat. We had a big hug, with the Principal looking on, slightly uncomfortable at my growing emotional state. Sally asked, *'Are you here for Zane or Jesse?'*

'Both,' I answered quietly. At this stage, the Principal thought I was here as a new prep mum.

She easily spotted my deer in the headlights moment and said, *'I'll be finished here in ten minutes. Come to mine for a cuppa when you are done.'* She hugged me again, smiled at the Principal and went back to her task.

The Principal looked at me, with questioning eyes when I confessed that yes, I certainly was here for my kinder boy, but also, I was seeing if there was a place for my eight-year-old son who was in Grade Two and had been constantly bullied. As I spoke he could see I was restraining myself against my tears. It was so hard trying to relay simple facts without becoming emotional. It's like when you are telling someone a story and you say, - *'I couldn't stop crying,'* and then you start crying! It's adding the emotion to the word that trips us up. Unless you have a heart of stone.

He was a professional and helped me out of the hole I almost fell into, letting me know there was probably, most certainly a place for you and he would ring me in the afternoon to confirm, stating if that was the case, you could start as early as next week. I thanked him, we finished the tour and I was on my way to Sally's.

I sat in the car for a few minutes, my mind a whirlwind of thoughts and hopes. Firstly, how I was going to convince you, once and for all, it was time to move on. By the time I walked up Sally's pretty garden path, she had the kettle re-boiling, with the sweet smell of French Earl Grey steeping in the tea pot. It was exactly what I needed. Sitting at her polished table, she asked, *'How did you go?'*

I nodded, my hands wrapped around a steaming cup. *'I loved it. It felt so right, it feels like such a great school. The Principal was awesome and said he would give me a call this afternoon to confirm if Jesse has a place as early as next week.'*

'How do you think Jesse will take it?' She asked offering one of her famous raspberry and white chocolate muffins.

I shook my head, smiling no, *'I don't know. He has been fighting us for so long not to move schools. It could go either way.'* I sighed, looking out at her English garden in the back, lined with pretty citrus trees. *'God, I haven't even told Jade. I need to ring him.'*

'Do it now,' she said kindly, *'before the Principal rings you back. That way you have kept him in the loop.'*

I took my tea and my mobile out the front to sit in her garden, as I called Dad. Of course, as soon as I mentioned I had done a school tour with the Principal at Karingal Heights, I burst into tears. It was such an emotional time. *'Did you now?'* he asked in a non-judging way. *'How did it go?'*

So, I told him all about it and I could hear the relief in his voice that it may be as early as next week that our new beginning may take place. We contemplated what I was going to say to your school and Dad said, *'You deal with it the way you need to.'* It was dealing with you we were more worried about. I paced as we ended the call. Then I rang Grammy to get her thoughts. She said as long as we could get you on board, that was her main concern. I'd have to wait till Nana Lyn finished work that night, before I could fill her in.

Sally came out with the tea pot to top up my cup and offered to pick Zane up from kinder so I could make a phone call to your school and explain my situation.

It was an uncomfortable phone call to make. I sincerely thought that once my child started at school, he would be at that school till the end. I felt like a traitor, like we were the ones doing something wrong. I think we have been blessed to have lovely office ladies at both schools and as one of the ladies answered the phone and I began to tell her of our situation, I became a puddle of tears. She knew our story as she had answered the phone the past two and a half years when I had rung, distraught and upset. She was a mother also and completely understood. I could hear the sympathy in her tone and she reassured me whatever decision we made, it was the right one for you. That's what I needed to hear and hanging up, I allowed myself a good cry in private before Sally arrived home with Zane.

We spent the rest of the day there, had lunch and contemplated how we were going to break the news to you that we were finally moving schools, whilst Zane was occupied with Emily's play doh and Mr. Potato Head. Then we had a light bulb moment, of taking Caitlyn's spare uniform and simply hanging it on the back of our kitchen chair.

I received a phone call from your new Principal with a yes, there was a placement for you and they were happy for you to start next week. I was beyond elated.

Zane and I got home twenty minutes before I had to collect you from school and we hung Caitlyn's uniform over the back of the kitchen chair. I knew exactly what I was going to say to you when you got home from school and I had my fingers crossed it was the right thing, with hopefully the right effect. Once we collected you, I asked you how you enjoyed your day. You were loving what you were learning in Science and chatted about that on the drive home and up into the house. You went to hang your bag up when you spotted Caitlyn's uniform.

'*What's that doing here?*' you asked.

'*Oh, Sally lent it to us for Zane to try on, as we are going to send Zane to Caitlyn and Emily's school next year.*' I went into the kitchen, pretending to shuffle around, my eyes not leaving your face, waiting.

You walked off into your bedroom to get changed out of your uniform whilst I got afternoon tea ready. Zane was chatting away about how he couldn't wait to start school. You both sat up at the kitchen table and ate afternoon tea. You certainly were quieter than when we picked you up from school. I waited you out, giving you time. You went outside to feed your animals, then jump on the trampoline before some ABC 3 time (ah the days before Foxtel!) and I caught up on some housework I had missed whilst being at Sally's all day, getting tea ready, my mind feeling like a ticking time bomb waiting to go off. It wasn't too long, before I felt your stare, watching whilst I stuffed the cannelloni with ricotta, spinach, and shredded chicken thigh. My stomach tightened, and I thought, '*Here we go.*'

I smiled at you as I washed my hands and sprinkled the top of the pasta dish with the pasta sauce and grated cheese, before popping it into the oven. '*What's up, mate?*'

'*I've been thinking.*' You were so serious. '*I think I better go to Caitlyn's school too, so I can look after Zane.*' Just like that! My heart nearly exploded with relief.

I told myself to be calm, do not act like an excited lunatic. '*Be calm, be calm.*' I nodded slowly, '*I think that's a great idea, mate, if that's what you want to do.*' Make him feel in control, like it's his idea! '*You are so clever. Why didn't I think of that?*' I smiled at you. You smiled back and came into my arms for a cuddle. Yes, of course, I swallowed back tears. This was it! It was really happening, and it was your decision! It's so hard to put into words the pure joy a parent feels, when the belief of all the negative pain will stop. That all the heartache is finally at an end and we can simply live like other normal families. (Yeah, I know there's no such thing as normal, but you know what I mean!)

When Dad came home from work, you bounced up to him, announcing that you were going to go to a different school. As he scooped you up for a big cuddle, his eyes met mine over your head. I nodded, a big smile on my face. His eyes shone with relief and happiness. This was it! A brand new fresh start!

You were to start the following Thursday, so I thought that by telling your teacher your last day was on Wednesday, that would give her plenty of time to throw you a going away party. After all, a few kids that had moved from the school for many reasons, had gotten a party. When I picked you up on your last day, I asked if you had a party. You said no, but your friends were sad to see you go. I thought poo to the teacher and good riddance anyhow! This was your new beginning!

2009 - KARINGAL HEIGHTS PRIMARY SCHOOL GRADE TWO: BREATHE

This was it, your very first day at your new school. I felt like a new prep mother all over again and justifiably so, my feelings of protectiveness were enormous. I was ready to rip anyone's throat out if they so much as looked at you the wrong way. Not that anyone would ever see that side of me. I was all politeness and smiles, wanting to fit in for your sake, as nervous as you probably were. I was so proud when you went into your new classroom, and hearing some of your old kinder friends exclaim in happiness, *'Look, Jesse's here.'* That's all I needed to hear to breathe easy and get on with my day. First up, with Sally and our kinder mums we went to Degani's for a cup of tea to celebrate your new day. Sally bestowed upon me, a gorgeous gift of a fairy statue, representing happiness and freedom. It was the perfect gift and meant so much that she would think to mark this wonderful day for us both, after you had been through so very much.

Grammy was travelling down to surprise you after school, wanting this to be a special day for you. When it was time to collect you, we walked past your teacher commenting to another staff member, *'I mean I really can't believe it, it was just disgusting, we often end up with the troubled ones.'*

My heart sank, I knew without a doubt she was talking about you. Not because of what she said, but the way she went bright red when her eyes met mine, and she realized she'd been overheard. Great!

I smiled at her and passed Zane's hand to Grammy as the teacher said, *'Oh, Michelle, can I chat to you for a second?'*

'Yes,' I replied, my heart sinking with a nervous drop. I had to remember I wasn't the one in trouble. But, we are a team. When you're in trouble, I'm in trouble. David Bowie's *Under Pressure* started playing in my head as I followed her into the empty classroom, as you were all out at sport. She began by telling me, that apparently, you told another boy, to go suck a big fat, well, unfortunately, a big fat dick! You were joking, but no one else thought it was very funny. I was dying on the spot. Absolutely dying! I couldn't have been more embarrassed if I'd farted loudly, shat myself and had diarrhoea running down my legs. (Well maybe I would have, it's debatable!) I tried to reassure her, that was just not you, and that it was my belief that it was first day jitters and you were simply trying to fit in. That you were, essentially a very good student and had never been in trouble a day at school in your short two and a half years! It wasn't the time or place for me to explain, we had not been *kicked* out of your old school, that it was actually our decision due to the terrible bullying you had endured. Didn't they do a background check? If they had, they would have found out you were a wonderful, attentive student, who had only been absent ten days in the two and a half years you were with your old school. I don't know what schools did in general, but unfortunately for some, if you didn't come

to them in prep, then you weren't considered, *'theirs.'* Ridiculous I know.

Taking you home that afternoon, in my embarrassment of having a talking to for the first time in your school life, I lectured you about your language and I didn't want to hear about you speaking like that again! The sparkle of your new day quickly faded as you went into your bedroom cross and unhappy with yourself. It was definitely not how I wanted your first day to go. It seemed to be the running theme for first times for you, and I could hear Freddie singing, *'Another one bites the dust.'* You didn't come out of your room for ages, and I decided to go in and talk to you whilst Grammy played with Zane.

I began by saying that I understood how you must have been so nervous and excited all at once, as I too had changed primary schools from Koroit Primary school to Woolsthorpe Primary School in prep. I reassured you I wasn't cross any more about your language as long as it did not happen again. You told me how happy you were that your old kinder friends made you feel welcome, but another boy who went to a different kinder kept calling you a freak and it hurt your feelings, so you told him to go suck a you-know-what. I got it. I really did. We had a cuddle, you had a late afternoon tea and then went and spent some quality time with Grammy before Dad came home from work. She was very relieved to see you happy once more.

I believe it was in fourth term, parent teacher interviews, that your teacher couldn't express her delight in discovering what a sweet, caring student you actually were. *'Oh, Jesse is just so lovely it is such a pleasure to have him in our classroom.'* A comment I had heard repeatedly over the years, it was no surprise to me, that an intelligent woman would finally come to this conclusion.

*****

It was such a peaceful time watching you as the weeks slowly rolled on, to see you coming home each afternoon after school, genuinely smiling. You become good mates with one of the boys you went to kinder with and after a couple of weeks, began to have play-dates at each other's house once a week after school. Zane's fourth birthday was such a celebration and it was so good to have your new friends over, plus Jarrod, to go crazy on the giant jumping castle with Zane and his kinder friends. What a brilliant day it was. The sun was shining, and looking back at the photos, I had titled the album, *'Life's Great.'* That's how good it totally felt; as if the clouds had lifted, leaving only warmth and a chance to simply enjoy the feeling of calm in our home after so many days, weeks, months, years of waiting for you to explode, cry, rage, despair. Finally, finally we had reached a tranquil platform that wasn't tilting us in any unfavourable direction. Dad and I, our arms around each other, so relaxed and happy, not a care in the world. Only three weeks at your new school and we were new people.

We were so happy with our decision to choose Karingal Heights Primary School. A little over 200 students it was small, welcoming and it did not take us too long to feel as if we were a part of the school's community. One thing I appreciated about the Principal; he greeted students and parents alike as they entered through the main building and at the end of the day, made sure to say farewell to as many students as he could as they left through the back gate. The staff was amazing and like all schools, different parents' personalities either collided or connected with the teachers, resulting in their own battles or smooth transitions as the school year went along.

Your Grade Three teachers were lovely, and you settled into your first full year at the school well, especially as Zane was now there, starting prep. He had his best mate Liam with him and started off his school life, fairly confidently.

At the end of each day, I enjoyed coming into the corridor and peeking through the classroom window watching you sit happily amongst your peers. Over the course of that year, as other mums peeked in at their children also, we would chat about our kids, what we'd been doing that day and general conversations you have with other parents you don't fully know but have the common denominator of being mums with kids at school. One lovely mother in particular stood out to me, with her softly spoken voice communicating gently her love for her partner and children. It took me months to build a solid and lasting friendship with this lady due to her shyness — *Jacqui Jefferson*. She is one of your biggest supporters, and what I loved about her, as we really got to know each other over the coming years with all your battles and heartache, her softly spoken voice was quick to vanish and turn to razor sharp icicles if someone as much as looked at you the wrong way. Loyalty. It's so wonderful to have for one's children, when others are so quick to judge and lash out. I'm sure many, many mothers can relate to this.

*****

Coming into September, Aunty decided to throw us a double birthday bash down in Drysdale. Her house was stunning with its beach views and short walk directly onto the open sands; it was pure paradise for adults and kids alike. Somewhere completely relaxing to sit quietly or enjoy a big social gathering with plenty of food, music, conversations, and laughter. It was on this occasion, well after midnight when most party guests had left and all you kids were sleeping; that gave Aunty and I some much-needed catch up and communication time. We talked about all our trials of motherhood and I relayed to Aunty all the emotions having to watch you struggle for years, with seemingly simple things, and how brilliant it was to finally see you be such a happy little boy once more. Aunty opened up about her guilt of not always being the most understanding aunt to you. Yes, she always loved you, but often couldn't figure you out and had difficulty at times, treating you the way you deserved to be treated as her little nephew. Sadly, some of the things she had said in the past, influenced the way Thomas treated you. Although it was good to hear her confess that she did feel guilty, it saddened me to a degree also. My sister had been through so much and life had not always been as kind to her as it should have. There were times as I have said, I was disappointed in the way she spoke to and treated you, but in many ways, she was a wounded little bird, simply trying to survive this world the best she could whilst raising her own babies and dealing with obstacles that life kept throwing at her. At the end of the day she was a survivor too. When she finally found her true, worthy love, my heart rejoiced for her as she became that whole, happy individual that was always there, just too afraid to come out and bloom.

I was always supportive of my sister, but because of the way she treated you at times as the years went by, I had built up a wall between us and did not often show her the real me, where I could sit back, laugh and be genuinely warm and honest with her. Half the time I felt she was not interested in a thing I had to say, especially if it concerned you; my wall would go higher. It took me a long time to forgive her, and when the day came, many years later, that she stood before me and said, *'Your struggle has been real, it has been such a long journey and I never knew how hard it was for you, or Jesse. I simply thought he was a little shit, the way he spoke to you at times, the way he was. I didn't understand, I didn't know. I never got him. They say ignorance is bliss but that's no excuse. Out of everybody in this world, I should have been there for you, for Jesse. I'm so sorry. I am here for you now.'*

Hearing those words, from my twin, who I loved so much, for me, was like world peace being announced. All the hurt and disappointment that had built up over the years, simply slipped away into a thick fog of forgiveness. To be able to put my arms around her, cry with her and feel all my love for her return was simply bliss. My heart was healed.

I apologised to her also. You were my son. She was my sister. I should have been there to look after and protect you both, be more aware and understanding of her mental health issues. *Like Aunty Louise says, we, all of us, have them at one point or another in our lives. Life's about conflict, resolution and if we are lucky enough, forgiveness.* And not just for the person we are forgiving, but for ourselves.

The Disney movie, Frozen, had a point. Theme Song*: LET IT GO!*

So, this particular conversation was two things, *very cleansing and extremely revealing*. Unfortunately, what was also said, was sad for me to hear as a mum, when my sister confessed to talking with some of my friends, who were not as loyal to you and I as I thought. It was heartbreaking for me to hear some of the nasty, petty, malicious, cowardly back-stabbing comments that had derived from some people's mouths. So-called adults. Debatable for sure. A couple of comments; *'You were nothing but a pain, always causing some upset no matter what the occasion,'* and *'There must have been something seriously wrong with you,'* they had said. That I was *soft* and allowed your behaviour to continue. Bad, weak parenting. Were they nuts?

As Aunty filled me in, letting me know some of my friends weren't the friends I thought they were, I had a flash back, to a moment, two years prior to this conversation. It hit me with such clarity. I was showing a group of friends a photo of you, your brother, and cousins at the Inglewood Christmas party— all your sweet happy faces looking directly into the camera as I had directed. A couple of my friends were saying how cute you all looked, when I pointed to your round little face smiling at us, saying, *'Look how happy Jesse looks here!'* when one of my friends said quickly and loudly, pointing excitedly to Zane, without commenting whatsoever about you, *'Oh, look at Zane, he's so adorable!'* Yeah. Thanks. So, one of my kids you like, so, that's ok then is it? Bloody hell, I remember at the time smiling as I put the photograph down to make the next round of tea, telling myself not to be hurt that she had overlooked you. But that conversation with Aunty, brought back a few painful memories of how some people had let us down over the years by simply being shallow, judgemental, unsupportive uneducated arseholes.

I remember the time I politely made the round of phone calls to said friends, to let them know yes, my sister had relayed their shared conversations over the past few years, where you and I had been spoken of unfavourably and in future if they had anything else to say regarding their thoughts on you as a child, and me as a parent, say it to my face.

All gardens need to be tended with care, love, and a certain passion for its survival, and at times need to be totally re-landscaped. Even the prettiest of weeds can be destructive to a well-bedded garden, and once removed allows the most beautiful blooms and plants to grow harmoniously together.

Friends are exactly the same. They come into our lives for a reason and for a time. If they are the friends we select as our family, they stay forever if we are blessed enough to have them for that long; their warm, honest blooms filling our lives with a sense of that sunshine we humans need to grow healthily and happily.

It's not about being cliquey, bitchy, cold, or cruel. It's all about selecting those you feel you can be the very best *you* with. Like Uncle Stuart has said often, *'If you lie down with dogs, you're going to get fleas.'* I discovered this to be very true at one, short stage of my life, before I took the pruners out and cut a particular weed away and did what I had to do for the happiness of myself and my family. I hadn't lost too many friends over the years. Some were simply poison and had to be removed. Others slipped away due to life's path, and those I miss to this day.

Theme song for removing unwanted, damaging friends; The Angels: *Am I ever gonna see your face again.* (Unfortunately, yet therapeutically, at my high school re-union in 2015, I decided, thanks to many glasses of red wine, to add on a couple of extra words after the famous, *'No way get fucked fuck offline.* I think my dear high school friends Robbo and Brendan, appreciated it at the time. Unfortunately, others did not. Sorry!)

*****

Your year in Grade Three was wonderful all in all and you celebrated your ninth birthday at Skate World surrounded by new and old friends alike. Looking back at the photographs, seeing your cheeky smile radiating with pride and joy, you were so happy with your new lease on life, which gave your Dad and I the same new lease. It was so lovely when most of our relatives mentioned to us how great it was to see you so very happy. I was constantly, mentally, high-fiving myself with disbelief that life could feel so easy breezy and chilled! There was absolutely no way my smile was coming off my face! The year continued along with happy school days and play-dates with mates, swimming or skating after school, beach trips and general kids' activities we continued with all our friends. We kept busy as a family on the weekends, where one day was usually spent on a day trip searching for crabs and exploring the rock pools along our gorgeous coastline and the other day was spent tidying the yard, and cleaning up after chooks, your pet rats, mice, rabbits and guinea-pigs, fish, cats, and several different breeds of birds, making sure to leave accessible water for the family of possums that lived in our gum tree, plus Summer! We even had a beautiful duck we allowed to swim in our old pool. She was my pride and joy and did not last longer than a week before I had to return her to the farm we bought her from, as she was a tad noisy, and Dad was worried she would upset the neighbours! Thoughtful man that he is!

That's something that worried you, even as a toddler. You always fretted that the animals were going to die. You were eight when our first cat Bonnie, had to be put down. You handled her death quite well and didn't seem too stressed at the time. But over time, as you got older, you constantly fretted that *someone* was going to hurt the animals, or if we were away on holidays, our friends wouldn't look after them properly and they would all be dead when we got back. You would become angry with me, if I didn't get the cats inside around five pm, saying, *'If anything happens to them it's going to be your fault.'*

You understood death. You were two when my Nana passed (Nana Lyn's mother) and of course, losing Aunt Dorothy. I believe most kids ask about death and it is normal to ask a lot of questions. Yours weren't really questions, more getting ready to blame me if anything were to happen to our animals. You never blamed Dad, just me. Always! But, I overlooked it all and moved on, as the sun was still shining so brightly in our direction, and if I knew what was coming, I would have basked, naked daily in its rays and soaked it all up for as long as I could without a single care in the world!

Let us reflect on an interesting word, that in the moment does not do us any good whatsoever and I am sure a lot of parents can rejoice in how meaningless this word is, right alongside me. Hindsight. I, with many of my comrades, discovered the uselessness of this word plenty in the coming years. Hindsight and mosquitoes. What good are they?

2011 - GRADE FOUR

Our beautiful, caring, funny, smart, stubborn nine-year-old. Another great year for you, with only a handful of disturbing episodes that trickled in to upset our new-found balance. One of them being a trip to the dentist. Zane was Grade One and it was his second trip to the dentist. You had been a couple of times for check-ups. Sitting in the waiting room you did not speak but sat very still with your arms folded.

Zane was snuggling in my arms, chatting quietly away about what he wanted to do after school that day. I quietly asked you if you were okay. You would nod, licking your lips not meeting my eyes. When your names were called, we walked in and my hopes for you being seen to one at a time, so I could support you individually, came crashing down as one nurse wanted to see Zane and another called you over to a separate chair. I was torn. How could I choose whose hand I would hold first? I could see you looking at me as the dental nurse continued saying, *'Come on, you're a big boy, you don't need Mum.'*

Zane was gripping onto my hand as he sat back in the big chair that consumed his little body. *'You'll be okay, mate, I'll be there in a minute.'* I smiled at you, feeling immediate guilt. Was this me choosing Zane over you? Please tell me other mothers had these thoughts too.

Holding Zane's hand, I watched as you slowly walked over behind the nurse and climbed up into the chair she pointed to. You sat back, answering a couple of simple questions calmly and did what she asked, until she leaned over you and told you to open up. You leapt off that chair faster than I could blink.

'No, no!' you repeated, in an unusually loud voice for you to use in public.

'Jesse, it's okay, love, she is just going to have a look at your teeth.' I tried to reassure you from across where Zane and I were.

You tried to walk over to me, when the dental nurse actually grabbed your arm and pulled you back towards the seat, sitting you back in it. I could see you instantly start to internally freak out. I squeezed Zane's hand and quickly said, *'I just have to help Jesse, love.'* He nodded, knowingly, his eyes wide as the other dental nurse had her hands in his mouth.

Quickly walking over to you, I grabbed your hand, trying to come between the abrupt dental nurse and you. *'I'm here, mate, it's okay.'*

'No, it's not, Mum!' you said angrily, as you tried to get up out of the chair.

'Oh, come on,' the dental nurse snapped out, *'you're supposed to be a big boy, stop fussing. Even your little brother is sitting better than you'*

My back went up immediately. Who did she think she was? Did she actually think this tactic was helpful? It was anything but! You yanked your hand out of mine and grabbed the arms of the chair trying to get up, but the dental nurse pushed her hand down against your chest, trying to pin you in place.

Your voice became louder, and seeing your tears of anger, I had more than had enough.

'No, we are not doing this today. Stop!' Was that actually my voice? Clipped with firm authority? Yes it was!

The nurse stood back, folding her arms giving me a look of disgust as I pulled you out of the chair and tucked my arm around your shoulders. I could feel you shaking and I wasn't too far behind. Walking over to Zane's chair, we waited until the nurse had finished his check-up. *'All good,'* the kinder nurse smiled down at you, *'maybe we will see you next time hey, mate?'*

You did not answer and as we left, you tucked under my shoulder, and Zane's little hand in mine, I heard the nurse say to the other, *'Pathetic, isn't it? Some parents wonder why their kids have crappy teeth!'*

My cheeks may have flamed to a bright red, but I still had enough fire in my belly to throw her my own haughty look of disgust over my shoulder as I hustled you both from the room. For the record, you had *great teeth.* Not surprisingly enough, your fear for the dentist did not dissipate as the years went on!

Some teachers need to retire about ten years earlier than they do. Some police officers should never have gotten past the Academy. Some people should never own animals and others should never have become parents. And some dental nurses should have become morticians as their skills with children were so poor! As Aunty would say—*'Just saying!'*

You were pretty upset on the way to school, yelling that the nurse had no right to touch you and you didn't even want to go in the first place! I decided the best thing to do, was stop off at Ballam Park for twenty minutes before I took you both back to school, hoping that would put a smile back on your face. It did in a way, but you spoke of the nurse in an angry voice at the dinner table that night, after Dad had asked you about how your trip went. Dad was not impressed and felt badly that you had had such an ordeal at something as simple as a dental check-up.

*****

Your Grade Four teacher was new to the school and she was young, kind, and full of so much enthusiasm for each and every one of her students and was so open and welcoming for parents to pop in with any concerns. Although you were enjoying school you were relatively quiet and still finding your way, like most boys on the cusp of turning ten, there was so much going on within you. You loved sport especially football and basketball, and it was so wonderful to see you still interested in reading. Your bookcase was full of an assortment of books that you enjoyed when you needed a bit of quiet time.

As always, we looked forward to our trips to visit our family, especially when it was one of the kid's parties and it was time for Ireland's birthday to kick off. It was so exciting to have all your cousins together and with Ava, Kiralee, Hannah and Wyatt plus Ireland's friends it was bound to be an epic day. Thomas had a group of mates over also and I was a little worried about one of the boys, who was there this day, as he contributed to throwing you into the creek a year ago. But, his mother was here and reassured me he had had a talking to about being on his best behaviour. So, things were looking up to simply being a sensational day, where there was plenty for all the kids of all ages to do and just have a ball, enjoy all the activities, and keep busy in a positive way!

You were in such a great head space and were full of laughter and simply wanted to enjoy yourself as a nine-year-old should. Ireland had a huge *Scooby-Doo* jumping castle with slides and you were completely in your element being the gymnast that you were, performing entertaining backflips and taking turns with Kiralee throwing yourselves down the blow-up slide.

The cupcakes were huge and delicious, perfect frosting and plenty to go around; lollies and fruit platters, marinated barbecued meats and salads with music flowing and plenty of beverages for young and old alike. As the day went on, my entire system started to relax, taking photos of all the kids having a great time together and joining the adults around the back of the entertainment area, catching up on any gossip I had missed whilst spending quality time with all of you kids.

I felt as I always did when there was a group of kids together, like I needed to keep one ear open in all of your direction, just in case an adult was needed. Paranoid? Not really. I have always been glad my *Nanny* instincts and radar have stayed intact over the years. I have heard my friends say over time, *'I didn't hear a thing, I just switched off!'* For me, when there is a group of kids around, it is impossible for me to switch off. I am always ready for anything; unpredictable little critters that they are!

As I finished my plate of food and a cup of tea, I decided to head back out the front towards the jumping castle area to see if any of you youngsters needed anything. I am so, so glad I did not wait five more seconds and kicked myself I hadn't left two minutes earlier.

What I saw saddened, shocked, and enraged me to my core. When the kids at school had bullied you, of course I was completely overwhelmed with feeling distraught that you had suffered, been in pain and felt such sadness; and that was just hearing about it, not witnessing it. Just like the compatibility of reading a disturbing chapter in a book, to watching the shocking scene in the movie; takes it to a whole new level when we witness it with our eyes.

As I stepped around the jumping castle, all sound escaped my ears. It was like I was seeing *all* with the volume turned down; an eerie, silent movie and everything was happening in slow motion. All your little cousins, along with Zane, were bouncing up and down on the jumping castle, their mouths open with such joy, but no sound coming out, the movements of Ireland's long piggy tails and all the other little girls with long hair, seemed to be going up and down in the slowest of movements, like gravity no longer existed. I know it wasn't more than twenty steps to you, but I couldn't make them fast enough, my feet feeling like the Italians of old had set them in concrete blocks. You were in the centre of Thomas and his four friends and they had you surrounded.

Your face a mixture of anger and utter sadness. Your hair soaked wet as the boys had shaken up their cans of coke, squirting it all over you. It was coldly, stickily, dripping down your face, your mouth open in utter unhappiness but I could hear no sound.

As a full can of coke was flung at your head, the universe turned its volume back on, allowing me to hear and see all, in its crystal-clear ugliness. And it was worse than when it was muted. When the can hit you solidly on your forehead, your angry cries at the boys to stop, fell on their deaf ears and as your anger turned to tears, their cruel laughter and horrid jaunts rang in my ears with such clarity, I felt consumed with a rage I was hoping I could control.

It seemed only minutes earlier I had seen you laughing with Kiralee and Zane, eating those delicious chocolate cupcakes, your smile so bright and carefree. And then *BANG!* Here you were, crying in discomfort, pain and probable humiliation, surrounded by a group of boys you trusted to simply be your mates when you were at your cousin's house.

If only I was a different person, I would have taken such joy in slapping their smug faces right off.

'HEY!' I yelled (probably screamed!) as I marched towards them, making some of the little kids jump as I walked past the jumping castle to get to you. *'Knock it off RIGHT NOW!'* Two of the boys had the decency to at least look a little guilty. Or they could have been shocked they were sprung in the middle of tormenting you. You stood, trying to stop your crying, your hands flicking the sticky coke off your face and hair.

I looked away from your sadness and felt like I was going to rip someone's throat out. I took a deep breath and my eyes fell on my nephew, whom I loved deeply, had helped raise for a handful of years and felt such disappointment in that moment. His handsome eyes stared right back into mine, waiting.

I couldn't help myself, I simply screamed out, *'I am DISGUSTED IN ALL OF YOU! How could YOU, you pack of COWARDS! What have you got to say for YOURSELVES!'* (I wanted to scream out they were a pack of F**ING little shits – but that's not cool, right?)

Was it too strong? I think it may have been to some people, but at the time they were lucky to escape with their lives. They were twelve years old. Some of them battling their own silent demons. But it's one thing I will never tolerate, bullying!

Bullying is a sad, cruel, disgraceful act! And what does the diction-ary say about bullies? —

To be loudly arrogant and overbearing.

To act the bully toward; intimidate; domineer.

A blustering, quarrelsome, overbearing person, who habitually badgers and intimidates smaller or weaker people

A couple of these children's fathers came to my mind. What hope did some of them have?

Thomas and his friend Harry were quick to apologise, as another mother came around to see what was going on. She was appalled at her boys and tried to pull them into line, apologising to you and I.

I had nothing to say at that moment, as I took you off into Aunty Leah's bathroom for a quick shower and change of clothes. It broke my heart hearing you finally release your tears of frustration and devasta-tion as you lathered yourself with soap bubbles, angrily saying, *'Why, Mum? Why don't they like me? Why are they always nasty to me?'* It wouldn't have been appropriate for me to say, *'Because they are thoughtless, nasty little arseholes.'*

So, I went with – *'I don't know, love. I don't know.'* I was about as helpful to you in that moment, as flea ointment was to a cat, when the dog had not been treated. I left you to shower and dress and pulled my-self together as Aunty Nadine came to see if you were alright. It was nice to have five minutes alone with her in the bedroom to swear and vent honestly about my thoughts on what had just happened. She was pretty upset for you, had a few choice words of her own and made sure for the remainder of the day that you were having as much fun as you could, keeping her eye on you, whilst Ava happily played with all the younger girls.

Having an aunt like Aunty Nadine, is like having a little guardian angel on your team. Always sweet, supportive, and not a bad word to say about anyone. (Not out loud anyway!) Love that girl. The shine of the day had faded greatly after that incident and although I enjoyed my niece's party as much as I could in the remaining time we were there, I could not wait to get home to Dad, for him to put his arms around you and make you feel safe and loved and as special as you deserved to feel.

*****

The remainder of that year flowed, with you turning ten and events that went smoothly, and had the occasional hiccups, as was required by life and all its valuable lessons that make us who we are apparently supposed to be. Thanks life! And a big Thank You to Grammy and Poppy, as they flew us all to Queensland at the end of the school year, for our first family holiday in many years.

It was a concern when Grammy first mentioned the trip, as you had always been terrified at the thought of flying. Always thinking the worst, saying the plane would crash. If we were to go on a boat, it would sink. So, when the day came to get on the plane, we were so proud that you got on, not saying much, as usual in public when you were nervous, but sitting in between two of your biggest fans, Grammy and Poppy, you enjoyed the flight with quiet enthusiasm.

Once you were settled and relaxed, I allowed myself to enjoy the short flight also. Having only flown three other times myself; Hamilton Island as a Nanny, and a trip to Sydney with Dad, and of course flying to beautiful Tasmania for our honeymoon, when you were three months old and growing safely inside me. To travel with a group of my favourite people and have everyone happy was a blessing.

The eight-day holiday in general was so good for us all, and the typical touristy trips such as Movie World; Wet and Wild; and Ripley's

Believe it or Not, was so much fun. Poor Grammy did her knees going up and down the slides at Wet and Wild, simply because you wanted her to join in on all the fun. And it was fun, until she got home and had to have knee surgery! All for the greater good of spending quality time with her grandsons. We packed in as many activities as we could in between Time Zone; Surfers Paradise beach; and walking the strip with all its many sights day and night. Having a night spa at our hotel's pool; watching the fruit bats fly into the palm trees as you, Zane and I would talk about our adventures of the day, whilst Dad caught up on news of footy and what was going on back in Melbourne. Zane turned seven on our third day in and received birthday wishes from Sally, Aunty Nadine, and Aunty Louise, and we celebrated the day capturing the moment at one of the old photo salons. You suited the old southern period perfectly, with your cheeky grin and a hat sitting crookedly on your head holding your vest with a little pocket watch. Zane had to hold a teddy bear, which he wasn't very happy about, after all he was seven now! But you both looked adorable to me, and it's a memory I am grateful to have had caught on film. Looking back at how young you actually were, *how happy* you really seemed. If only I could press *pause* in that moment and keep that cheeky grin on your face, that twinkle in your eyes.

2012 – GRADE FIVE

Nana Lyn's 60th was an epic event. Lunch in Terang at the Wheat-sheaf Hotel. Locals called it, *the Wheaty*— beautiful meals and a comfortable country atmosphere where I felt right at home. After lunch Dad took you, Zane, Thomas, and Ireland out to the park whilst the rest of us had drinks, before returning home to Nana's in Glenormiston South, where the haystack from our childhood called us back, to show you kids how it was really done! Climbing on the huge rolled hay and up the rectangle bales in the shed. There is absolutely nothing better than being with a group of family members, getting together in the fresh air, laughing, and simply taking joy in watching our children follow in our past footsteps, whilst reflecting back on our happiest childhood memories. Life passes us all too quickly.

Not only did Nana turn 60 that year, but Aunty and I celebrated the big 4-0. And of course, the country mouse and the city mouse had to celebrate our birthdays twice, in our own fashion; I had a gathering at our home, having lunch at the *Langy* better known as Beretta's, followed by family and friends relaxing in our backyard, with Aunty Louise flying down from Mildura. It was a typical *me* get together; kids everywhere, food a-plenty and everyone welcome. Nana Lyn made my night, after a few glasses of red wine, with Abba blaring trying to teach some of my girlfriends how to correctly dance the *old fashioned* way. All of you kids thought that was funny until you walked past and she grabbed a hold of you. And of course, not wanting to hurt her feelings, you danced along with bright red cheeks of mortification!

Aunty Leah's party was held a month later, as she took herself off to Thailand to celebrate as only Aunty can, whilst we had Ireland stay with us for a fortnight. Aunty had her party catered for beautifully, with over 80 guests and a DJ which allowed me and my friend Bec, to dance our feet off till 2am. I had such an amazing time and it was only the next morning watching Aunty pull a pork-slider out of her serene fish pond with the comment, *'What inconsiderate fuck-wit wasted this?'*

'Shit, that's a bit harsh,' I thought to myself taking a mouthful of tea, as a quick flashback occurred in my foggy, morning brain; the memory of dancing to a fine beat alerted me to other happenings of the epic night before. (I clearly did not get out enough, and perhaps should have had my first alcoholic beverage before I turned 35!)

I pushed my bacon and eggs around on my plate as the chatter of the night's events were happily discussed with remaining guests, who had spent the night. Apart from Ireland, it had been a *kid-free* event and I enjoyed my party time perhaps a little too much. What's the expression, *'Go hard or go home?'* Jesus Joseph and Mary, I went hard alright! I poured as much tea down my throat with the painful thought of driving back to Melbourne soon. Thank God, I had Bec for company and we had more than one McDonalds, to drive through on our trip home.

As Aunty joined everyone at the breakfast table, with Aunty Nadine and Kylie heaping more bacon and eggs on people's plates, she commented once more, about the rude fucker that had thrown the slider into her pond.

I noticed Bec going a little red, her eyes flickered in my direction and then, horribly it came to me. I recalled a waitress had walked past with a tray of the sliders, that looked so good and juicy at the time, only after biting into it my thoughts were, *'this sucker is dry!'* I remembered shrugging at Bec as we danced along, and pitching the slider over 80 odd guests' heads, towards the back fence, not knowing my aim would be so precise and land in the pond. To this day, I don't think Aunty Leah knew it was I, who ashamedly threw the dry slider into her precious fish pond! Sorry Sos!

For me, as your mum, as an adult, I enjoyed those three social gatherings that year. It allowed me to be with family and friends, kick off my heels and let my soul party. To be able to celebrate life while you were in such a happy place made the celebration all the more enjoyable. How did we get so lucky? To be able to live, breathe and not fret every single day that some incident may knock you off balance and throw you into a dark hole.

Speaking of balance, Uncle Cameron who had continued teaching Martial Arts over the years, (along with boxing, and personal training, talented man that he is) had opened a new training program for adults and kids alike, Combat Kai. Both Zane and you were so proud of yourselves when you had your first class. Liam and his brother Tyler and their sister Gracie, joined along with you, which gave you that added confidence to attend. It was such a joy being able to sit and watch you develop the skills of a beautiful style of Martial Arts, such as Wing Chun. Some parents joined in the class, I preferred to sit with a cup of tea and chit chat with Bec while we watched you all. You were hesitant to put your hand up and answer any questions that Uncle Cameron asked the class, and although he was wise enough to know that you wanted to stay under the radar, he would ask you anyway, bringing you out of your shell a little more each time. You didn't realise how talented you were as a Martial Artist.

*****

Your Grade Five Teacher was a sweetheart— *a real modern day Mary Poppins.* It was a good school year for you, where you also met and made a couple of good mates - both boys from different schools that transitioned to Karingal Heights. Noah would come and spend weekends where you would take off on skateboards to the park or our local milk-bar and he would join us when we had parties during the holidays. He was a confident boy that was kind to Zane and any of our number of friends that were welcome to visit at any time.

He played football for the Karingal Bulls and you all often had a great, spirited game going at school during recess and lunchtime. It was during one of these games that you went to mark the football when it hit your little finger straight on the top, breaking it.

So, what did you do? Did you do what most ten-year-old boys would do? Perhaps let the teacher know, as class resumed, that your finger was throbbing painfully? No, no you did not. You sat down in your seat and got stuck into your work. Not only was your finger throbbing, but it had swollen to double the size. When your teacher walked behind your seat and noticed it swelling like a balloon, she asked you, *'Are you alright, Jesse?'*

To which you replied, *'Yes.'*

'What happened to your finger?'

'Nothing, the football hit it.'

'Well, it doesn't look like nothing. I think we better send you to the office and ring Mum.'

And aren't we grateful she insisted you go to the office and I receive a phone call. I collected you and after a trip to our Doctor then to the X-ray peeps we headed off to hospital where it was confirmed you had broken your little finger. After a week, seeing a specialist, we were lucky you did not require surgery. There's a reason why I mentioned your broken finger, and that will be addressed later.

The year flowed by, as the years do. Aunty Leah presented us with two brand new little kittens that needed a home. Dad named them Hakuna and Matata. (We did see the Lion King three times when we started dating back in the day). I was hoping to call the cute brothers Starskie and Hutch, but the boys soon became Koonie and Tardwell. Koonie definitely has his own theme song— Day Dream Believer, and he also became a big hit on Instagram. I adore all animals, but these two furry little guys were my saviours at a very dark time. Animals really are therapeutic, magic for the soul.

You turned eleven, and you and I had some test of wills. You were still such a good boy at heart, it was just your attitude and the way you spoke to me, like I was the maid, or your sister. Not the person who stood by you, supported you, and gave you my all. In front of Dad, Grammy, Uncle Grant, Nana Lyn, or Aunty Nadine, you were a real sweetheart. But with others, such as Aunty Leah, Sally, Aunty Louise, or Aunty Rachael, you would let me have it, and they would see the real *us* in action. And at times I'm ashamed to say, it wasn't very pretty. Like all parents, there has been many times I wish time machines existed and I could zap us back where I would be more aware of your emotions and more equipped to handle you in a mature, loving manner; where I didn't feel like an abused, unappreciated mother, like I'm sure so many mothers feel at one stage or another.

One thing many noticed was how particularly clean you kept your room. Others, with kids the same age, had their own tips forming, with rotten food, mouldy milk and half the cupboards worth of dishes, collecting their own kind of funky bacteria, shoved under beds. You had always hated any one sitting on your bed, especially after you made it so meticulously, with not a crease in the covers, but now, you even hated anyone eating in your room, in case they dropped crumbs or wrappers and didn't pick them up. You even began vacuuming your room before and after you knew people were coming. One major thing I noticed, if you were in a particular headspace, was, you would pull absolutely everything out of your room, (minus the bed), dust, mop, vacuum, rearrange your bookcase, then put everything back the way it was, or totally rearrange your entire room's layout. It was a total bonus that you loved to keep your room so tidy, apart from the stress you would feel if others messed it up.

Having deeper conversations with my close girlfriends and family members, there was a reassuring comfort amongst us, when we shared our darker thoughts on motherhood. How it made us feel at times when our children challenged us with simply being children, or a rudeness we never thought we would hear come out of our children's mouths. It always lessened the burden when you'd hear another mother explain her deplorable actions or comments when she was pushed to her limits when her own child had been a *horrid little turd ball* and busted her chops. We knew, as adults, we were in the wrong. We would try harder to change our actions and words, when faced with a similar situation next time. It's always easy to say this when you have shared the burden of your wrongdoings with a loved one, when your bad parenting has been turned into a comical scene, and hysterical laughter has taken place of your shame. But when you are in the moment of a battle, with that human being you give so much to, and they are ripping your soul into tiny, little worthless pieces, all the common-sense parenting in the world flies right out the window.

I mean, are we bad parents if we are so worried about it in the first place? Would we share our stories and confessions of shame whilst offering each other support? I guess that's debatable?

2013 – GRADE SIX: THOU SHALL NOT JUDGE

What an epic year this was to be. Our beautiful eleven-year-old. You were so happy and excited that this was your last year of primary school, and very excited at long last to have a male teacher. You made good progress with your Martial Arts and continued your close friendships with Noah and your two other mates. Life was pretty good. It really was.

Then it all changed. Two weeks after you turned twelve and I don't know why I ever complained about motherhood and its difficulties till now. One thing we should all try to remember, it can always, always, be worse. The icing on my nightmare was about to begin. Is that too dramatic? No. Because living with the new Jesse was like Dr Jekyll and

Mr Hyde on Ice, and the egg shells I was previously walking around on, had turned to sharp slivers of glass, waiting to pierce through any of my protective armour.

There was the at school, at Martial Arts, at family functions, in public, Jesse: polite, friendly, quiet, agreeable. There was the Dad's at home and awake Jesse: fairly agreeable, a little bit cheeky, testing the boundaries like any twelve-year-old boy. Then there was the Dad's asleep Jesse: total unpredictable nightmare. Rude. Angry. Aggressive. Unbearable. Pushing boundaries like never before.

To explain to someone that has not been in our home: we live in a small house. Actually, that's an understatement; it is the tiniest house ever. I like to think it has a warm, welcoming feel to it and thanks to Pinterest has charming qualities here and there. We have a large yard with gardens to embrace all, offering a feeling of tranquillity with several water features that include bird baths, fish ponds and other pots of water that hold lilies, duck weed or clean water for birds and possums to drink. It had a decent entertaining area with a fire. Out the back we have a pool, large trampoline, and plenty of space for the many kids, of all ages, we have over. Sometimes the backyard looks epic when the lawns are mowed and all is kept tidy, trimmed, weeded, and pruned. When it's not, well it's a jungle out there.

But our actual living area was small. Adults' room is down the front of the house secluded away with a master bathroom. In the main living, my writing area, open plan lounge and dining are in between your and Zane's bedrooms at the other end of the house. Due to Dad being a painter, our walls have seen many colours over the years from sunshine yellow with blues, burnt orange and green feature walls, to now antique white, with a warm chocolate feature wall in the lounge area.

Yes, I embraced the provincial farm feel and after many years of trying to convince Dad we needed to paint all our beautiful mahogany and wooden furniture to rustic white, I succeeded. I was living the dream in that moment of surrender.

Floor to ceiling windows that allowed the feel of the garden to come in with a soothing quality. The kitchen with its Granny Smith apple-green counter tops, still belonged in the 1970's, and despite its tiny size, three adults were able to function and move in and around it on Christmas day, without anyone ending up in the emergency unit at the Frankston hospital. Those that have seen it will marvel at this statement!

Both your and Zane's bedrooms are small but roomy enough as you don't over-clutter with stuff and can sleep six kids, packed in tight, when the need arises. Like all Aussie home owners, our renovations never seem to end, due to time and money and unlike some women, I am not demanding or fussy. If it's clean, looks presentable and is welcoming, I'm happy. If there is somewhere to sit out in the garden for entertaining or simply to relax, I'm happy. Yeah sure, I'm still dreaming of the extension of the French doors leading out onto the entertainment area, and a waterproof roof to replace the shade sail, so I can sit out in the winter time in the pouring rain, with the fire blazing without having to wear dad's waterproof poncho! That will come.

Of course, as you grew and changed over the years, so too did the overall appearance of the walls, with grubby fingers marking them, along with Summer dragging her backside against them trying to scratch her persistent fleas. The freshly varnished floor boards that were done when you were growing safely inside me were no longer shiny and new thanks to the wear and tear of normal foot traffic plus the occasional motorised child vehicle that some relative bought you when you were two, which you would hoon up and down the corridor till the battery ran flat.

Although the floorboards are well worn, it makes for a homey feeling. There's nothing like seeing a stain where Summer had the trots and it had soaked into some worn parts of the wood that had been etched into, by the life of the house! (Gross I know, but Glen 20 was invented for a reason!) Skirting boards being dug into whilst Zane tried to master his Hover Board. Some of the windows no longer whole thanks to a skateboard, a football or a broom going through them.

Some of the maintenance was cheap and easy. For the walls a quick wipe down or a paint job. The skirting boards, well they have been painted but still a bit bashed up here and there. As for the windows, many of them have been replaced over the years, and some have not. For example, in your room I thought I would be cleverly artistic by creating a spider web with industrial duct tape to hold your window together. You had put a rather large stick through it, pretending it was a Harry Potter wand when you were six.

So, in explaining the sheer tiny size of our home, in this new, trying time of you turning twelve, I was often grateful, amazed, and stupefied at times that Dad could sleep through War of the Worlds that occurred between us. Probably due to his complete exhaustion and a couple of beers at the end of the day. Being an early riser for many years, Dad's day could start with him rising anywhere from 5.00 am, getting to work, putting in eight hours' (or more) physical labour, as a painter does, and getting home to his family. He would then spend time taking you to the park after school, watching you do Martial Arts, or escaping for some man time. Twelve years being a hands-on loving, entertaining and supportive father, husband, and family member to those around us, a full-time employee for 20 years and generally busy, active guy; would make anyone want to sleep well at the end of the day. So, why toot the horn of my husband? That's so easy. It deserves to be blown, honked or whatever you want to call it and I know there are going to be a lot of women and men reading this, nodding their heads in agreement to their loved ones who support them without regard to themselves, that just get on and do what they need to for their loved ones. I am beyond grateful for the home I am blessed enough to live in. When Dad and I decided to have children, we also agreed to not put ourselves in the position of having a crippling mortgage where we would both have to work full-time and have you kids in day care. When Zane started school, I worked during school hours cleaning, and then moved onto health and beauty working with Australia's own, Larissa Bright selling gorgeous aromatherapy products, before turning 40 and being given an iPad. This allowed my fingers to keep up with my thought flow and construct a story I had always wanted to write. And, *The Given* was born, in between you being a settled sweet school boy, to an absolute demon on ice. Harsh, but felt like my reality at the time. There was no beautiful one day, perfect the next, it was all hell on earth rolling on and on to what felt like an eternity of – '*I want to shoot myself.*'

Sadly, it was not just me who suffered from your hostile, angry, abusive attitude, but poor little Zane also.

And how do I describe the depth of pain you caused in the seven odd months that your body was adjusting, testosterone flowing and personality forming? I'm not really certain I can be so wonderfully descriptive on what a complete horrid little arsehole you actually were. That I struggled to recognise the person you had become and who I became while you broke my heart into a million pieces each night as I questioned myself as a mother more than ever before. But I will try.

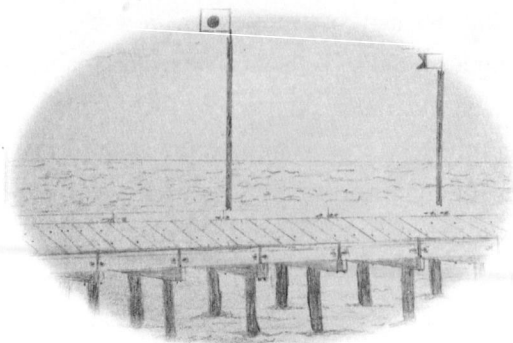

ABUSE

The days were as busy as always. Work for Dad, school days for you boys, friends and activities in between Kung-Fu and weekends away, and perhaps I wouldn't have been so tired after shopping, housework, cooking and simply just existing if I didn't sit up till 2 or 3 am writing my heart out. But I was suddenly so aware that this was my calling. The need I felt to put down on paper every character and story-line that popped into my head, and create a world away from my own, was such a peaceful, therapeutic tool. It really was a time in my life when I felt that this is what I was supposed to be doing, that fingers crossed I could be good at it, and if just one person would take away some joy in what I was writing, well that would be reward enough for me. So, I was feeling blessed in this life with the fact that I was able to write and look after my family as best I could.

And there you were, a smiley sweetheart in your Grade Six sibling photo with Zane, both of you looking like the happiest, loved little brothers in the world. You were. Then night-time came. You usually had an early dinner Tuesday and Thursday nights before Kung-Fu, so it would have time to settle before your class started, then home again to shower, catch up on any homework before an hour of relaxation then bed. Dad normally went to bed in your hour of relaxation as the house was quiet and it was time for him to turn in anyway, so it worked out well for us. I would set up for writing, boil the kettle a million times over and pop on some quiet, relaxing music that usually flowed in our household after hours. You both had your own rooms with plenty of space and alone time in them during the daylight hours. But for whatever reason, you had decided to sleep on the top bunk above Zane's double bed. So, when it was time to call lights out, you'd both snuggle under your covers, the soothing music caressing you to sleep as I typed away at my keyboard, enjoying the stillness of the house, and escaping into the world I was creating.

Sounds perfect for a few seconds, doesn't it? And for a few seconds it was. Then it would begin. Zane would want to ask me a question, or tell me about his day, to prolong the night so he wouldn't have to sleep, and to have some snuggle time with me. I enjoyed the night time chatter, and Zane still reveals his entire school day to me to this day. I hear all about what the teachers say, how they make him feel, who's the best teacher, who's the meanest, and all the gossip on his school mates. It can take anywhere between 20 – 45 minutes. Sometimes it's intriguing, sometimes not. I did fall asleep on him once! He was not impressed. I was too exhausted to care!

My eight-year-old needing me for a time during bedtime was certainly not a problem for me. That's my role, to comfort, communicate and listen to my children. Speak nicely to me and I am your slave. On one of our trips to Inglewood, Hannah and Zane decided it would be a great idea to hide behind the couch whilst Uncle Darren made a coffee, before he resumed his movie. Unfortunately for Zane, that movie just happened to be *Lord of the Rings* with all the horrifying Orgs and battle cries. Zane has always been a brave lad and enjoyed *Harry Potter* movies at three years of age, but *Lord of the Rings*, although one of my favourites, is definitely not suitable for a six year old! Hence, Zane's fear of being alone in the dark began. So, if he needed to talk to me until he was sleepy enough to fall asleep, well that is what I would do.

This of course, gave you ammunition to call down from the top bunk, *'Zane Lover .'*

'Okay, Jesse, that's enough.' I'd say in a calm, quiet voice. *'Go to sleep.'*

'You go to sleep, stupid.'

I froze, wondering if I'd heard that right. *'What did you say?'* I was hoping you wouldn't let me down. You did. Quite confidently I said, *'You go to sleep, stupid.'*

Zane started fidgeting and getting upset. *'Don't talk to Mum like that!'*

'Shut up you dog poo muncher!' came your retort from above.

I kissed Zane's hair before rising and looked you dead in the eye. You were grinning like a cheeky monkey, but I far from thought you were funny. *'What's going on? Why are you being so rude tonight?'*

You simply laughed and ducked under the covers. *'Right, that's enough now, shut up and go to sleep.'* I went back down to the bottom bunk and gave Zane a cuddle before going out to the dining table to start writing, after making a cup of tea. The light from the dining area reflected in Zane's room making him feel safe enough to sleep, with the music quietly floating in.

Night two was a step closer to being more unappealing as night one was, with your new found attitude. I decided to play a bit of *Candy-Crush* whilst I snuggled beside Zane as he settled into sleep. I asked you if you wanted to talk about anything, which you replied, *'Nah.'* So I continued playing the mind-numbing game of matching candies and getting excited when I entered the next level. It was relaxing, and I almost fell asleep myself, before someone slapped the top of my head from above, followed by a fit of laughter.

I was in shock for about five seconds. Not yelling at you as I would have liked, I stood, placing the iPad on Zane's desk, and whispered angrily, not wanting to wake Dad, *'What the hell did you do that for?'*

I couldn't believe it, you were actually smiling. Full of pride like this was the best game ever. You simply stared at me, making silly noises, like a one year old that didn't know any better.

'Pull your head in and go to sleep, and if you do that to me again, it's going to come back at you like a boomerang!'

You muttered something under your breath as Zane began to stir. I bent to rub his hair and he settled, then I took the iPad out of the room and leant against the wall, away from your view. I could not believe you thought it was funny to hit my head. My mind raced back to the past few weeks, searching for anything I may have said or done to upset you. I could think of nothing. You wanted to go to *Stacks Pancakes* for your twelfth birthday, with Uncle Grant, Dad, Zane, and I, which we did. Dad went back home afterwards as you wanted to see a movie, and by the time it finished would have been too late for Dad who had work that Saturday. So, Uncle Grant, you, Zane, and I went on the watch *Pirates of the Caribbean*.

School had been going well and I was simply doing my own head in, wondering what was going on in that head of yours. Dad got home from work the next afternoon and jumped in the shower. I wanted to give him time to relax and unwind but often found this hard to do when I had so much to off-load from the day, or in this case the night before so I quickly got around to telling him about what had occurred the night before and he was not impressed whatsoever.

Once Dad was out, dressed, and had afternoon tea, you arrived home from the basketball court where you had been playing with Tyler, Liam, and Noah. *'Hi Dad,'* you said quite happily reaching for your water bottle.

'Hey, mate. Did you have a good day?' Dad's voice was silky and calm, full of fatherly love. You had no idea what was coming. I almost felt sorry for you.

'Yep!' You slugged back some water and then ran your hand over your lips, slamming the water bottle back down on the bench with an *'Ah.'*

'So, you slept well, mate?' Dad hugged you as you walked into his arms, like you usually did when you saw him after he got home from work.

'Yep!' You hugged him back before starting to walk towards your room.

'Jesse, if you ever hit your Mum again I'm going to be so disappointed in you, plus you'll lose your Xbox for a week.' That stopped you in your tracks. I don't think you thought I would have told Dad, as often when you and I had a to-do, you ended up apologising and begged me not to tell Dad. And because I didn't want to burden Dad with our *nonsense*, often would simply deal with whatever situation alone that I had to. And that had nothing to do with Dad, it was simply me trying to solve it on my own, protect you and leave your Dad in peace. Yes, it was a bad parenting move. Another lesson learnt. Although I didn't completely learn it yet!

'Did you hear me, Jesse?' Dad said firmly.

You turned around, looking past Dad at me, before returning his gaze. *'Yes, Dad.'*

'What do you say to Mum?'

'Sorry, Mum.'

'That's okay. Is there anything you want to talk about?' I hoped you'd give me something that may explain your behaviour.

'Nah. Sorry.'

'It's all right, just don't do it again,' Dad sighed as you walked off into your room, closing the door. He turned around and looked at me, shaking his head. *'I was a real little shit to my Mum too when I was his age.'*

'Well, I'm sure you never whacked your mother on the head,' I replied.

'No, I wouldn't be alive today if I did. Hopefully that's the end of it.'

'Yeah.' I said, as he walked outside to find Zane on the trampoline.

As I turned to start dinner, I heard the vacuum fire up, as you began to clean your room.

Surely that's that.

*****

The afternoon, after night thirteen.

Out and about, having a picnic with friends and some of their acquaintances, apparently, calling out to both you and Zane as you whizzed down the path on your scooters, I did not call out as nicely to you as I did Zane. Another mother who I had only met a handful of times, turned her cold, beady eyes on me and said, *'It would be nice if you spoke to your eldest, as lovingly as you did your youngest.'*

I looked at her, too tired and stunned, at her *balls* of steel comment, to respond, that it is in fact easier to speak nicely to someone, when they haven't been abusing you for a couple of weeks on end.

Meeting Sally's eyes as she pushed a bowl of potato salad in my hands, I turned and walked over to Jacqui and dolloped a violent scoop of the creamy salad onto her plate. She squeezed my wrist and whispered protectively, *'Ignore the silly bitch.'* Which of course I did! We communicate to our nearest and dearest of our pain and heartache and general problems in life. Not mere acquaintances that won't be around for the long haul. But they are always around in the background, with a negative opinion, judging without knowing the full story. That's life.

Night Fourteen:

Zane was trying to tell us about his day when you kept reaching down trying to play with my hair, while making animal noises. *'Jesse, you can talk about your day in a moment, but bloody stop hanging over the side of the bed. You will fall over the edge.'*

Zane was starting to get frustrated, twenty minutes in he hadn't even gotten past recess, I was getting tired and as we were two weeks into your feral behaviour, it didn't take me too long before I was super pissed off with you. Yeah sure, at this stage you were simply stroking my hair, probably trying to have a nice mother-son moment; but I was beyond anything to do with you touching me, as the night before you head-butted me hard coming over the side of the bunk, laughing your head off thinking it was the funniest thing since *Billy Connelly's* last tour.

My tolerance for you in that moment, and sad to say, many moments in the months that followed, was almost zero. What was I missing here? Yes, we had had our ups-and-downs over the years, our relationship may have been a roller-coaster at times, but our bond and my essential love for you ran deep.

You reached your hand down again to play with my hair making a silly sound which you thought hilarious. Zane had enough, calling out quietly, *'Shut up, Jesse!'*

'You shut up, you dog crap!' you unintelligently responded.

'Right, that's enough, both of you, now shush so you don't wake up Dad! Zane, finish your day at school quickly so you can both go to sleep.'

'Most boring story ever,' you scoffed from above. Which resulted in Zane telling you to shut up again. And then there we were, the Australian Open of 'shut up - you shut up - shut up - you shut up - shut up - you shut up', and as Aunt Dorothy would say, and so on and so forth!

Yes, it seemed we were raising intelligent, kind-hearted boys!

'Can you please both of you shut up! For Christs sake! That is enough.' Seriously, why did this have to happen? *'And Jesse if you*

can't shut up and simply be nice you can piss off into your bloody room and sleep in your own bloody bed!'

Yeah, I was a bit over it all by this stage. Seriously over it and not feeling like mother of the year whatsoever. With the added pressure of Aunty Rachael and the kids coming down in a few days' time for the school holidays I was praying you would pull your head in and return to the not always perfect but easy to live with Jesse.

'You piss off to your own room,' you replied. Wow. Not even close.

I stood and slapped your leg through the doona cover. It hurt my hand.

'That didn't hurt.' you said.

'Oh, really,' I thought, this will, and whacked you as hard as I could through the doona once again. Yes, a real proud moment as I heard you cry out, *'Stop it, you stupid head.'*

I took a deep breath trying to recall I was your mother through my red haze of anger, wondering if I should call *DHS* on myself.

'Mum,' Zane called sadly.

I shook my head and sat on the bed, head in hands. *'I'm sorry, Jesse, I should not have done that.'*

Nothing from you. Not a peek. I stood and looked at you, but you had wrapped yourself up tight, like a moth in a cocoon. Well, at least you were quiet. I snuggled down beside Zane and whispered, *'Just go to sleep, Baby.'* I felt him nod as he rolled over, and let my thoughts wander to you.

We got through the next few nights, unhappily. And Aunty Rachael's visit was one of the first ever where I couldn't wait for everyone to go home again as having people witness your deplorable attitude after weeks of you running me emotionally into the ground, was tough.

Aunty Rachael had organised to take us all out on *Puffing Billy* for a day trip. Wyatt may have been a little over a year younger than Zane, but his love of trains was on par with the *Fat Controller's*. Everyone was excited about it that morning as we organised our picnic and thermos. You continued repeating the same questions over and over, *'How long's it going to take to get there? Where is it? What happens if it crashes?'*

Both Aunty Rachael and I answered your questions calmly at first, but as the hour went on and your questions did not change, I could see my cousin raise her eyebrows and look grateful that we had to take two cars to get there, allowing her to have an hour break from you.

'Jesse, please get your shoes and jacket on, and relax. It's all going to be fine. The train won't crash, it only takes an hour or so to get there, and we are going to have a fab day out.'

'Yeah, but what if it does crash? Will we die? How fast does it go? Who's going to feed the animals if we die?' you persisted.

'We are not going to die,' I tried calmly to reassure you.

'How do you know? You don't know everything!' You stood there staring as the other kids bustled around getting shoes and jackets on. I snapped at you then, telling you to chill out and go get your shoes and jacket organised and stop with the questions as you were driving me crazy.

'You're bloody crazy,' you screamed and stormed down to your bed-room, yelling at everyone to stay the hell out, and then slamming the door behind them all. We could hear you pushing your bed up against the door, so no-one could get in, while you yelled and punched the door.

I marched down to your room, yelling out, *'Jesse knock it off!'* It wasn't helpful of course, but my cousin was looking at me as if to say, *'He needs a whack and you're letting him get away with being a shit - head.'* (I know this for a fact as she told me towards the end of her stay that perhaps you just needed a good hiding.)

You did come out of your room after a little while, yelling at me that I was the worst mum ever and so dumb! I felt so bad for Zane, Kiralee, Hannah and Wyatt. We all usually had the best holidays together, filled with fun activities, laughter, and chill out good times. They were seeing a brand-new side of you on this get together, and none of them were enjoying it. Can't imagine why?

I rang Grammy in tears, debating whether to go at all, in case you ruined the day for everybody else. She was the voice of reason stating, you either behave and have fun, or you stay home on your own and get over it. Well, you were twelve and I wouldn't leave you home alone, but I knew what she was getting at.

After you and I had a screaming match, which left me in tears again, we finally got in the cars and left for what was actually, an epically relaxing day. I watched you sit beside Kiralee and Hannah, a happy boy who didn't have a care in the world, all of you kids had your legs hanging over the sides of the open carriages and the stunning landscape of open green fields to forests of ferns whizzed by us, the fresh air blowing our worries away. I sat with a cup of tea in my hands and tears of gratitude in my heart for Aunty Ray, who persisted that I bring you. And here we were, enjoying our time, seeing you laugh with your cousins and brother, erasing all traces of your earlier anger as if it hadn't happened. Aunty Rachael gave me the warm hug I so desperately needed, and we laughed and quietly swore about the so-called joys of motherhood. Whenever I look at the photo of you between Kiralee and Hannah, Zane and Wyatt standing near the stream, where the ducks joined us for hot chips, to go with our packed picnic, I marvel at two things: how very young and absolutely happy you looked. A proud, confident little man standing with a few of the people in this world you totally adored. And secondly, what took place two hours prior to that photo being taken - how angry and out of control you were. Swearing, crying, punching, and kicking your bedroom door. How did we get here? Why? Was this how it was going to be from here on out? You being angry and hurtful and explosive over what seemed like nothing?

What was I missing, because I sure as hell was missing something? The nights rolled into weeks, months, and every night was the same or worse than the night before. You started getting tummy aches every Tuesday and started missing a day of school once a week, to once a fortnight.

After another worrisome night, where we were both lucky to escape with. A: You - your life. B: Me - my remaining sanity, I found myself sitting on the back porch steps the next afternoon while everyone was doing their own thing. I had five quiet minutes to myself before someone wanted a Nutella sandwich or ask a question, to dob on someone, report an incident that happened at school or just needed Mum. I sat there, glancing out at my yard I loved so much, wanting the tranquillity to soak into my shattered, parental confidence with fat tears silently running down my cheeks, as Shannon Noel continued whispering quietly in my ear— *What about me, it isn't fair!*

Yeah, I was feeling like a bit of a woe-is-me loser for a split second and as much as I loved Shannon I was desperately trying to hear Robbie sing me something inspirational.

I was trying to sort out in my mind, where we were going wrong! You didn't live in a household where you were neglected or abused, so I just couldn't grasp where your anger was coming from. We had stayed away from any social gatherings, where we knew Thomas would be, to give you space, and let your injured confidence around him flourish again. I had been doing more girl weekends away to Aunty Leah's, not only for my own sanity and peace of mind but to leave you in the safety of our home with Dad, where no one could speak to you or parent you the way they thought they should.

But the constant worry of your growing anger loomed in my mind. And as angry as I got with you when you disrespected, abused and generally were a horrid son to me in those moments, I still felt an over powering urge to protect you from all, and at times that included Dad. Yes, he was your other parent, but I could still see through my anger, you shut down, and go into a shell and become a different boy when Dad raised his voice and repeated to you, over and over how he expected you to behave. As soon as his voice hit that pitch of — *You're in trouble*— you immediately closed off and blocked everything and everyone out.

Thank goodness for other women venting and reflecting their family business. It's in this way, women hear from another source that they are not alone in keeping the odd swear word their child has blurted out from their husband. That, they too, only tell their husbands what they need to know and not overburden them with unnecessary, often petty, arguments between children and mothers. I thought it was just me, wanting to handle things the best I could. After all, Dad went out to work each and every day, sometimes even when he was ill. Bills had to be paid, life rolled on. And here was I, living the dream, raising my children, and generally feeling pretty blessed all round.

So, if I had to carry the burden, discipline the best I knew without turning into a raving lunatic and hold down the fort at home, concealing ugly arguments and ball-breaking moments between you and I, well, I would certainly try my best to continue to block life's bullshit with kids (just you really!) from Dad. But it wasn't just that. I think for us mums, (or dads) who do the full-time parenting, not being at work, we build a kind of resilience to a degree to the way our kids speak to us over time. We tolerate a lot, whilst we discipline, and know when to let certain things go and not press the situation making it worse. For me, keeping certain things from Dad was my way of protecting you all really, and giving myself less anxiety, worrying how Dad would deal with you and how you would react. It wasn't right of course, but it's what I needed to do for me at the time!

As the weeks rolled into months and the days would often be as diabolical as the nights, I knew I needed answers as to why we were heading down such a destructive path, and fast. In these months, I had finished writing *The Given,* moved past *Dark Angel* and was two thirds of the way into *The Guardian,* whilst entering the unknown, daunting world of looking for a publisher and all the do's and don'ts getting your first book out there. I was as terrified as I was excited, and thanks to a handful of honest people who had read the manuscripts through, I felt I was on a very good wicket with the story-line I had created. Like everything in life, time would tell, and if I didn't try I was only letting myself down.

Night 160-something!

You had had a quick chat about your day before Zane started in on what he had been up to, and as the night was winding right down without an incident thus far, I was feeling fairly confident we might have a quiet one and escape any drama. That was my first mistake, feeling confident, followed by thinking we could escape any drama; you were after all, related to Nana Lyn, Grammy, and Aunty Leah. All of whom could be wonderful Drama Queens at the best of times. (Some Women!)

Listening to Zane's breath start to slow into an almost steady rhythm of nearly asleep, I slid my finger along the colourful candies, stuck on a high level I was struggling to get passed. I enjoyed playing for the five or so minutes at your boy's bedtime before I got on with writing.

'Look at you playing that stupid game,' you scoffed, hanging over the bed looking down at me with a grin on your face that spelt trouble.

I took a breath trying to steady the flutter of — *Oh shit, here we go* — and simply said, *'Okay, mate, don't bother starting any nonsense, just go to sleep.'* I resisted the urge to slap your arm away as you decided to hang lower to put your hand in front of the iPads screen, blocking my colourful diversions to life.

'I don't know why you play that anyway, stupid Candy Crush.' You reached over and tapped my head gently.

I pushed your hand away. *'I play it because it's relaxing and I don't need to think about too much. You don't have to play it so don't worry about it being stupid. Now go to sleep.'* The next tap on my head wasn't as gentle and I could feel my emotions brewing in a negative direction. I simply wanted all the bullshit to stop once and for all! Unhelpfully, I slapped your dangling arm, hard. *'Please knock it the fuck off!'* (Sorry, couldn't help myself!)

'I'm going to tell all your friends you're the worst Mum ever! Stupid head.' You tapped my head again, repeating, *'Stupid head-Stupid head,'* like it was your rhythm and my head was the drum.

'Jesse, I swear to God if you don't stop that and go to bloody sleep, I'm going to lose it!' My twelve-year-old son was literally making me want to pull my own hair out. Feelings of exhaustion, a sense of sadness mixed with the overwhelming feeling of unwanted repetitiveness was taking me to the edge of an unhealthy numbness.

We verbally hurled immature comments back and forth for a few moments, although your behaviour was unacceptable, it was age appropriate, but I was forty years old, and each time I said something hurtful to hopefully shut you up, it simply made matters worse. I hated what was coming out of my mouth, and as angry and pissed off as I was at you, for sending me into this shitty mental state in the first place, I was even more angry and disgusted at myself for not having the power or strength to handle you in the way you so obviously needed to be handled. It was like this: when you behaved, I could be the sweetest mother ever. I was kind, loving and yes okay, - who am I trying to convince in this moment? When you didn't behave, I too became an arsehole of gigantic proportions!

As you reached to slap my head again, yelling out I was the worst mum ever, I proved you right and grabbed your arm and yanked! You almost came over the side crying out in fright. All your laughter had stopped in that instant, and as it did, angry comments replaced your silly ones.

'Jesse, please bloody stop it, if you wake up Dad I'm going to be so upset with you.'

'He'll be upset with you for trying to pull me out of bed!'

'Well I wouldn't have tried to pull you out if you hadn't been hitting me on the head!'

Our tennis match resumed, as Freddie began singing to me about wanting to break free. I decided to close my eyes and hum a few bars, which did not suit you whatsoever.

'If you don't stop singing I'm going to wake up Dad.'

I thought that highly unlikely and continued humming.

With that, you banged the wall with your fist. Hard!

And what happened in the next moment is difficult to define whom got the biggest fright as your Dad snapped on the light and said in a voice filled with as much anger as I had ever heard, *'What the hell is going on in here?'*

I don't know, my startled inner voice thought. *What's been going on for months almost every night while you've been sleeping peacefully, unaware that your son is a serial arsehole come night-time, and your wife is an emotional-abusive-basket case*!

To which I replied, *'Oh Hun, I'm so sorry we woke you.'* Wrong response as it upset your Dad, all the more. I should have stuck with the above reality.

'I don't want you to be sorry that you woke me; I want you to be sorry that this is going on! Jesse, I have been standing in the corridor the whole time listening! This has all got to STOP!' I knew he was referring to you being out of control, and me not handling it in the correct way. His raised voice, the late hour, and the fact that we both knew we had done wrong, left a silent, hollow feeling echoing in the room once Dad was done. My eyes met his, wanting to say a million things but knowing any of it would come out wrong if I opened my mouth. He looked back up at you, where you were silently perched, said goodnight firmly and left the room.

I could hardly move, my shame had me immobilised. It was one thing, me verbally venting in a disgraced fashion to my twelve-year-old boy who was breaking me down with his own anger and confusion, but to have my behaviour witnessed by the man I loved so completely, deflated me to a whole other level. I ran my hands over my face and glanced over at your brother, who was sitting up and had pushed himself into the corner of the wall, a sad look on his face. My heart dropped as his big eyes said it all — *Why does this keep happening?* My guilt at being a lousy mother magnified.

'I'm sorry, mate, I'm so sorry!' I said quietly as I reached over and wiped his fringe off his smooth forehead as he came into my arms for a cuddle. I wrapped my arms around him as we slid down under the covers. I gently pushed his one ear against my chest so he could hear my heartbeat, and placed my palm against his other ear to block out the world. As you were silent and Zane felt like he was asleep, I slowly released my breath and whispered out loud, *'I'm sorry, Jesse.'*

'You should be.' Your reply was flat and sad.

'Yes, I really am. But I hope you are too?' I waited, as your silence continued for a few more minutes.

'Sorry, Mum. I love you.'

'I love you too, mate, I just want us to get along and have some happy, peaceful night-time, day-time and everything in between. Do you think we can start to do that, mate?' I must have said every other night.

'Yes. I love you, Mum.' You dropped your hand over the side of the bunk, wiggling your fingers for me to take hold, which I did, linking my fingers through yours I stroked your hand until numbness took over the length of my arm as the blood flowed back down pooling uncomfortably in my arm pit.

'I love you, Mum,' you repeated.

'I know, I love you too. Now go to sleep, mate it's getting late and you've got school tomorrow.'

'Okay. Sorry, Mum, I love you.'

'Yes, mate, I love you.'

You continued saying sorry and I love you for another few minutes until you finally fell asleep.

I pushed myself off Zane's bed and stood in the middle of the room, the dining room light sending in soft shadows here and there. I stood there for a few minutes, listening to the breaths of two of the most important people whom I loved more than anything else in this world and felt mixed emotions from sadness with the way I spoke to you, embarrassment that Dad had witnessed my demise through months of battling with you, and gratefulness that everybody in this house was asleep, and

I finally had some alone time. I sighed quietly as I walked from the room to our tiny kitchen, to pop on the kettle, reflecting back on a recent conversation I'd had with a group of mums, including Noah's, about pre-teen boys.

They were all saying how much more vocal their boys had become and not in the nicest ways. Argumentative, rude, stubborn, abusive, and some of them even violent. A lot of it was absolutely normal teenage behaviour. Boys getting ready to grow into men, finding their way, battling through so many diverse emotions. I was thinking, I had it pretty good considering. Yes, your rudeness had certainly reached a point I never thought it would have, and your cheekiness had exceeded all points of no return in some conversations. But you didn't swear, you didn't push or hit with your fists. We were doing okay in the grand scheme of things. We were all alive and breathing, loved each other, were sorry when we knew we had done the wrong thing and tried to improve our ways. Until the next emotional, abusive battle. That's life isn't it, when you are caught up in the red haze of anger of —— *I can't believe this is happening - that my child is speaking to me like this - that I am responding in such a negative, possibly damaging way* — And then those moments where you'll tell yourself next time, you'll be in control in a mature, loving way.

In those moments when everyone in the house was asleep, and I had the relaxing company of Koonie purring contently in my lap as my fingers raced happily across my keyboard and Sade sang, *Love is Stronger than Pride,* I would be at peace and say to myself, *Tomorrow* is a new day. I will be a better, more understanding, loving, calm, supportive mother tomorrow. And I sincerely meant it at the time.

That's the thing with emotions. When you are in a happy calm place with positive affirmations floating in the air around you like bright coloured balloons, with no one around to pop or deflate, you can believe it all.

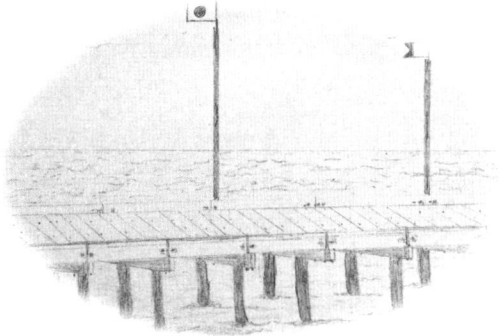

ALMOST THERE

As we drew closer to the end of 2013, Grammy organised a camping trip to Mallacoota. Despite the fact that it was a six-hour drive to get there, it was the most epic trip, and for me personally, I enjoyed it more than our Queensland trip. We were camped right in front of the river inlet with the ocean in our view. Our own little pier that we fished and dangled our feet off while we chatted in the early hours of the morning, with a cup of tea warming our hands. There was no such thing as a sleep-in with the dozens of pelicans and galahs flocking around the campsites, looking for a tasty morsel, with the never-ending flock of seagulls, imitating a scene from *Nemo* calling out to their mates — *mine, mine, mine.*

It pretty much rained the entire time we were there, but it was my kind of weather. We all huddled under Grammy and Poppy's deluxe camper-trailer annexe, playing copious games of UNO, cooking on our little gas stoves, and simply spending hours of quality time with you boys. The fact that Uncle Grant came along with us was so much fun for you and Zane. I know it meant a lot to Grammy and Dad to have his company, especially as he had just met a lovely young girl, Nicole, and still wanted to spend time with his family. Those who put family first, Legends!

Uncle Stuart came down for one night also, to go for a spear fish with Dad. Eight days of total relaxation in the fresh air, doing physical activities such as snorkelling, fishing, scooting at the local skate park, and bush walks, either as a group or splitting up for some quiet time. Grammy organised a treasure hunt in the nearby bush, which was a bit of educational fun and being the wildlife carer she was, relished any opportunity to discuss the Australian bush and wildlife that lived in it.

Poppy wanted to take both you and Zane out on his canoe for a paddle on the calm surface of the river's inlet. You said, *'No thanks, I don't want to get eaten by a shark!'*

Poppy replied, *'That's okay, mate. I'll take you out whenever you are ready.'* You and I knew, that wouldn't be anytime soon. So, Poppy took Zane out, while you and I stood chatting away with a cup of tea in our hands, standing at the end of our little pier.

'How are you enjoying our trip, mate?' I sat down on one of the little chairs Grammy had placed at the end of the pier, you sat on the other as you replied, *'I'm having fun. I love fishing. It has been my favourite thing to do while we've been here.'*

'Me too,' I smiled at you, secretly glad we hadn't caught a fish yet. The action itself was therapeutic, but the thought of a catching a beautiful creature, struggling for its life at the end of a hook didn't really sit well in my stomach. Grammy had been Vegan/Vegetarian for over forty years and her influence was great! (I say that, yet my mouth waters at the thought of crunching into pork crackling!)

We could hear Grammy call out excitedly, and as we looked over to see her pointing in Zane's and Poppy's direction, we followed her finger pointing to see a curious seal, swim alongside the canoe.

It was that kind of holiday. Full of surprises. On the last day, you, Zane, and I, had gone to the top of the lookout so I could record you both practising your Wing-Chun form with the serene ocean view as the background, with both of you fighting the gusts of wind trying to topple you over from the high point. As the heavy rain drops slowly started to ascend upon us, we made our retreat to get down the hill, passed the toilet blocks back to our campsite. Only as we approached the toilet blocks, and the little gateway back to our campsite, Skippy-on-steroids was blocking our exit. The three of us froze as Skip's eyes penetrated ours, waiting for our next move, when you whispered to Zane and I, *'Drop and look at the ground!'*

The three of us knelt together, our eyes remained down, which was difficult as I loved looking at the beautiful creature that was the Australian kangaroo, and once he established we were no threat to him, bound off in the direction we wanted to go. As we hit the campsite, many campers were exclaiming about the sheer size of the male roo that had just bounced along the front of their camp sites so brazenly. You had a big smile on your face as you relayed to Grammy that we had just met Skip at the loo block and had instructed Zane and I on what we should do. As usual, Grammy was very proud of her eldest grandson. We went out to tea on our final night where Poppy shouted the entire group a delicious meal, and you ordered chips with an extra serving of broccoli. That's my boy!

*****

We all settled back into our routines after we returned home and it wasn't too long before your attitude, although not as bad as before, returned. One morning getting you boys organised for school, you declared that you couldn't go in this morning as you had a sore tummy, and looking as pale as you did, I did not argue the point and sent you back to bed telling you we would make a doctor's appointment once I got Zane to school. It was probably your 22nd day off in the past six months and I was feeling a little bit overwhelmed as a mother, that you were having so many days off school, as we had had a pretty good attendance record up until this point.

It hadn't been a particularly pretty night, the night before, so walking into your Grade Six teacher's office the next morning I was trying to compose myself with a smile that said, *'All is well in my world'*

When Mr. S asked how you were, after I had informed him you wouldn't be in today, I looked at him speechless for a few moments. Is this where I was to reply politely how wonderful you were, the apple of my eye? I knew that's how he and all your past teachers saw you, as you never put a foot out of place in public. Or should I take the honest road and disclose not all was peaches and cream?

He continued looking at me, as I felt my bottom lip start an embarrassing tremble of its own accord, and my mouth overtook my brain and words tumbled out on top of each other: that I didn't know what was going on, you were breaking my heart, being rude, argumentative and not the Jesse I knew and loved!

He was a young teacher, probably fifteen years my junior and to his credit, stood there professionally and calmly and offered me a seat, to which I embarrassingly replied rather loudly, *'God no.'* What I meant to say was, *'No thank you, if I sit down I will fall in a heap and not get up.'* But, in these circumstances it is difficult to convey what one really means! (Please tell me I am not alone in this!)

After a few minutes discussing that it was normally a Tuesday here and there that you had been absent, Mr S mentioned that you had a reading helper who volunteered at the school every second Tuesday. He wanted me to go home and ask you about him and see what your response was and if you were comfortable with him. He asked about your mates and social life outside of school in which I informed him about Wing-Chun and that you preferred having mates over, rather than going to their homes and that you did enjoy coming home from school most days to have quiet time in your room. He replied, he had been exactly the same at your age, and even more so now he was an adult with a family of his own. It was interesting to listen to his opinion, about what you were going through as a pre-teen boy, and funnily enough, the next day he pulled me aside to mention, that he had had a chat to his own mother the night after he had spoken to me, about what he had been like at the same age as you, and had apparently given her hell. I could sense he felt a real connection with you and wanted to do all he could to help you. Yes, we discovered you were very uncomfortable with the reading helper, who actually was a lovely guy, only with your short-term memory and sometimes struggle with certain words, you were embarrassed to read out loud to him. Mr S rectified that situation and in no time, you were no longer missing any days for the remainder of the year. It was that simple.

*****

Your Grade Six Graduation was a celebration to be sure. Grammy and Aunty Nadine came down to take photos and simply be there to support you. It was a nostalgic moment watching you sit amongst all your peers, some of whom were very excited, patting themselves on the back for being the true legends they thought they were, others getting by the moment as quietly as you were. Many of you had gone to kindergarten together and now, here you were at the end of your primary school journey, about to embark on another chapter of your young lives, sitting in the hall of McClelland College. I told myself I wouldn't cry, but of course why did I bother? When they put on the slide show of you and all your friends throughout the years, along with a piece of music about friendship, it was designed to bring all that possessed a heartbeat to tears.

2016 - CHANGES

Here I sit, closer to the end of our story than at the beginning, yet it is our actual beginning that brings us where we are today. Tardwell curled up in a tight ball of grey fur at my feet, quiet chill-out music on, taking me to a place I really need to go, candles fluttering their calm light over my desk. Zane and you in your own rooms, communicating with your cousin in New South Wales via none other than Xbox live! Dad has just gone to bed. Labour day tomorrow, Dad is going off to work but Zane is thrilled he has the day off school.

A lot of this story has been difficult and painful to write and at some stages I have sat over my keyboard crying my eyes out for things I didn't see and wondering, why the hell am I writing this in the first place? (Also, walking in the garden with a Baileys and iced coffee has helped some of the more painful memories flow into a comedy of words that will hopefully make sense to other mothers, parents and carers out there, that will be able to relate to some of these experiences!)

Why am I sharing with the world, my moments of failure as a mother and all the times I have been clearly blind-sighted to what was the early signs of your anxiety? It was only researching the journals for this book that opened my eyes wider to — *Holly Hell I remember that*— and then many things fell into place. Yes, I have been beside myself with guilt many times, wishing I had seen, understood, and done more. Been the mother to you I used to be when you were two and tiny, adorable, and not an unkind thing to say. But that's not reality, is it?

Thanks to online support groups, I know I have not been alone in my thoughts, along with thousands of other parents who have experienced what we experienced with you. Children simply growing, trying to figure out their place in their family, fitting into school and the world around them and depending on their personalities, coping with thoughts, feelings, experiences, and life around them, in their very own individual ways. Parents blaming themselves for everything whilst trying to make sense of it all. In the end, we searched and used every resource available to us to help find the answer we so desperately needed at the time. What exactly was going on with you and how could we possibly help you?

Like that wonderful expression that Aunty Louise uses often, *It takes a village to raise a child,* it also takes an army of extraordinary individuals to want to support any soul that suffers from any form of mental illness. When they extended their helping hands beyond you and to our family, it really made the world of difference in our ability to support you.

These were ordinary people living their own lives, while having that extra ability to be dedicated, passionate, loyal, and simply sensational as individuals who cared for us all whilst we were trying to deal with so many unknown obstacles that were standing in our way to understanding what was going on with you.

And we were so very blessed and lucky to find the help that we needed to fight the unpredictable battle. So, like all things in life, there is a balance. The Ying to the Yang, the chicken crimpy to the French Onion dip, the rain to the sun and well, you get my point. If I had the skills of Sun Tzu, I would go on. I do not, so I shall spare you all.

What I'm trying to say, with the next phase of our lives, is that we were faced with both positive and negative reactions to the growing predator that consumed you and our family so wholly for the next 24 + months before the clouds parted and we felt like humans once more. It was during that difficult time that individuals' own strengths and weaknesses, and how they viewed us as individuals, and as a family unit, were revealed to us. It was both interesting and heart-breaking; we saw people for who they really were and some of them weren't so pretty. As Robbie said, *'What a shame we never listened.'* And some of them never did, spending a lifetime ignorant. One Aunt questioning, *'What's wrong with him?'* in an unfavourable, judgemental way, with the answer never being good or clear enough, and she would raise her eyebrows and look down her particularly dry nose at me, as if I too, were an unknown entity that needed to be dealt with. Unfortunately, you cannot pick your relatives!

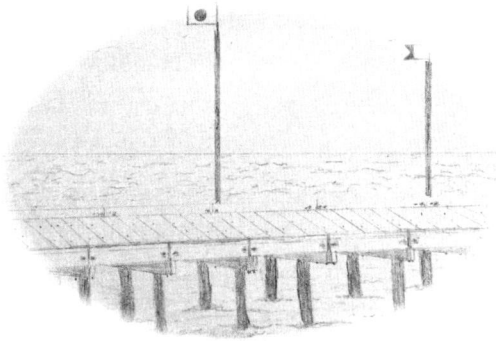

2014 - MILK BAR

The school holidays leading up to Year Seven were pretty amazing. We took the eight hour train/bus trip up to Mildura and had an awesome week with Aunty Louise, Rylan and Taylor, filling in the week stay with plenty of fun activities before heading back to Frankston to catch up with Sally, Aunty Nadine, and Aunty Leah. Grammy and Poppy came for a quick visit before they took off on one of their epic travelling adventures around Australia.

The usual fun with friends coming over for days, filled with pool and water-slide action, walks to the park and milk bar where you stuffed yourselves with sugary drinks and junk food; pre-teens living the dream. Until you weren't.

Two weeks before your Year Seven high school days began you and Noah grabbed your skateboards and headed out to hit the pavement for some chill out time. Zane was watching a DVD, Dad had just made lunch and I was reading a book in between cooking pancakes and a casserole. From our kitchen window, I had a clear view of the carport and driveway, where the basketball ring hangs and the driveway slopes down gently for some good speed on the skateboards.

I finished a riveting page and flipped the next batch of pancakes before they got too black on one side, and popped the casserole in the oven contemplating pouring a glass of wine, when I looked out the window and saw Noah standing alone in the driveway breathing heavily, looking sweaty and staring in the direction I was hoping you would be any second now. Turning the gas off I went to open the front door as Noah walked in.

'Are you okay, mate?' I asked as he walked by me and headed off into Zane's room. He mumbled something and disappeared. Noah was always such a polite kid, so I knew instantly something wasn't right when he vanished into Zane's room without so much as a feasible word. Dad came into the room looking at me.

'What was that all about?'

'I don't know, but I want to know where Jesse is,' I said as I walked over to the window and looked out again, with no trace of you to be seen. I then walked down to Zane's room, knocking on the door as I pushed it open. There was Noah, mentioning something about a group of brothers, close to tears.

'Noah, where's Jesse?' I walked over to him, rubbing his shoulders, not wanting to embarrass him by putting my arms around him. We were pretty comfortable with each other, but teenage boys when emotional and when they are not your own, are scary and unpredictable little creatures.

'He's behind me,' was all Noah could say.

'Are you okay, mate?' I tried again.

He looked me in the eye and responded, *'Not really.'* His voice broke and he cleared his throat.

My thoughts were racing as I was wondering what the hell was going on, and where were you? Dad walked up behind me, asking Noah if he was all right when we heard the front door open and slam shut, and heavy footsteps approach. We turned to a sight I will never forget. Your face was filled with diverse emotions of sadness, rage, and turmoil.

'*What's wrong, Jesse?*' I asked as I walked towards you, you looked like a ticking time bomb, wanting to go off but not knowing how to, and then *BANG!* You went off into an explosive rage of verbal ranting, and it looked like you had no idea where you wanted to go; your body vibrating in anger as your fists opened and closed, your eyes flashed bright and teary.

'*Those stupid ugly bitches!*' you practically screamed, as you banged your fist on the wall. I knew instinctively something was beyond off as Dad came up on one side of you, I on the other and we put our arms around you as you started shouting, swearing and was close to exploding. It was the first time we allowed you to swear your head off and let it all out, although at this stage we had no clear idea what had happened, our arms created a safety net around you keeping you from self-harm or any possible holes in our poor old walls!

As we kept you firmly in our embrace, letting you know it was all right, with kisses on your head, we listened to Noah telling Zane about a family of four brothers that had basically attacked you at the milk bar, as they thought you boys had upset their little brother, who was in fact a year older than you. Another boy from school who had been walking out of the milk bar, made a passing comment to the little brother as you and Noah walked into the milk bar, and by the time you both walked out with your goodies, the little brother had run into his big brothers and they all assumed it was you two that had upset him. Brainless enough not to do their research correctly, they attacked you both. I will be completely diplomatic and won't refer to this family by any sort of name. Only to point out sadly, ours was certainly not the first family they had scarred deeply with their inbred, derelict ways.

(Although this must seem like a harsh comment, I believe it is just. I don't know what these people have gone through in their own lives and I hate to judge, but my belief, religion, and value in life is, treat others how you would like to be treated. These people are the worst kind of humans. They have no reasoning skills, and their instinct is attack first and don't ask questions at all. Stupid, stupid people).

They surrounded and towered over two twelve-year-old boys taunting and threatening to punch your faces in because you said *boo* to their little brother. Noah tried to explain that neither of you had said a thing to their brother, but the older boys, along with the brother, did not listen whatsoever.

They threatened you both with bodily harm, and poor Noah having older brothers himself, believed them and fled as fast as he could back to our house, leaving you behind to face the band of cowards on your own. They wrestled your skateboard off you, flinging it across the road yelling at you, *'If we ever see you around here again we are going to break your face.'*

I can't imagine what you must have felt. Pure anger at the unjust situation, and of course you would have been frightened. Facing these idiots alone, having them physically wrestle your skateboard off you that Uncle Grant had only bought you weeks before for Christmas, and watch it get launched across the road whilst they threatened you some more. For me, imagining you crossing the road, fear in your heart to collect your now broken skateboard, and run the five minutes home to safety as fast as you could, breaks my heart for you. And holding you in my arms, angry and crying, listening to both you and Noah vent your stories, made my blood boil to a new level.

My eyes met your Dad's across your head as you quietened and after we reassured you everything was going to be okay, Dad went to comfort Noah while I texted his mother, Michelle, to let her know what had happened.

I rang the police and gave them the rundown of what you boys had said had happened. The officer I spoke to had in fact heard of this unfavourable family, and was as equally unimpressed as I was, with what you boys had been through. Unfortunately, there was nothing we could do that did not involve taking you down to the station to give a statement. Even then nothing was set in concrete that these people would be dealt with. After asking if that's something you wanted to do, you exhaustingly responded no and along with Noah's mum, we left it at that.

Their threats of *breaking your face* stayed with you for a very long time. And it was in fact over two years before you went to that milk bar again, when Noah came back for a visit from Queensland, you both went for a walk, ending up at the milk bar. What I did not know at the time was that you carried in your jacket, a pocket knife that Uncle Cameron had gotten you for a thirteenth birthday present, for protection. That says a lot in itself.

2014 - MCCLELLAND COLLEGE: YEAR SEVEN

Taking that first photo of you the morning before I dropped you off at school was a moment I proudly enjoyed as a mum. Seeing you standing there, hands in your pockets of the smart grey shorts, the purple spray jacket giving you a burst of colour and your cheeky grin as you laughed into the camera, set the tone of the day perfectly. You looked so cute and handsome all at once. I was so excited for you! This was going to be an epic year for you, I just knew it! (In saying that, I actually know nothing as it turns out!)

Dropping you off at the back car park, watching you get out with your heavy bag I said, *'Have the best day, mate. I love you.'*

'Love you,' you mumbled as you swung your bag onto your back closing the car door.

'*See you later, mate,*' I called in a happy voice oozing with '*You're going to have a great day*', through the car window, as you walked off waving your hand quickly and walking towards the stairs leading to your Year Seven building known as '*The Max*'. I drove off slowly, watching you in the rear-view mirror for as long as I could, as I exited the car park, enjoying the moment that my eldest son was starting high school. I had a few minutes to enjoy my proud, happy tears before I pulled myself together to go and get Zane organised for school.

You settled in well the first few weeks, making new friends and enjoying catching up with your old mates. You were, as always, easy to get along with, well-liked and appreciated for the good-hearted little soul you were. You saw a lot of old faces from your first primary school and some of those kids remembered you well. Thankfully all was going smoothly where you enjoyed your teachers, especially one of your Year Seven Co-ordinators, the enthusiastically, dedicated Ms Craig.

You loved the fact that you weren't sitting in one classroom all day and the variety of subjects excited you. You were learning the trumpet and as Dad played the guitar, harmonica, and drums, took great joy in watching you sit out in the garden whilst you blew away on your borrowed instrument.

As much as Noah and you were still good mates, you saw less of each other as he formed friendships with some other boys, which his mum wasn't so impressed with as they were a bit of a bad influence on his usually good attitude. You became close to a boy named Tide who had recently moved from Alice Springs, with his twin sister, Tilly. Your friendship became something closer to brotherhood. You were so similar in many ways and like most parents, Dad and I were always pleased with your choices to have *nice* friends hanging around, considering how often we had them in our home. You continued with your Wing-Chun training Tuesdays and Thursdays, so on the quiet afternoons I'd take you all swimming after school or you'd skateboard down to the park where you'd meet up with a group of mates to play basketball. Every second weekend Tide would come for sleepovers where we'd get the fire going in the backyard and you'd hang out talking late into the night. He was a pleasure to have, especially as he got along so well with Zane also. It certainly made having an extra body as often as we had Tide, that much easier.

It was close to the halfway point of term one, where our usual smooth sailing mornings altered. You were getting a bit grumpy and unreasonably rude as we would get ready to leave the house. I put that down to tiredness. And then our three-minute drive to the school, was no longer three minutes of peace. You were rude, and no matter how nice I tried to be, remaining calm and positive was no longer an option with your angry, aggressive mode and I too, turned into a nasty banshee, dropping you off with cruel words between us. As soon as the car door closed, and I watched your back get smaller as you walked away, I would feel immediate guilt, wanting to call out, *'I'm so sorry, I love you, have a great day.'* All I wanted was for you to be happy, feel loved and have a good day at school. I wondered if you felt as sad as I did that we fought. I know the overwhelming feeling of guilt, (coupled with the fact that on these occasions I was in fact a shit mother), remained with me for the entire day.

Watching you walk towards the car in the afternoons after our horrid mornings, I could hear Julia Andrews singing out about her favourite things, reminding myself you were definitely one of my favourite things, and I needed to pour some good old-fashioned love and positive energy into you. After apologising to you we hugged it out and all was well.

Yes— bickering, arguing, and disagreements are all part of *some-kind-of-normality* between kids and parents. Families growing and learning to come together. It's all a bit like a brilliant piece of artwork that can take ten to twenty years to complete. Starting with some awkward, fumbling, harsh strokes before it turns to smooth, flowing, soothing corrections before it can be perfected. Parenting— it's all an emotionally draining yet positive work in progress.

And for the most part term one was positive. You were thriving and we had a lot of comments from family and friends that noticed your confidence increase through your general happiness. You had mentioned only twice the entire term of the two occasions that had upset you. The first incident was Music. Your band was supposed to perform at an assembly in front of the entire school, which freaked you right out. You weren't too confident on the trumpet and had trouble reading the sheet music. Where was Aunty Kylie when you needed her, with her Grade Eight classical pianoforte, and Grade Six theory classical!

You asked me if I could talk to the music teacher so you did not have to play, which I did. Lovely guy and understood your stage fright, suggesting we perhaps put you at the back of the band so you would not feel so noticeable. That was not an option you liked, so we agreed you could simply sit in the audience with the other students, until next time where you might like to give it a go. This resulted in another class-mate from band, calling you a *Pussy Gay Faggot* because you were too *'scared'* to get up and perform.

The second incident you would prefer me not to write about, so I shall not. Needless to say, it involved some silly boys with too much time on their hands, and not enough information floating about in their brains. We were lucky on both occasions to speak to the lovely Ms Craig and although the incident was quite unsettling, all was dealt with accordingly.

As much as we loved McClelland College at this stage, we were yet to know the full power of its extraordinary capability to support a thousand or so families, yet make you feel like yours, and yours alone, truly counted for something within their community. Like meeting a quality friend for the first time. You know they have something special about them, you just haven't figured it completely out just yet, as it takes time to discover their admirable qualities. That's what McClelland became to us in the end. A dependable friend with a hand extended to help in any way they could. I'm sure there are a lot of schools out there that feel they can say the same. All I can say, in our time of crisis, bleakness, and despair, is I'm so very glad we chose McClelland College to be yours, and Zane's, stepping stone from childhood to adulthood.

TERM ONE HOLIDAYS

As always, we loved our holidays together. Family time, to re-connect after the busy term settling into new routines. We had our relaxing, wind down days, and others filled with catching up with family and friends, doing plenty of stimulating activities to keep our group of thirteen plus kids happy, from the ages of seven through to fifteen. On the Friday before school resumed we went to Jacqui's to have a barbecue lunch. We all loved going to Jacqui's, as she along with her husband Tom, made all feel welcome and at home. Zane felt like Harry Potter around Jacqui, and called her his *Mrs Weasley* as she treated you both like long lost sons when you walked in her door.

Sally was off in Hamilton, so it was just Bec and her three, Jacqui and her three plus her niece and us. Another bonus of going to Jacqui's house, was that she lived a street away from Havana Crescent, which housed Karingal Heights Primary School, your old kinder, a newly built park and a milk bar. And although you had not been back to our milk bar the past two months, you felt comfortable going with the larger group to Jacqui's. So, after a game of soccer at the oval, we all had lunch and afterwards all you kids grabbed some loose change, your scooters and headed off to the milk bar and then the park to hang out for a bit, which allowed us girls a chance to sit back and chat in private about things and life in general, a glass of wine in hand and everyone happy.

After twenty or so minutes, our serenity ended with Rebecca and Zane running in shouting out about someone stealing your scooter. You walked in behind them with all the other kids, looking frustrated and angry.

'*What happened Jess?*' Jacqui asked, '*did they pinch it while you were inside the milk bar, mate?*'

Before you could respond, Gracie stepped forward. '*No, these three boys came up to us and told Jesse it looked like the coolest scooter ever and one of them asked if he could have a go.*'

All eyes went to you and I knew straight away with your trusting, kind heart that you had let the boy try your scooter. 'Aw, Jess. Are you okay?'

You shook your head. '*I just thought he'd have a go and give it back, but he kept scooting off, and then they all just ran for it.*'

I gave you a squeeze and rubbed your arm, as all the kids started talking at once, answering Jacqui's questions about whether or not anyone knew who these boys were. We all decided to go off and do a manhunt to find the thieves, unfortunately we did not, and stopped after thirty minutes walking and driving around the local area to see if we might get lucky. You were very upset, and your trust in people began to break. Tyler commented how he would never let some idiot he didn't know borrow anything of his, and Bec replied we were all different and Jesse's faith in people to do the right thing was strong.

It wasn't after that day. And sadly, I played a huge role along with Sally, in breaking your trust in people even further.

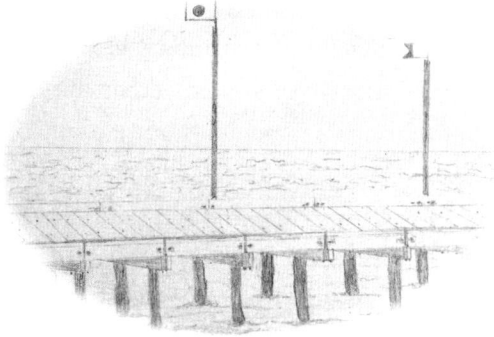

TERM TWO

Despite the scooter incident, the holidays had been great, refreshing, and gave us all that little recharge to get ready for term two. Although I missed you and Zane when the school day commenced, I also loved the balance of life the routine of school gave us all. Once you were off, I had the chance to blitz the housework, get any shopping done, cooking, research publishers, get on with writing, and if I was lucky enough, catch up with my girls for a much-needed cup of tea, before school pick up and my time with you boys and your after-school activities resumed.

Yes, two weeks in and I was feeling really good about the direction life was taking us all. I was about to start a part-time job in sales to take some of the financial pressure off Dad, that worked around your school hours, and fitted in perfectly with me being able to write my heart out after hours. You and Zane had gotten your red belts in Wing-Chun and you had the dream of black belt in your sights.

So, one morning walking into your room to wake you up for your morning shower, you informed me you weren't feeling well and you had a terrible stomach ache and couldn't go into school today. *'Okay, mate, just go back to sleep,'* I had said after noting you didn't have your usual colour about you. Getting Zane up and in the shower before breakfast with some cartoons, I rang McClelland's absence line and left a message saying you would be absent this day due to a stomach ache, and took Zane off to school, before my usual day began. When Sally popped in for a cup of tea mid-morning, you were vacuuming your room. She walked down to your room to see how you were feeling and was genuinely concerned you weren't well.

When Dad came home from work, I told him you missed school today due to a tummy pain. He went down to your room to see how you were, and was happy to see you happy, with good colour in your face, laughing about something with Zane.

The following morning was exactly the same, and for the next two and a half weeks, ground-hog day was on repeat in our house. For fourteen days, I rang the absence line, and each day was harder than the next, constantly trying to sound convincing as I repeated, *'Jesse Weitering of Year 704 won't be in today due to a stomach ache. Thank you.'* Of course, sometimes I'd try to spruce it up a bit, say you had a headache or a really bad case of hay fever. I mean could I be that convincing and say, two weeks in a row that you had a tummy ache? Yes, it may have been the case but for me having to repeat it I was thinking, *These* people are going to think I'm a pushover! How could one child have a tummy ache, fourteen days in a row? Simple really, but it was too simple at the time to see it for what it was. Anxiety was coming into play big-time, right in front of my face.

My little man was suffering, depleting of self-worth, and all I could think was, *'What's your Dad going to say tonight when I tell him I couldn't get you to school again?'* I couldn't handle seeing him roll his eyes or shake his head. I didn't want to appear to be a slack or lazy parent that couldn't be bothered getting their child to school. On the third week, ringing the absence line I remember waiting for the voice on the other end to finish it's recording of, *'Please state your student's name, class, and reason for absence.'* I paused at the end of the recording thinking, *What am I supposed to say today?* and in a flat, almost breaking tone, I mentioned you had a stomach ache once again.

For those three weeks, every morning I would wake you up, praying this would be the day I could get you to school. That all would be well and back to normal. *'I can't, Mum,'* you would say.

And I, in a very unsupportive, ignorant way, would un-elegantly scream, *'No-one's going to believe that you've had a bloody stomach ache for bloody three weeks in a row! Get your lazy butt out of bed and in the shower NOW! This is serious business you are in HIGH School Now!'* If I could have slapped myself in the face then and there, with a huge *'HELLO! SOMETHINGS NOT RIGHT!'* sign, I would have.

The day would continue, and once you knew the school day had started, you would slowly emerge from your bed and get on with your day and as the school day drew to an end, and it was time to collect Zane, you were once again in your happy place. It was so frustrating, and I would think to myself, *'Yeah, you really had a stomach-ache.'*

Sally would pop in each morning to see how you were, clearly concerned, and I'd try to keep it together. It's so hard to explain how I was feeling: lost - I didn't know what was going on; frustrated - I didn't know how to help and motivate you; sad for you - as you were missing out on fun, productive school days with your mates. Basically, I took it all personally, and felt like a complete failure as a mother, not being able to get my son to school. I was really getting concerned that something was seriously wrong.

It was in those three weeks I lost the sales position, as clearly, I couldn't be counted on to be available when they needed me, and sorry I was not about to leave my twelve-year-old son home alone any time soon!

Towards the end of week three, I was so happy to see you get out of bed when I called, in the shower, dressed, (*Praise the lord!*) grab your school bag and off to the front door we trundled, beyond excited that you were heading off for school. It was the Grand Final and we were running through our team's banner, on our way to victory!

On reaching for the door handle, your school bag slipped from your shoulder and hit the floor boards with a thump. I looked down at you as you turned to face me, and I was shocked at how pale you actually were.

'*I need to go to the toilet,*' you quickly said as you turned and bolted towards your and Zane's loo.

'*Okay, mate, hurry up, we don't want you to be late,*' I replied, concerned but not wanting to admit defeat just yet. In the amount of time you were on the toilet, I got Zane organised for school, dropped him off and returned home. You were still on the toilet two hours later, stinking up the place. Needless to say, we lost the Grand Final that day, and I rang the absence line once more, to state that on this day, you at least had something different, diarrhoea.

For the next week that's how each day went. You would rise, shower, dress, state you were not hungry and we would get to the front door. That's as far as you would get. '*Mum, I don't feel well.*' Your paleness was one thing, your tears another. It broke my heart and on top of no sleep say, for the past twelve years, I was close to breaking myself. You would dash to the loo and I would get on with getting Zane ready for school. He would say quietly, '*Is Jesse going to school today, Mum?*'

I would always reply with a smile, '*I'll see if I can get him there after I've dropped you off, love.*'

I felt like I said that day after day to your little brother for years whilst he got on with things and trundled off to school. As much as you were brothers, with the typical love/hate relationship, Zane was one little individual that was always sympathetic, supportive, and loyal to you and your cause, no matter how many times you broke his heart. Of course, you didn't see it like that, but that's okay. That's life.

During those first few weeks, Sally continued being the supportive friend she was, and would also witness your physical demise in the mornings. Once she had her three off to school, she would pop in before helping out at one of the many places she volunteered at, to see if there was anything she could do for you. It was two things, having my dear friend witness you and I at our worst. Firstly, she validated that I wasn't going crazy, that she too, could see you not coping physically in the mornings. That you were not making it up, and that I was not covering for you. Secondly and irrationally, I would find it embarrassing and frustrating that I couldn't get you to school, no matter what I said, how I tried to encourage or yes, even bribe you.

At the end of week three, seeing Dad's exhausted and questioning gaze each afternoon when he came home from work, and every morning, Sally along with a handful of other friends questioning if I got you to school that day, was like a pressure cooker ready to explode in my head. I was feeling the pressure build with every day that passed, every question asked and I knew I needed to get some answers myself before I internally exploded.

BEYOND BLUE

Before Uncle Grant met the love of his life, he dated a lovely lady whom I became friends with over the years, Julie Winter. A New Zealander by birth, she had travelled the world and worked as a counsellor with Kids Helpline and Beyond Blue. I knew I needed help but did not want to be judged in my fragile state. And yes, I was feeling fragile and exhausted. Put me as an individual, a girl, a woman through any kind of hell and I will and have survived. But if that Hell involves watching my child go through any kind of torment, then as strong as I am, my heart will be bleeding. Case closed. End of story. Watching you suffer with this unknown entity was killing my soul. As Julie had met us, as a family on many occasions, I wanted to run our situation by her. After she graciously gave me an hour of her precious time off, listening to me give her the run through of the past few weeks, let alone term one, not wanting to perform in the band, both the milk bar incidents, you leaving the house less and less, and becoming angry and upset more easily, she asked many questions and gave her opinion, with her years of experience, that it sounded a lot like you were suffering from anxiety. She then gave me Headspace's number in Frankston and suggested I give them a ring immediately.

I graciously thanked her for her time and verbal support, and after taking down the number, gave myself five minutes to get my composure together, before giving Headspace a ring. After speaking to a lovely gentleman, Greg and giving him a basic run down, he also said it sounded very much like you had some form of anxiety, but of course he couldn't state for sure until he could meet and chat with you, along with another member of the Headspace team. I made an appointment for the coming week, hung up and felt like I'd just climbed out of Mount Noorat after being on the wine all night after my high school reunion!

I took a few breaths and walked on down to your room where you were sitting on your bed, patting Summer. You looked up, I knew you'd heard me on the phone and I smiled at you, hoping it was a reassuring smile, filled with love and support. *'Julie says hello, love, and hopes you are well.'*

You nodded. You had always liked Julie. *'Who else were you talking to?'*

'Oh, a friend of Julie's, a man named Greg. He wants to talk to you and help you get back to school.' I was hoping that didn't sound creepy.

'I don't need help to get back to school. I'm going back when I feel better, I just can't go today.' You sounded calm enough for me to gently press on.

'I know, mate, but it's close to five weeks into term two and we need to get you back ASAP so you don't fall too far behind with the work!'

'You don't understand,' you screamed, pushing me out of your room and slamming the door in my face. You were right. I did not. I was a rotten mother. All I could feel was the pressure of Dad's questioning

gaze, of the school asking how you were, of friends seeing if I got you in today, with family wondering what I was doing about your school absence, and the pressure cooker was about to burst.

*****

I arranged a meeting for you and me to go into McClelland to have a chat to Ms Craig and the Vice Principal at the time, Mr Capp. When the day arrived, I could not get you out the front door. What was supposed to be a gentle, persuasive talk about getting you into school for a chat, turned into War of the Worlds, with you just about hyperventilating with anger. So, I went alone and sat in the office waiting for Ms Craig to call my name, trying to compose myself and get the angry, sad image of you out of my head. Once Ms Craig came to collect me and take me to Mr Capp's office, I was on edge and repeated to myself — 'Don't cry, don't cry, speak calmly, and don't get emotional.'

Ms Craig asked where you were and said she would have loved to have seen your face today, telling me she adored your cheeky grin when she had the opportunity to see it. I explained I could not persuade you to join me this morning.

Walking into the office, Mr Capp walked around his desk and reached out his hand for me to shake, with a polite smile on his face as Ms Craig introduced us. He was a friendly guy and I felt calm immediately as he pulled three chairs close together so we could sit as an informal trio. I appreciated it immensely and felt completely at ease to tell your story up to date in a calm, narrative way in the hope that he and the school would support you and the fact that we wanted you at school; we just couldn't get you there at this stage. It was my biggest fear that you would no longer be a part of their community if we could not get you back in their gates as soon as possible. The more I spoke of how I saw your decline each morning, your struggle, I could feel myself break and hearing Sully's voice from *Monsters Inc.* calling out *Keep it together, man!* did not help, and I lost it towards the end, retelling of how I saw you collapse at the front door too many mornings to count. Both Ms Craig and Mr Capp were so supportive of you, and Mr Capp mentioned how he would love to meet you, so you would have another familiar face at the school to come to if you needed to. He mentioned getting you into see his mate Pellegrino, the school's Psychologist, for a chat once I organised a Mental Health Plan for you with our doctor. A Mental Health Plan!

I hugged Ms Craig when I left, and thanked Mr Capp, from the bottom of my heart. And on the short drive home, I could hear the words, mental health plan, mental health plan, mental health, mental, mental, over, and over in my brain. Like, it would not stop. Mental, Mental, Mental!

Pulling up in the driveway, I told myself to chill the hell out. A Mental Health Plan was a positive, productive direction.

You were waiting inside the front door for me, saying how sorry you were that you didn't come to the meeting. I told you it was all alright, giving you a hug as you cried and said how sorry you were that you didn't come.

'I'm so sorry, Mum, so sorry, I love you. I love you, Mum.'

'I know, mate, it's okay, I love you too. Look, don't be upset. Let's have a cup of tea and chat.'

'Okay, Mum, okay. I'm sorry, I love you. I love you, Mum,' you repeated once again.

'Jesse, I love you too, mate, it's okay. Now let's put that kettle on.' I unlocked the back door so the fresh air would stream in and walked into the kitchen to light the gas under good old *Russell Hobbs*.

'Come on, let's go sit out in the sun,' I said to you after I pulled our cups down and threw an Earl Grey tea bag into each one waiting for the kettle to boil.

'Am I in trouble?' you asked as we walked out into the sunlit garden full of autumn blooms.

I sat down near the pond, watching the gold fish glide around the lily pads, enjoying the serenity our garden always gave me, and taking a leaf out of its calmness, I turned to you and gave you my most reassuring look and said, *'No of course you are not in trouble. In fact, Mr Capp and Ms Craig want to do everything they can to make you feel safe and happy to come back to school and Mr Capp has a friend that you can chat to about getting any help you need to get back to school. How does that sound?'* I watched you become more closed off; the more I talked, especially when I mentioned you chatting to Mr Capp's friend.

'I don't want to talk to anyone, Mum.'

'I know you don't, mate, but we need someone's help to get you back to school and Mr Capp's friend will do that.'

You stood up and shouted, *'I said I don't need to talk to anyone and I'm not talking to some stupid Paedophile!'*

I stood to as a car pulled up in the driveway, my blood pumping faster at the look of outrage on your face. *'Jesse, calm down. It's okay.'*

'NO, IT'S NOT, MUM!' you screamed before racing inside, slamming your bedroom door as the kettle joined in your screaming; Sally was knocking on the front door and the phone started ringing.

'Come on in, Sal,' I called, forcing out some cheer I did not feel, as I walked into the kitchen to flick the kettle off, grabbing the phone from its cradle, I smiled at Sally as she walked past me towards the bedroom as I sang out, *'Hello, Michelle speaking,'* and Aunty Nadine's sweet voice brought me to tears as I explained you were still not at school. She firmly told me, *'Mickey, you need to get onto this immediately. Something is not right.'* I almost laughed through my tears thinking— *Really? I had no idea, please, tell me something I don't know!*— But I knew deep down she was coming from a good place, and I was on an emotionally overrun roller-coaster with a few cracks in the tracks that needed some good maintenance. It was easy for me to think I was being judged on my parenting at this stage, and always the happy person I usually was, did not see my own decline of depression sliding into my life. It took me until I was, my very happy self a year later, to recognise and admit I had overlooked my own depression.

I told her about my earlier meeting, and listened to her thoughts about our situation, in-between trying to listen in on Sally's conversation with you. After a few minutes, we ended our conversation with words of love and support between us. Aunty Nadine was dealing with her own battles with your cousin Ava, and in the end, we were both blessed to have each other to bounce ideas off, thoughts and general frustrations through tears and laughter. Blessed as we were, like I said, life is hard when you watch your own flesh and blood suffer.

THE DAY BEFORE YOU
TURNED THIRTEEN.
HEADSPACE.

What was supposed to be a special day was in fact, an absolute night-mare. Your last day of being twelve, and I ruined it. Completely! Just for something different! Our appointment at Headspace was at 1.15 pm. The only reason I was able to get you to leave the house so willingly this day, was that we were going to shop for your thirteenth birthday present. You wanted a new Xbox 360 game from E.B Games, and I would have given you the world if I could; I felt that guilty I was trick-ing you to get you into Frankston's Headspace.

I was also your mother enough to know, if I didn't make up some sort of story to get you there, I never would. And I was unashamedly, completely desperate. So, our day was all about shopping for your birthday, which it kind of was, followed by a visit to Bec at Strandbags where she worked at the time, then we drove through the McDonald's drive thru on our way to Headspace. Once you were happily stuffing your face with a cheeseburger and fries, we drove into Frankston. Pulling up into the Headspace car park you asked. *'Is this a Doctors, Mum?'*

'No, it's not,' I replied. I wasn't lying. *'It's an information centre, and I'm helping a friend out by getting some pamphlets for her daughter.'* That sounded pretty good to my ears. Certainly convincing, as to why we would come here. *'Do you want to come in with me?'* That's it, I thought to myself; make him believe he has a choice!

'Well, I'm not staying here by myself, who knows how many paedophiles are around here!' You said this like you knew what the hell a paedophile was. I needed to know who you had been getting your information from and clarify, if you knew what it was in fact you were talking about.

We walked into the building and my gut was clenched in knots, hoping they wouldn't call out your name as I walked to the information wall and started collecting leaflets on anxiety, depression, and a few others I thought might be useful for Dad to look at later. I knew he had started his own research on anxiety, but it's always good to have a paper trail to share with others that don't have internet access. (Nana Lyn!) I told you to take a seat as I walked to the counter, praying the girl would not say your name until I could quietly let her know who we were and why we were here. Of course, luck was not on my side, as I stepped closer she smiled brightly and called, *'Jesse Weitering.'*

'Yes, that's my son,' I said quietly as she passed me an iPad to start filling in our personal details. I gave her a small smile as I took it from her and turned around to go sit by you. The next 20 minutes were amongst some of the worst I will ever have as a mother. The look of betrayal on your face as I sat beside you, as I started clicking on answers and typing in details. You were disgusted. *'You are a fucking liar! I am*

getting out of this shit place, it's full of fucking paedophiles.' You sat rigid, your face as angry as I've ever seen it.

I was shocked at your public outburst and devastated by your reaction. I wasn't expecting you to be overly pleased that I had gotten you here by deception, but I wasn't expecting this heated attack either. *'It's going to be okay, mate. We're here for me as much as you, so I can help you.'* I tried to sound calm, reasoning as my own panic began to set in. I could feel my heart try to claw its way out of my chest.

'I hate you! You are nothing but a fucking lair! You are the worst mum ever!' Your voice was full of so much anger, hurt, resentment and devastation. Although at the time that wasn't what shocked me to my core. It was the fact that, although you were sitting so rigidly, you were swearing your head off in a public place, almost politely even, as you hissed the words out quietly. Not quietly enough that the receptionist didn't hear you, or a few other clients that had wandered in. The receptionist gave me a sympathetic look as I handed her back the iPad.

I took a deep breath holding myself together as I walked back over to you. I'll admit it was one of the hardest things for me to sit beside you, watching you fight back the tears of fright, as you continued hating me verbally. I completely understood where you were coming from. I had lied to get you here. But how the hell else could I have done it? I knew if I told you, I would not have gotten you in the car. Simple fact! I was a desperate mother that wanted her son well, sorted and back to school. *Was I so wrong?* Yes, apparently, I was. But *bloody-hell*, I was doing the best I could with what I knew! It obviously was not enough.

I could only take your hatred for a few more moments before I quietly choked out, *'That's enough Jesse! I have brought you here today because we need some help getting you back to school and happy. That's it! Please calm down!'*

'I hate you, I fucking hate you and this stupid place!' Your voice broke, along with my heart.

I got up and walked across to the other side of the room, arms folded, forcing back the sobs that wanted to escape my tight throat. *Look up, look up!* I repeated, stopping the tears that desperately wanted to fall to cleanse my soul, trying to block out your brazen, quiet swearing from across the room. My god you must have been in so much pain! With my arms folded, I pinched myself as hard as I could as I walked around the large waiting room, reading about all the wonderful things Headspace could do for you and others like you. It seemed like such a wonderful place that offered so much. Your name was called and I walked over to the open doorway that led into the offices. A tall, thin man stood, looking across at you. Sitting there looking small and cross. I walked over to him and reached out my hand. *'Hi, I'm Michelle, I'm Jesse's mum.'*

He shook my hand meeting my eyes. I could see he was taking in their red glow and teary surface. *'I'm Peter,'* he said gently, calmly, his eyes returning to you as he let go my hand. *'And is this Jesse?'* He offered you a smile you wanted no part of.

'Yes,' I replied, turning my own gaze in your direction. It was hard for me to meet your eyes. The distant look on your face. In trying to help you, my eldest son whom I loved so much, I had completely broken us. I wanted to burst out crying then and there, my pain was that deep!

Peter was asking you if you wanted to come with him, which you flatly ignored him. It was so unlike you to be openly rude. It was one of the biggest signs for me that things in our universe were completely out-of-whack. You turned your gaze away from us both, and Peter looked at me. *'Will he run away from here if I bring you back into our rooms?'* I wanted to laugh and tell him there was no way in hell you would leave this building, as you were too afraid of the people 'out there,' but simply replied. *'Trust me, Jesse will not leave without me.'* Yes, I was that sure. Even though you hated my guts in this moment, I knew you hated the world out there more. You would not leave without me. It had to be a mother- son thing.

Peter mentioned something quietly to the receptionist, probably to keep her eye on you and asked me to follow him. I glanced at you. *'Are you sure you don't want to come, mate?'*

You shook your head as Peter said, *'You can change your mind anytime, Jesse. I'll have a chat to Mum, and if you want to join us later, you can. Okay?'*

You nodded, saying nothing.

It pained me to walk away from you, yet I was happy to have a moment away from your hateful stare. Following Peter into a small room and taking a seat, I tried to keep it together as constant thoughts flowed around my brain— *'He hates you, this is your life now, you suck!'*

Peter snapped me out of it, asking me questions and taking down notes. And what do we, as parents do in these situations? Clear our throats, answer in our polite, public voice as elegantly as we can, so as not to be judged as an unstable parent doing damage to their child. I never thought I'd be in the position where I felt I had to justify my parenting, along with Dad's. But in these circumstances, it's like you are pledging your case.

'Please Sir, we are wonderful, loving parents, and have not intended to do any harm to our child, but he has issues regardless and we really need your help!' Of course, it's not like that at all, but like I said earlier, when you are at your lowest point, and although grateful for any help you are about to receive, regarding the wellbeing of your child, it is hard not to take absolutely everything, including every mistake and wrong decision, so very personally.

After I gave Peter as much information as he asked for, he was finally able to convince you to come and join us for a chat. Your eyes remained downcast, your answers as brief as you could get them. After half an hour, Peter said he had plenty of background information and asked if he could do a follow up call, which of course I agreed to.

Saying thank you and goodbye, we walked quietly back to the car. Getting in, I glanced in the review mirror, wishing I hadn't, as a large gob of mascara, stuck to my eye lid, greeted me. I looked like the wreck

I felt. Pushing the mirror away, I rubbed my eyelid, as I glanced across at you.

You reached for your coke that you had left in the cup holder when we pulled into the carpark earlier.

'*I'm so sorry, Jesse. I didn't want to lie to you*'

'*Then you shouldn't have,*' you replied, sucking on the straw.

I know, mate but if I hadn't, I wouldn't have gotten you here and I really needed some help to get you back to school.'

'*Yes, I would have. If you had of just told me the truth, I would have.*'

I didn't want to argue with you anymore. I knew for a fact, I would not have gotten you in the car if it hadn't been for your birthday and the promise of a McDonald's feed. You had not left the house for the past five weeks. I started the engine and we drove home in silence.

That night, after I had given Dad the information, I broke down explaining how devastated you were, in me betraying you. '*Why didn't you just tell him?*' Dad asked.

I shook my head. '*There is no way he would have left this house if I had told him.*'

Your Dad wasn't so sure, but he had not seen you react physically to leaving the house the past five weeks. Seeing it and hearing about it weeks on end were two completely different things. And many weeks into our draining saga, it became frustrating to me in the end, when Dad still questioned your anxiety, to the point of asking Sally one day, '*I just wonder how real it is?*'

There's nothing more exhausting, as not being on the same page with your partner in life. When you are fighting the battle, protecting your country, and giving your army everything they need to survive, and your other commanding officer is not in agreeance. The war cannot be won.

We all gathered around you for your thirteenth birthday and managed to get you to Gravity Zone along with Tide and a couple of your other mates from school. Plus, Sally's, Aunty Nadine's, and Aunty Leah's crew. When we first arrived, you did not leave Dad's side for the first half an hour, which left you a half hour jumping time with all your friends. It was enough for you, and you were exhausted by the time everyone came back to our house.

A couple of days later, we received a follow up call from Peter to see how you were going and if you were back at school at this stage and after asking more questions, suggested it sounded very much like you had Social Anxiety.

Funnily enough, I had made a call to Beyond Blue the previous day, as I felt the need to speak to someone about our situation, and they suggested the same thing. So, we were all on the same page. It was a good start.

ANXIETY

Signs of Anxiety: The symptoms of anxiety are sometimes, not all that obvious, as they often develop gradually and, given that we all experience anxiety at some point, it can be hard to know what's too much.

What you might feel: If you are experiencing anxiety you might feel anxious, on edge or worried most of the time. Feeling overwhelmed, frightened, or even panicked is also common.

You might also experience a range of physical symptoms when you are anxious like your heart racing, butterflies in your stomach, muscle tension, shaky hands or perhaps feeling nauseous.

What you might think: A common feature of anxiety condition is, to think a lot more than you would normally. You might also notice that what you are thinking about is unhelpful or perhaps even irrational or silly, but you are unable to stop these intense sometimes overwhelming thoughts.

The thinking tends to be repetitive and often negative in nature causing your feelings of anxiety or fear to get worse.

What you might do: Our natural instinct is to avoid situations that cause us anxiety or stress. When an anxiety condition develops, you might begin to avoid lots of things and/or whatever causes you to worry, may it be places, people, or specific situations.

Beginning to avoid things might mean that you slowly spend less time with your friends. You might also find going to school, university or work becomes challenging. You might find it hard to sleep because of your constant thinking and worrying, leaving you tired and lacking energy. Not enough sleep can often mean that it's harder to think clearly about things that are on your mind.

I began jotting down everything I felt related to you.

COMMON SYMPTOMS OF ANXIETY

Hot and Cold flushes. Chest tightening. Obsessive compulsion. Racing heart. Snowballing worries.

FEELINGS: Overwhelmed. Fear - particularly when facing objects, situations, or events

Dread - something bad is going to happen. Constantly tense, nervous and on edge.

Overwhelming panic!

THOUGHTS: I'm about to die. I'm going crazy. People are judging me. Finding it hard to stop worrying. Unwanted intrusive thoughts.

BEHAVIOURS: Withdrawing from, avoiding, or enduring with fear situations which cause anxiety.

Being startled easily. Difficulty making decisions. Not being assertive (i.e. avoiding eye contact) Urges to perform certain rituals in a bid to relieve anxiety. - (And here I thought of you vacuuming and tidying your room.)

PHYSICAL: Shortness of breath. Increased heart rate/racing heart. Vomiting, nausea, pain in the stomach. Muscle tension pain (e.g. sore back or jaw) Feeling detached from your physical self or surroundings. Sweating, shaking, dizzy, lightheaded, or faint. Difficulty concentrating. Hot or cold flushes. Numbness or tingling.

TYPES OF ANXIETY

Anxiety is different for everyone, however there are common types based on people's experiences.

Six of the most common are as listed: Generalised Anxiety Disorder. Obsessive Compulsive Disorder. Panic Disorder. Post-traumatic Stress Disorder. Specific phobias. Social phobia.

And I sat there, crying my eyes out, for what you had been feeling. I read how a person with this type of anxiety has an intense fear of being criticised, embarrassed or humiliated, even in everyday situations, such as public speaking, eating in public, being assertive at school or making small talk.

Research suggests that you can only be diagnosed with social phobia if the problem is disabling or distressing and when avoidance behaviour isn't attributed to a substance-use problem or a general medical condition. If you're under 18, you may be diagnosed with social phobia if you've displayed symptoms of the disorder for at least six months.

WHAT CAUSES SOCIAL PHOBIA?

Temperament – Social phobia generally begins when people reach their mid-teens. Adolescents who are shy or socially inhibited are particularly at risk. In children, clingy behaviour, shyness, crying easily and excessive timidity may indicate temperaments that could possibly put them at risk of developing social phobia.

Learned behaviour/environment – Some people with social phobia attribute the development of the condition to being poorly treated, publicly embarrassed, or humiliated (e.g. being bullied at school).

Family History – In general, anxiety disorders can run in the family. A predisposition may come from having a family history of anxiety disorders or learning an attitude or behaviour from family members.

I thought of Grammy with her anxiety, and cousin Kylie. Even little filters of Nana Lyn came to mind. Wow! Simply wow and there you have it.

I felt over the years, Dad and I had set a good example. Get a good night's sleep, think positive, exercise, get involved in a sport and be the best you can be. It wasn't enough.

I immediately felt overwhelmed with the flood of information one could get at one's fingertips on Google, and once I put all that information beside everything that had been going on with you, my mind could not take any more and I shut down the screen. I don't know how long I sat there, unproductively staring off into space, regrettably thinking about all the mistakes I had made in not supporting you, due to the fact that I simply did not know. How I had made things ten times harder for you. I pushed myself away from my desk and walked out into the garden and tried to stop the guilt from swamping me.

Yes, I'd stuffed up, but now I could start to do everything in my power to make your life easier. To understand what you were dealing with on a day to day basis. I raised my face to the sky, allowing the crisp breeze to carry all my worries away. It was time for positivity and nothing else. It was time for me to *step up* and be the mother to you I always thought I would be.

*****

We received the advice, to gently encourage you each day to get to school, and Sally was my support in this each, and every day, as she continued offering any help she could. As always, she was the calmer force with you, not being your mother and one day, managed to get you dressed in your uniform, with your school bag and into her car. *'We are just going to drive to the school, Jesse. You don't have to get out of the car.'* She believed it when she said it, and off you went.

I had left earlier for an appointment and had finished when I received a call from Sally. She sounded excited. *'Mickey, I got him into the car and we are parked outside the school! I'm at the office waiting for Ms Craig to come to the car and say hello to Jesse. Can you come?'*

'Yes, I've just finished my appointment I'll be there in a minute.' I hung up and drove out of the car park, excited that after several weeks, you were in your uniform and out the front of the school. I was feeling so proud, thinking—*This is it, finally! Back to normality!*

A few minutes later I pulled up behind Sally's car and jumped out of ours and got into the back seat of Sally's, smiling at you sitting in the front. *'Hi, mate! I'm so proud of you, you look fabulous in your uniform, how do you feel?'*

You shrugged, looking pale, and we glanced outside the window as Sally and Ms Craig arrived at the car. I got out and walked around to them, saying hello to Ms Craig. She smiled at me as she leaned down to you and Sally opened the car door.

'It's so good to see you, Jesse, how are you?'

'Good.' You didn't make eye contact with her but stared straight ahead.

'Are you going to come out?' she asked.

'No,' you replied shortly, your voice shallow.

'Oh, come on, Jesse, you can do it. Come on,' she encouraged. *'Just come into one class.'*

You got out of the car and Sally handed me your bag. *'I'll come too, mate.'* I said carrying your bag, thinking, *'we are on a-roll!'* Of course, I could see that you were unsure and nervous, but I was thinking maybe you needed this little push, it couldn't do any harm. (Of course, I was wrong once again!)

Walking with you into the gate and towards The Max, Ms Craig turned to me and said, *'Give Jesse his bag, Mum, it's all right, we'll take it from here.'*

I passed you your bag and you took it, your eyes begging me to understand the panic you were feeling but could not communicate. *'Mum, please,'* you said quietly.

'It's okay, mate, you can do this. I'm so proud of you.' I squeezed your arm, feeling another kind of panic begin to grow inside me. Before I had the chance to say, *'It's okay, that's enough for today, let's go,'* Ms Craig continued walking with a chirpy, brisk, *'Come on, Jesse, let's go.'*

You looked away as you swung your bag on your back and followed Ms Craig to the Max. I stood for a few seconds, swamped with guilt and the look on your face as you begged me to understand with your eyes. The quiet, desperate pitch of panic in your voice, as you had said, *Mum, please*— stayed with me all day and I could not wait for school pick up time.

After you had vanished from my sight, I sat in our car and rang Dad. *'He's at school. Sally was able to get him dressed, and out the door. He's in the classroom now.'*

'Oh, that is great!' Dad was extremely pleased and relieved.

Apparently, all your friends were so happy to see you and have you back in the classroom with them and that was enough for me to be able to get you into school again the next morning with a little persuasion. I promised you, if it got too much and you wanted to come home, I'd arrange Ms Craig to ring me and I would pick you up immediately. By 10 am you were not coping and ready for me to collect you from the car park. Unfortunately, my message to Ms Craig was not clear enough, and you spent the rest of the day in classes you were not comfortable in or coping with, whatsoever.

By the time I picked you up, you were a nervous wreck, crying and angry. Of course, I was to blame, understandably so. I was also a liar and couldn't be trusted. I couldn't say sorry enough and felt sick to my stomach that you had been so unhappy all day. I don't think I will ever get over the guilt I felt about taking you into Headspace, so anything on top of that, I wasn't coping with myself.

204 · MICHELLE WEITERING

Once we were home I heard the vacuum go on in your room, and knew to leave you alone.

****

We were introduced to a friend of Aunty Nadine's, Haley and her 16-year-old daughter Kerri, who had been dealing with her own school refusal due to depression and anxiety. Up until the year before, Kerri had been an *exemplary* student with high grades, involved in her school's netball team and had a good group of friends. In the first few weeks of Kerri's school refusal, Haley had told me she had become so frustrated with not being able to get Kerri into school and feeling pressured from the Year Ten Co-ordinator of their school; had taken the tactic of physically forcing Kerri into their car and driving her to school.

On the 10-minute drive from Mount Martha to Mornington, Haley was screamed at, sworn at, punched, and scratched whilst she tried to do what she thought was the right thing for her daughter. She was amazed they had not had an accident on the way. When they reached the school car park, Haley was an emotional wreck and had to leave the car and walk for twenty minutes to calm down and cry in private. Returning to the car, Kerri was beside herself with guilt and her own fears, sobbing for her mother's forgiveness, and begged her to drive her home. Haley said it was one of the worst days she had experienced as a mother and had a scar along her cheekbone to remind her every day that she had pushed her daughter too far, instead of really listening and understanding Kerri's fears.

I felt for her completely. The things we will do as mothers, when we are trying to do the right thing by the system and our children. It can be frustratingly unbearable at times.

Although we did not have the physical experience as Haley and Kerri, you felt as traumatised as Kerri in those moments where we had forced you into an uncomfortable situation, and you did not leave the house for over six months after that day. Sadly, you did not trust both

Sally and I for a very long time, which shattered both our hearts. We understood where you were coming from and although we thought we were doing everything with only the best of intentions, it was too late.

TERM THREE

The days rolled on into one big ball of bleakness. No matter how much sleep I got, it was never enough once the alarm sounded of a morning. I had my routine where I liked to freshen up, brush my teeth and open-up the house as the kettle boiled. One morning walking into the lounge area, I noticed a very large goldfish, at least 16cm in length, laying at Koonie's feet as he looked up at me with his large green eyes, his long fluffy black tail swishing to-and-fro, seeming extremely proud of himself. *'Oh Koonie, why'd you get Mama's fish honey, you know I love my fish, mate.'* I had no idea they had gotten so big as you can never really tell their size as they swim around under the pond's surface. I bent to pat Koonie's smooth head, his eyes blinked in appreciation. I sighed, walking outside to the pond to count the fish. At the time, I only had three fish, and of the three, I could only see two, and rubbing my tired eyes and looking once more, the third fish slowly swam to the surface, only half the size of the one in the lounge area. I blinked, thinking, *'I only have three fish so where did that one come from?'*

He was a beauty, and I did feel such guilt that Koonie was a trouble-making hunter. Tardy was such a giant, grey, gentle creature that never did any harm. I owe one of my neighbours a goldfish! It was our cats and my fish that gave me great comfort in those trying days. Animal therapy. It's underrated.

For you, it was your friend. Mostly you were quiet, seeming unhappy, lost and only animated when Tide came over after school or on weekends, which sadly became less and less as the months rolled on. You became extremely angry when any talk of school or counsellors were mentioned. After you had *emotionally exploded*, and your anger had been expelled, you became overwhelmed and seemed to fall into a pit of despair once you calmed again. To witness your utter sadness was unbearable at times.

When Grammy, Poppy or Uncle Grant and his girlfriend, Nicole, came over for a family visit, you briefly came out of your room, but for the hours of time they were here, you would remain in your room. Sometimes Grammy would be able to tempt you out, asking if you could show her a new trick you could do on the trampoline, or Uncle Grant would get you to play a bit of footy in the backyard, but it wouldn't be too long before Zane, Dad or myself said something that would set you off, and back to your room you would go. It was sad and frustrating, especially as none of us ever said anything that was untoward. But you simply took the tiniest things so personally. If you kicked the ball into my garden I'd say, *'Great kick Jess, but please watch the tomatoes!'* Off you'd go to your room.

If we'd all be sitting around playing a game of UNO, and Zane had to pick up 12 cards, we'd all laugh kind-heartedly, and you would sit there grinning, saying, *'Ha Ha you fat rat!'* Which is standard for an older brother to stir his younger sibling. If either Dad or I would say, *'Righto, Jesse there's no need for that.'* You'd quietly drop your cards on the table and off you'd go to your room. If you and Zane were argu-ing and I told you both equally, to knock it off and speak nicely, you'd go off to your room, screaming over your shoulder, '*You Zane lover, you always take his side!*'

Seriously, was I speaking a different language that you could not hear me say the exact same thing to both of you? It was interesting how you actually believed we were never on your side. For days on end, where I was trying to do my best for you and support you, you still felt I let you down. That I wasn't there for you! That I never believed you! As a mother, I was obviously not saying the right thing, or communi-cating my love and concern for you the correct way. I became so frustrated that you couldn't hear what I was feeling or thinking, as I obviously could never say what I was feeling accurately. At times, I would hear myself talk to you and think, *'Hang on, it didn't sound like that in my head.'* But you'd intervene with a comment that was either unhelpful, rude or cross and I would go off the rails to a negative desti-nation and take us both to the wrong side of the tracks. I didn't like the mother I had become, and that was depressing enough to face. I would never throw in the towel, but on those many days I would hear the tiny whisper of, -*What's the point? What's it all about?* Yes, I would punish myself because I felt there was nothing I could do to help you really know, how much I loved you and how much I wanted to help you.

Interestingly enough, years later, a friend gave me an article to read, from an Anxiety site for Parents with Anxious Kids. It was titled — *Being a good parent will psychologically destroy you, new research confirms —*

I had to read on. It stated: Kids with empathetic parents have well-documented advantages: less depression, less aggression, more empa-thy themselves. Parents also report better self-esteem when they make the effort to understand their children's feelings. But inside, it's tearing them up.

I totally understood what message they were trying to get across, and as I read on, I related all too well.

A team had examined the hidden costs of parental empathy. They found that while the children of empathetic parents are better off physically and emotionally, *the parents' cells reveal chronic, low-grade inflammation.* When their children suffer psychologically, empathetic parents' immune system takes a hit. As their child's depressive symptoms increased, so did empathetic parents' inflammatory markers. The findings were consistent with previous research showing that the caregivers of people with chronic illness develop chronic inflammation and elevated stress hormones over time.

That's it I am screwed and doomed for an early death, I thought to myself, and read on.

Empathy requires us to push our own feelings aside and focus on someone else's, an effort linked to increased stress and higher inflammation. Empathetic parents may also be more willing to sacrifice their own health for their children's sake, forgoing things like sleep, exercise, and other activities that could mitigate the stress of care giving.

It made a lot of sense. Some nights I would get into bed and not be able to switch off, tossing and turning till 2am. Or, I would fall asleep and wake at 2 am, and not be able to return to my desperately needed sleep till typically twenty minutes before the alarm sounded. I was tired all the time, as I'm sure many can relate to, having too many thoughts pounding the inside of their minds, like tiny miners picking at the walls, searching for the right answers to the never-ending questions of, *'How do I help him, protect him, make him see everything is going to be all right? How can I get my family to understand, to not judge? I need more help, where will I go and will he be willing to talk to someone?'* These questions rolled on and on, with so many others, and thoughts of occurrences that happened daily in our family's life. Finding a lump on my breast didn't help my sleep situation, and going through the procedure of a mammogram, check-ups and a biopsy over a period of a fortnight, left me feeling like one of the Walking Dead. I was blessed to find the lump was just that and nothing more sinister.

****

It was another one of those mornings, that I woke before the alarm went off, to Buddha's chanting, and although my eyes were still closed, unhappy, tired tears of *'What's going to happen today?'* made their exit. It was a grey, rainy morning as I dropped Zane to school and I arrived back home to a voice message on the answering machine from a counsellor stating his name and when he was available to speak to you. You also heard the message and stood in the hallway watching me.

I turned the machine off once I wrote down the number and bent to pick up Koonie who was meowing at my feet.

'Who was that?'

I could hear the resentment in your question as clear as the day was not. I brushed my fingers in Koonie's soft fur, taking comfort from his purr against my chest. I didn't want to answer your question and instinctively knew it would not end well.

We stood there, in a kind of face off just looking at each other and you asked again, *'Who was that?'*

I did not want to answer your question, I knew what would come if I did. But you stood there waiting, asking again. I kissed the top of Koonie's head before gently placing him on the ground. *'That was Graeme.'* Short, and sweet.

'What does he want?' Obviously, you were not going to let my easy answer go.

'Oh, he's going to come over to have a chat to you and me about some things to help us understand how we can help you.'

The look on your face. I thought I had seen it all. You threw your head back and screamed in anger,

'I've told you! I don't want to talk to anyone! I don't need to see anyone.' You started crying as you screamed through your tears, *'Why are you making my life so hard? I hate this! I hate it! If you make me talk to anyone else, I'm going to KILL MYSELF! I'M SERIOUS, I CAN'T TAKE THIS ANYMORE! I JUST WANT TO KILL MYSELF.'*

Your screaming sent Koonie flying through the cat flap and I stood there, too numb to be shocked. Your screaming turned to sobbing and you ran down to your bedroom and slammed the door. Kicking, punching and verbal venting was inflicted on your bedroom door for a few moments, before deep sobs filled our otherwise deadly-silent little house.

I slowly walked towards your room, knowing you would not kill yourself. Knowing it was said in fear and desperation. But it was a blow for a mother to hear all the same. I wanted to give you space, but I needed to let you know I was here for you also. *'Jesse, it's going to be all right. If you don't want to talk to anyone, I'm not going to make you. Okay?'*

Your sobs were deep, and I wasn't sure if you even heard me. You were calling out, *'I hate my life. I hate it.'* Over and over between your sobs, a desperate, hollow chant.

I closed my eyes and leaned my forehead against your door, allowing my tears to flow. I was silently agreeing with you for the moment. I was hating life too! It sucked in a big fat, ugly way and I didn't know how to fix it. What could I do? I knocked gently, calling out your name. You begged me to leave you alone, and that actually suited me better at the time. I was lost and failing, and basically making everything suck ten times more than it should have.

But I knew what would help. Well, at least help me anyway! I walked into the kitchen and grabbed the box of matches, lit the flames under *Russell* and walked outside into the rain to light the fire. The shade sail didn't offer full protection from the rain, but it was a bearable drizzle that fell softly down from it. Whilst the fire blazed away, I walked into my room and grabbed Dad's poncho out of his side of the cupboard. Pulling it over my head I flicked the screaming kettle off, only to hear your sobbing turn to quiet cries.

Pouring a cup full of boiling water, I grabbed a tea bag and walked out to sit in front of the flickering flames. I didn't care that the seat I sat on was drenched, I had a hot cup to hold, flames greedily licking the sides of the grill and Dad's poncho allowed me to sit in the rain comfortably. I was living the dream in that moment. Not a great dream, but not a solid nightmare. I don't know how long I sat there exactly. But I knew it was a couple of hours. Thinking so many thoughts, not all of them helpful. I am not a person capable of self-harm, but the pain I was feeling that day made me think about grabbing a knife from the kitchen drawer, and plunging it into my leg, for just a second, to take away the internal pain that was drowning me. No, it wasn't worth the extra trouble, I'd have to bear the pain and get on with it!

I continued to sit there, blaming myself, trying to figure out the answers to so many questions. Always, always thinking. Not getting anywhere fast. Going over and over the information given to us regarding the best way to help you, whilst feeling a little numb with our present situation. This was it. This was our life and yes, we were all living, breathing and I was grateful for all of that. But I was in pain. Absolute heartache. I thought about ringing Grammy or Nana Lyn. Usually I rang Aunty Louise as I knew our conversation would lift me, and we would both crack each other up in perfect, inappropriate laughter in no time. But I could feel myself slowly withdrawing from people. I didn't have the heart to communicate and my heart was usually so full and beating at a healthy, steady pace. Not today. Not lately.

'Mickey! Mickey!' I don't know how many times Sally called my name and it was only watching her reaction to my state, that I realised I was sobbing myself. So, that was me back in the day, sitting in the rain crying to myself. Sia was right about one thing, big girls do cry when their hearts are broken.

And how lucky was I, that Sally wasn't the type of friend to politely knock on the door and wait for it to be answered. No, I was blessed enough that she knew she was family and could walk right in, front door or back gate at any moment, and simply be a part of the furniture. Sometimes we all need our friends to take charge!

Sally pulled me inside out of the rain and told me she had already been down to have a chat with you. You had just finished vacuuming your room. *'I'll put the kettle on and make us some toasty sandwiches, you go down and see Jesse',* she said kindly.

I nodded and after blowing my nose, went down to knock on your door. I walked in to see you lying down on your bed with a book in front of you and Tardwell asleep beside you. I reached down and ran my hand over your hair. *'Are you hungry?'*

You shook your head no. *'Can I play Xbox?'*

I nodded, *'Sure, you can, mate.'* What was I going to do, make you write lines? The last few weeks I had gotten you to write a page a day, on something you were interested in. Years ago, Grammy had given you an awesome encyclopaedia about animals. You copied pages from that and added extra if you felt like it on the day. I was pretty proud I could interest you enough to do that.

'Yell out if you are hungry.' I walked over to the door as you scooted off the bed to turn on your Xbox. Your face pale with red, puffy eyes. *'It's going to be all right, mate,'* I said softly.

'I love you, Mum.'

'I love you too, mate.' I swallowed down my tears and forced a smile before I closed your door and went down to the kitchen as Sally poured the tea and popped hot toasted sandwiches onto plates. I thanked her as we sat down to eat as she chatted about what the kids had been up to, taking my mind off my troubles for a bit. I chewed away, noting for the first time that day I was starving, and burst into tears of gratitude that Sally had made me something to eat, and commented through my tears, how delicious these sandwiches were. For whatever reason, we both cracked up laughing and continued doing so for the next few minutes. It was a desperately hard day, amongst many of them. I did not mention to you for some time about talking to anyone.

*****

Half way through term three, Mr Capp and Ms Craig came for a home visit after I had sent an email explaining how you would not leave the house whatsoever, and how I was still desperate for you to be a part of McClelland's community and not be thrown to the wind. They sat at our table and chatted to you about how they wanted to support you in any way they could. I nearly cried with relief when Mr Capp explained to you how he understood about anxiety. That he did in fact totally get how hard it was for you, and that although you can see when someone has a broken leg or arm, you can't see when there is a break in the mind, and he was here to support you in any way he could, on behalf of the school. I sat there, keeping it together and watched you nod to the things he said, pale and licking your lips, forcing yourself to make eye contact. I wanted to clap and cheer that finally, another person understood that what you were dealing with was as real as the cup of tea in front of them!

Yes, there are so many wonderful support groups out there, and I didn't know about half of them until we started our own journey, but it still blows my mind, in this day and age, the ignorant that still question anyone who has a mental illness. A relative informed me, only two weeks prior to this meeting, that you simply needed to toughen up, get over it and get back to school. No matter how much I tried to explain it, or offer any information they would not be swayed. I simply gave up on them in the end. They weren't my problem to solve.

Towards the end of our chat, Mr Capp told us about one of the programs the school has for students that have trouble getting to school. The Outreach program was run by Steve Reid, and Mr Capp assured you he was a wonderful teacher that would look after you. He asked you if that would be okay with you, which of course you politely responded yes.

I thanked both Mr Capp and Ms Craig as they left and turned to you as the front door closed after them smiling. *'I think that went really well. How did it go for you, mate?'*

'Good.' You sounded like you really meant it.

'*Do you think that you will feel okay with Mr Reid coming in to teach you some maths?*'

'*Yep, as long as he doesn't expect me to be good at it.*'

I nearly laughed. '*Don't be so hard on yourself Jess, you'll just do the best you can. That's all any of us can ask you to do. I'm proud of you and the way you handled our visitors today. I know it's not easy for you.*' I gave you a hug and was pleased when you squeezed me back. We were going to be okay.

It's always good to remain positive.

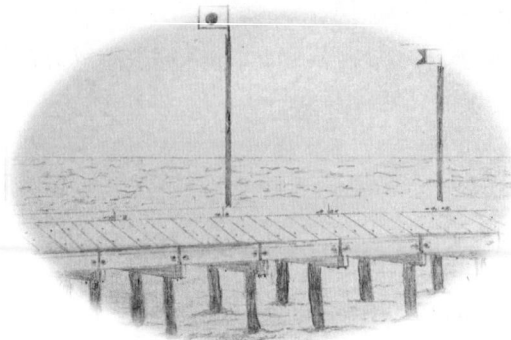

MR STEVE REID

I missed the first call from Mr Steve Reid and imagined what he looked like, as I listened to his educated voice on my voicemail. A clipped, dry tone, I envisioned a serious looking man, very professional, probably mid-fifties, tall, thin, handsome with salt and pepper hair. Mr Reid was setting up a time and meeting place for you and I, to get together with him to discuss your future with the Outreach program. He was smart enough to hold the meeting at McDonald's. A place to entice any young boy out of his lair. Only Mr Reid had not met you yet. And when I rang him back, I heard his clipped, professional voice state, if I could please leave a message, he would return my call as soon as he was able. My message was, we could not meet at McDonald's at this particular time, and if he could please call me back so we could arrange another meeting.

I knew of course, no matter how many meetings we arranged, that were not in our home, I would have to cancel every single one of them.

When I put another meeting day at McDonald's to you, you lost the plot and exploded into a hysterical rage, screaming, *'You don't understand anything, Mum, it's not that simple! You just don't get it!'* Fight reaction, followed by flight as I watched you storm off, slamming your door, crying in desperation to your situation, which of course had me at breaking point when my mobile decided to ring. *'Hello, Michelle speaking.'* I held it together and thank god for it, as Mr Steve Reid and I finally connected for the first time.

'Hello Michelle, this is Steve Reid from McClelland College, how are you this evening?'

'Good, good Steve, how are you?' Take a deep breath, don't let your emotions show. Keep it together so this man does not think you are a basket case. (Oh, the pressure!)

'Good thanks. So, I'm wondering if we can set up a meeting time at McDonald's, so I can meet Jesse?'

My heart was in my throat, and I wondered how I could explain to this serious sounding man that the only way he would get to meet you was if he came here to our home. I could hear you going off in your room, Dad was in the shower and Zane was singing along to Adventure Time, which was blaring in the lounge area. The lack of sleep and my emotional state of mind, of late, had me agree to another meeting time the next day, without verbally committing to facts; like there was no way in hell I could get you there. After thanking Mr Reid for his time, I stepped out the back door pulling it shut behind me and sat on the back steps and cried. Not the loud *boo-hoo* kind of cry, just the silent tears that flowed out of nowhere and I honestly didn't know if they would ever stop. I felt so flat, and knew I would have to ring this poor, obviously busy man, the next day and cancel again. Surely, he would think, I was the most hopeless mother ever. I certainly felt that way.

Well it certainly couldn't be helped. I sighed, dried my eyes as I heard Dad come into the kitchen, forced a smile, and walked inside the house to get everyone's dinner ready.

I had cancelled on Mr Reid three times in the end, when he realised the only way to meet you was in fact, to come on over to us. It was three or four weeks till the end of term three, and Dad and I were so excited you were finally going to get some school work. You weren't too excited about the work part, but once you met Mr Reid it was clear to me that you liked this man, that you were comfortable enough with him to be able to learn from him.

He was not tall or thin, and, did not have salt and pepper hair whatsoever. But he was professional, in a very down to earth, comfortable kind of way, mid-forties (guessing) an athletic type and yes, he was handsome. What he was, as a person, was a legend! He was patient with you, which was what you needed after months of no schooling, and not much confidence. Although you were quiet around him, he broke through your reserve and made you smile often and laugh occasionally. Being with you for only an hour or so once a week it took a couple of months for him to get your dry humour, but once he did, I think he really appreciated you for the kind-hearted, funny boy you were. Yeah, stubborn, and disagreeable with anything I said, but I think he could see what a good kid you essentially were. Mr Reid would spend time going over certain maths problems, set homework for you to do during the week, chat about life and then go. It was so wonderful to have a teacher in the house once a week. I certainly felt better as a mother, that we had at least one positive step in the right direction. That you weren't being *abandoned* and *forgotten*. That you were being educated.

The extra homework was very much appreciated. The only problem being, you would have a panic attack if you didn't understand what you were supposed to be doing. So, I would put on some calm music, and if it was a sunny day, drag the maths books and plenty of spare paper outside, into the garden and sit on the bench with you. *'Okay, let's read what we have to do.'* I'd start in my calming, we can do this, voice. My mistake was mentioning the word *read*.

'Just tell me what to do. Don't read it!' You would screech at me like a mangy old man.

'I have to read it to know what to do, mate. I haven't done maths like this in years, and I wasn't that great at it then, so if I'm going to help you, I need to read it clearly don't I?'

Then I would start to read the question over, while you would yell at me in exasperation, *'Just tell me what to do!'* Then I would yell back, *'I'm trying to tell you what to do, but I need to bloody read about what we need to do first!'*

Yeah, we would go on like that for a bit, you would stalk off and I would try to get on with a hundred other things and would finally start making progress with at least one or two of them when you'd come back out and say,

'I'm ready now, can you just tell me what to do?' And we would continue with the maths, two hours from when we first began. Let's just say, the maths put extra stress on our already strained relationship!

But I did re-learn some cool maths stuff that I had quite forgotten. One particular question, you couldn't quite get, and I thought, *'I've got this.'* Only, I wrote down the wrong answer didn't I, and the following visit, Mr Reid went through your answers, which most of them you had correct, and then he got to the one I thought I had so cleverly answered.

I went to put his cup of tea in front of him as he said to you, *'Good effort mate but this one's wrong.'*

You kindly said nothing, but the quick look you gave me made me almost laugh out loud, for you knew I was the one that had stuffed it up. As much as I know I annoyed you as a mother in general, your loyalty in that moment was like a hug full of love then and there.

Although the addition of Mr Reid to our party was marvellous and very much appreciated, our day to day dealings with you and your anxiety was stressful, and I had lost a bit of my spark throughout the year. Seeing one's child fight the battle for days, weeks, months on end and push himself to the point where it makes him sick, crying or becoming so angry over what may appear a very small obstacle to someone else the same age. My motto of *fake it till you make it* became weak after a while and was not as believable even to my own ears. To have one of my closest friends ask me, *'Where have you gone? I'm worried about you,'* made me realise I had to snap the hell out of my own headspace, and, find the *real* Mickey ASAP.

It was mid-November when the publishing company I decided to take a chance on, contacted me, to state if I wanted *The Given* published and available for sale before Christmas, I had to act now and get any editing changes done. I'll admit, it had been a slow year for writing, and I was enjoying any spare time I got to spend on *The Guardian*, and I had not re-edited The Given since I had first sent it to the publisher's editing team. I only had a handful of days, and sat up late into the nights making changes and corrections, slightly worried that the Xlibris editors hadn't picked up on more, as I was certainly finding plenty to be concerned about. I gave it my all, and enjoyed the changes, hoping whatever mistakes I may have missed, the editing team would definitely pick up before it went to final print.

I can only say I adored writing *The Given*. I love all the characters and am excited about the direction that Books Two and Three take. What I was not so impressed about, when I finally held a copy of my first paper baby in my hands, was the final editing. I believe there was actually no editing done whatsoever. Considering I emailed my draft of acknowledgements off the moment I wrote it at 3 am, hoping to meet all the criteria of my deadline. So yeah, I cringed a bit when I saw *woman* instead of *women*! *Waist* instead of *waste, (I really cringed and snapped the book closed thinking at least the font is pretty! I had to take something positive away with me!)* But no-one died except a small piece of my pride. I will revise *The Given* when I am in a better position as an author and give my dear readers a copy their hands deserve to hold and their eyes to roam. If we don't have goals to better ourselves, what's the point. *Live and learn people*, I certainly did. Note to self: Don't rush editing on your first book. Don't edit when you are depleted of, well yourself! And smile and say thank you when someone compliments you on your book, don't immediately rush in and apologise about the editing! (Bloody hindsight again!)

****

There were many days that I felt the darkness, reaching out its arms to collect me and drag me down to its eternal abyss of unhappiness. I can honestly say as an individual, 2014 was one of the bleakest years of my life.

As a mother, it just about destroyed my soul, to hear my son threaten to end his life because he was so overwhelmed with fear, regarding so many things in his life that he felt he had no control over. We can all say, *'Oh, he wouldn't really do it,'* but what parent wants to take that chance? Male suicide statistics in Australia are grim, and suicide is the leading cause of death in men between 15 and 44 years of age. – Black Dog Institute- *blackdoginstitute.org.au* (2018) That is beyond overwhelming to think about. Although it was my belief you would not self-harm, there is no way, as your mother I would take that chance. Yes, there were days I would watch you like a hawk, and tip-toe around on egg shells, trying not to do or say anything that would upset you, make you feel less than what you were already feeling. I was on guard to jump in between you and Dad in any circumstance, if I believed he was using the wrong tone or being completely, unintentionally insensitive to your thoughts or feelings. I became that over-protective mother wanting to shield you from anything and anyone, even the man I loved so deeply. He was your father, but I lived with your emotions 24/7 without a break (and I don't call going off to do the shopping, peeing in private, or having an hour's cup of tea with the girls, a break!) Throughout our screaming matches and battles, you and I became a force to be reckoned with, the more I learned and understood about what you yourself were dealing with every minute of every day.

It put a strain on my relationship with your Dad for a time, which killed my heart and I'm sure he did not recognise the giving, loving, carefree young girl he once fell in love with either. So, amongst all my anguish, I felt like I had lost my best friend for a time also.

The day he was on the same page, understanding your anxiety, after hours upon hours of researching, reading, and educating himself, plus communicating with other parents online through a support network that we had joined, was the day he became my Henry Cavil once more. I can't tell you how I felt, when the boulder of stress was removed from my chest, and Dad and I became a real team once more.

After our year of ups and desperate downs, as much as I had your back, it was time that you felt I had your back. I needed you to know that, to feel it, to believe it. I wanted to put 2014 behind both of us, for Dad and Zane, you, and I to come together as a family. We needed to heal and move forward for all our sakes, and I believed we could. We loved each other, had the support from several marvellous family members, divine friends and a school who proved their ongoing support.

2015. Bring it on. I knew it wasn't going to be all sunshine and lollipops, but I was more than ready for it.

2015 – YEAR EIGHT

Over the summer holidays we had many visitors, took a trip to Inglewood, and had Tide stay with us for three weeks.

We had several parties, which was my way to get you socialising with your age group, and most of the time it took you at least two hours to settle in and be relaxed with everyone. There was one day Caitlyn was chasing you around the house, out the front door, around the side and through the back gate and back inside. It was all fun at the start, with Adam, Gracie and Emily joining in the race to see who could catch and tickle you first. I was so enjoying seeing you run around laughing and it was good for Caitlyn too, who worried about you. The past year at school she had dealt with so many students coming up to her asking if you were *okay*, concerned you had dropped off the face of the earth. Some were even worried you were sick and dying! So, to watch the two of you running around laughing your heads off, gave Sally and I a few moments of pure joy. It was so nice to have our group over and all our kids just laugh and enjoy each other's company. And as most of you had grown up together, you did.

Sally turned to me smiling, *'It's great to see him so happy.'*

'I know. I love these moments. I only wish he could see how great he is.'

Of course, that's the magic of the universe, we spoke too soon and five seconds later we heard you hit the wall, screaming in anger as you had tripped over Dad's Wing Chun dummy, hitting the top of your head on the hard wood as your foot caught on its leg trying to escape Adam's tickling fingers. You tucked yourself away for an hour, Sally making sure you were okay after a little while, and we got you an icy-pole to cool you off, along with an ice pack for your head. You were embarrassed that you fell in front of everyone, and angry. As Sally walked out of the room, I double checked if you wanted anything else before I left.

'Just some luck,' You said. It wasn't unusual for us to hear you say, on many occasions, *'I've got the worst luck in the world.'* It wasn't you being negative, it's just the way you felt.

After time alone to gather yourself and your thoughts, you came out and enjoyed many hours of fun with all the kids, and they were happy to have you back in the fold.

Normally our gatherings involved eight to twelve kids, always with plenty of activities on the go like basketball, a game of chase-hide and seek, or a bunch of you would jump on the trampoline or rope swing and talk for hours, the other kids filling you in on all the other kids at school. Who were still jerks and who were still cool. On one occasion, all the kids wanted to scoot off to our milk bar, and although we had a large group you were not interested in going. As they took off down the drive way, you stood alone with the basketball under your arm watching them go and turned as Jacqui approached you.

'How are you, mate? Are you having a good day?' she asked you, in her friendly, Kiwi accent.

You smiled at her, nodding, *'Yep.'* Short and sweet.

'You didn't want to go to the milk bar with the others?' She caught the ball you tossed at her, bounced it, and went for a goal. Missing the ring, you retrieved it as it bounced towards the sloping driveway, looking at her with such a serious expression.

'God no, there's too many paedophiles out there!' You answered, as if thinking there was something wrong with her to even suggest such a thing.

She wanted to laugh, not because it was funny, but you said it with such conviction and with an adult tone. You chatted some more before she returned to our group of friends and let me know what you said. She laughed quietly re-telling it, saying she could not believe how serious you were. Yes, at this stage there were not too many people you trusted whatsoever. And sadly, as much as you loved Sally and me, you did not trust us to take you anywhere. If it was a Friday afternoon or the weekend, I was starting to get you into the car for short trips, but only because you knew I couldn't take you to school.

****

One afternoon, Tide's aunt came to pick him up after a four-day visit, as his parents were overseas for a month. It was the third time I had met her. Over a cup tea, she began asking about whether you would be going to school this year.

'Things are looking good,' I said, blowing on my hot tea as you boys were getting out of the pool and inside for a last hit of Xbox before Tide left. *'Jesse seems really positive, when we talk about it, so that's encouraging.'*

She looked at me, puffing away on her cigarette. I was sitting far enough away I didn't have to inhale any of it. *'You know, he's always happy when Tide or Tilly are around, and Tide says he laughs a lot. Do you think he's just doing it all for attention? I mean, it sounds like an attention thing to me.'* She inhaled again, and I realised as little as I knew this woman, I really didn't like her whatsoever. She stared at me, squinting her eyes as she blew out more smoke. I could feel the judgement in that stare.

'No!' I said shortly. 'It is not an attention thing.' I stood and tipped my remaining hot tea on my poor agave, hoping she would get the point and get up herself and get the hell out of my house.

'It's just that he is always happy and laughing when I see him.' She stood and shrugged. 'I know a lot of kids do stupid shit to get attention and I think this is his way of getting attention.'

'Look up anxiety!' I said, sadly furious. I turned to her and tried to be calm. I snapped out my hand and tapped off my fingers as I said each point.

'Social/Separation Anxiety: At home, laughing, confident, running around making up silly songs, letting off steam in his place of safety. In public: Don't look at me! Don't make eye contact! Don't ask me anything! Don't touch me! On a forty-degree day, wears a jacket with a hoody pulled so low, so no one can see him! He does not want to be noticed and begs to go home! Does that sound like someone who wants attention! I mean, in Grade Five, he sat there with a broken finger that was swollen to triple the size because he didn't want to tell anyone about it because he DIDN'T WANT ANY ATTENTION!' I was more than a little pissed off at this stage and she wasn't the first person I had to justify our case to.

It was one thing explaining anxiety to someone, who really wanted to understand, so they could be of some support, but on the other side of that fence, sat exhaustion and justification. And I wasn't exactly an expert at this stage, I was simply trying to understand, and educate myself in any way, to further help you manage your anxiety. It's that stigma, ignorance and discrimination associated with anxiety. Knowledge helps people's attitude only so far, in the way they behave towards an individual or any of their family members, with anxiety or depression.

After having a conversation with Aunty Nadine one afternoon, about less informed, uneducated, and judgmental people, she sent me a link to a site she had joined called, *Children with Anxiety/Anxiety Disorders.* It's a site I will be forever grateful for, and there was one lady who reached her arms across the oceans, and gave me so much support, all the way from England. Helen McDonald was her name, and her issues had been great. She had lost so much over the years, dealing with her son, James, and his anxiety, before time became her friend again, and life navigated her back on track. As it does with us all.

I would sit over my computer screen, reading hundreds of individuals' stories, and cry my eyes out, for what their families had been, and were going through. Many of their stories were identical to yours. It actually blew me away if I were to write a post, either about your successes or attempts to push yourself forward to leave the house for a small amount of time, someone would write back and say, *'it sounds like you are describing my fifteen-year-old daughter'*, or *'twelve-year-old son'* and so on and so forth. It was a site where you were supported, by hundreds upon hundreds of people that immediately *connected with, and understood you*, completely. Reading their journeys and battles, I would reach out and offer anything I could. What little words of wisdom I had dealing with your anxiety, words of comfort and encouragement. It was a place to go to celebrate others' achievements, and support those that were cut off from family and friends that no longer offered them the support or belief of their circumstances. It was therapeutic to sit, read and cry for the people that were lost, confused, conflicted, and were still begging for some answers as to what was going on with their child. I was not alone in my tears for these strangers.

3368 plus people and counting, and I wish I could hug them all, tell them they are complete legends because at the end of the day, they are giving their all to their children. Some of them exhausted and desperately sad beyond belief. I want to say to them, *'You are a rock star; you are doing everything you can. Be kind to yourself, it WILL be okay in the end.'*

There were days I was beside myself, and having those people, with words of, *'I totally get what you are saying/going through/feeling,'* made the difference between being hard on myself, to cutting myself a bit of slack and saying, *'I'm doing the best I can today. I've got this!'* Helen was one of those people. Thank you, Helen!

*****

In the middle of January, I took Zane, Tide, and you to the PARC for a swim. Sometimes it would take you a good ten to twenty minutes to get into the water, but I didn't care if you stood there for an hour— *you were out of the house.* You usually stood beside me and sussed out the lay of the pool and headed off in the general direction that had less people. The three of you had a great time together and thought you would have a quick splash in the toddler pool on the way out (it was always warm, let's not question why!) I stood with all your bags, knowing you would all have a quick shower before we headed off to the car park, and I was keeping my eye on the time, thinking about the parking ticket about to expire.

Glancing down at you all, I noticed a little toddler rolling around on her back, kicking her legs and reaching out her hands in the water, clenching and unclenching her little fingers. Her little face was above the surface and I thought, *interesting technique.* I glanced around for a parent and looked back at the toddler. She had rolled onto her tummy and was sinking lower, legs thrashing. I glanced over at the life guard whose eyes were focused elsewhere and looked back at the little girl. I felt a kind of panic set in and as Tide was standing an arms-length away from her, I yelled out to him.

'Tide!' He couldn't hear me. *'Tide!'* I yelled louder. He glanced at me and I thrust my finger at the drowning toddler, ready to jump in fully clothed.

He glanced at the little lump twisting in the water and moved away from her. You looked at her, then at me as I said, *'Jesse, she's drowning, help her!'*

And in five lunges from where you were, you dove down and grabbed her, bringing her to the surface. I was so relieved and beyond proud of you. She was snotting herself something awful and it took her quite a few seconds to let a blood curdling scream out, followed by hysterical crying.

And you just held her, trying to comfort her saying, *'It's alright, it's alright,'* as you patted her on the back. I could see the disgust on your face. Not the screaming little body, but her snot. You hated germs and anyone's spit or snot was a no-no. (God I am the same, even writing the words, I have to swallow hard, and try to think of something else. Writing a scene in The Guardian, I just about brought up my Rice Bubbles! I can't even handle it when the footy players spit on the field after a drink!)

I finally got the docile life guard's attention and he took the little girl from your arms, thanking you.

As we were leaving, you were thanked once more; they took our statement and told us, the parents were off in the adult spa section, whilst her five-year-old cousin was supposed to be looking after her. I kept my thoughts private about the imbecilic parents, got you all hot potato cakes and headed for the car, praying we did not have an overdue ticket.

I did a *Proud Parent* Post on Facebook, as many of our friends and relatives knew of your battle, and I was so impressed with them reaching back, and letting you know what a champion you were. Reading some of the comments to you, you sat on your bed, quietly looking proud of yourself. It was a good moment for you, to realise you were the champion we all knew you to be.

2015 -YEAR EIGHT

I told myself not to stress about the first day of school. As much as I had my fingers crossed you would go, it wasn't life or death. You would either be able to go or you would not. Tide wanted to sleep over the night before and that was perfect, having him there with you, gave you that safety shield that helped you get there. And for the next two weeks you did.

The third week you got in a couple of days, and then one afternoon, sitting at my table with Jacqui and Sally over a pot of tea, chatting about how proud we were of your efforts, what our other kids had been up to and life in general, Sally was looking at me carefully and commented, *'You look grey Mickey.'*

'I'm fine, just a bit tired,' I said rubbing my lower back that had been paining me for weeks on end.

'Is that pain still there? I thought you were going to get someone to look at it?' Sally was like Mother Hubbard at times, and I loved her for it.

'You really should see someone, that's been going on for a while now,' Jacqui voiced her concern.

'No, you know me, I'll be fine. It's all good.' I was the kind of woman that did not dash to the doctors for anything bar the usual women's health check-up every two years, and had never been to hospital outside giving birth to you and Zane. My pain threshold was high, and I was as stubborn as Nana Lyn. I could put up with a lot, and my lower back pain and nagging sharp pain in my tummy was something I had been dealing with for many weeks. I was simply happy to sit with my friends and celebrate the fact that you were at school and things were looking so bright. Yes, it was all sunshine and lollipops at the moment, and I was loving it!

We strolled around the garden, picking tomatoes before school pick-up when Tide rang me on his mobile, asking if he could spend the night. I was happy to have Tide 24/7, especially if it meant getting you to school the next day. I would do whatever it took.

I hung up the phone, getting a little short of breath as I rubbed the pain that stabbed me in the back. *'Are you okay to have Tide tonight?'* Sally frowned.

'Of course. If I've got my two, what's one more?' I forced a smile. *'Best pick them up.'* And off we went to collect you all.

An hour after school pick-up, I had to go and lie down as I felt like I was going to pass out. Thank goodness you were all settled in with afternoon tea after a swim in the pool, followed by an hour or

two worth of Xbox. The three of you chatting away through dinner and bedtime.

I got up the next morning, sitting over the side of the bed with the kind of pain that was making me see black and white spots dance in front of my eyes. I forced myself to stand, more intrigued than scared about the amount of pain I was experiencing and determined not to let this stop the routine of school, pushed on towards the kettle, knowing Tide liked a hot chocolate before school. And I knew he would get up and be in the shower before you. So, I woke him first as the kettle boiled, and after his shower, handed him his hot chocolate, hiding the fact that I was in internal torture. Seriously, child birth was more bearable. I got you up, and in the shower, grateful I had another twenty minutes before I had to wake Zane.

I walked into the lounge and made it to the couch before the blackness completely stole my vision, and finally admitted to myself, something was seriously wrong. I pushed myself up when the spots cleared and made it into mine and Dad's room, bending over as another wave of sharp knives began attacking my insides, sending me sprawling out onto the bed. I closed my eyes and thought of you in the shower, getting ready with your mate, to head off to another successful day at school. I could not interrupt your progress.

I stood and grabbed my black skirt I put out the night before and went to pull it up as another wave stole my breath and it was so severe I felt the urge to vomit. I made it into the toilet, but on my empty stomach, nothing but desperate sounds came out.

'Get a grip, get a grip,' I repeated as I wanted to cry. I stubbornly refused to call Dad. Sally was on breakfast duty at the primary school, Bec was at work. I recalled Jacqui's sweet voice say to me the afternoon before, 'If you need me, call me.' I didn't think I'd make it to the phone, but I grabbed it as the black and white spots performed their own version of River Dance in front of my eyes, and once again made it to the couch.

Hearing my friend's warm voice on the other end of the phone overwhelmed me, and I whispered, 'Jacqui, I think I'm in trouble.' My friends rarely hear me complain let alone ask for help, so she immediately knew this was serious, and seeing me the day before, she knew something wasn't right.

'I'll call the ambulance and be right with you, love,' she said, and hung up the phone.

'*Shit,*' I thought and looked around the lounge. Ambulance people! Thankfully, in my everything- has- to-be- in- its- place state, the room was fairly neat. But I glanced down to see that although my black skirt was on, it was unzipped and my nighty was not respectable for public viewing. I pushed myself off the couch and stumbled towards mine and Dad's room once more, hitting the wall a couple of times, but that was good, it was keeping me upright. I stubbornly ripped off my nighty, snapped on my bra and pulled my zebra tee shirt over my head. I almost blacked out and stumbled back out and down to you boys. I leant outside your door, listening to you and Tide talk about what class you had first as I took a few deep breaths, running my hands over my hair and tried to smile as you opened the door. I must have looked like a crazy person, but luckily you didn't seem to notice. Tide on the other hand did.

'*Are you alright?*'

'*Well, mate, I'm actually not feeling that great, so Jacqui is going to drive you to school. Is that okay?*' Please say yes and close the door before I pass out right here.

'*Yes,*' you answered together. I smiled and shut the door in my own face and stumbled back into the lounge area. I hit the floor like a sack of potatoes and crawled to the toilet as I felt I was about to disgrace myself.

A few minutes later, with no disgracing occurring, I made it to the couch as Jacqui burst in the front door like Lara Croft, the paramedics three minutes behind her. They asked a lot of questions and were sweet, considering they do this kind of thing day in day out. I was vainly hoping they didn't think I was some sort of junky having a bad moment! When one of them handed me a green stick and told me to suck on it deeply, yet gently, my first thought was, '*What the hell is it?,*' but in my state of pain, and concern that we had to get you to school, I didn't ask, I just started sucking.

I saw you standing there, taking in the scene, and was about to ask you a question when the world began to tilt in a very cool direction, and all I could hear in that moment, was Jacqui's little voice repeating over and over in her accent, *'It's just like Bondi Rescue Mickey, Bondi Rescue- Bondi Rescue,'* as she stroked my hair.

I was in a haze of; *'What is she talking about and why is this stick making me feel like I am taking a flight off this planet?'* I saw Zane walk out with his Carlton pyjamas on, rubbing his little eyes and Jacqui went to give him a cuddle and quickly explain I wasn't feeling too good. He actually showed more concern than you, but that was as always. You kept your cards folded close to your chest.

Things moved quickly, yet in slow motion after that, and I was whisked away in the ambulance (It pays to have ambulance cover people!) without the chance to say to all you kids, *'Have a great day.'*

As the ambulance made its way to the Frankston Hospital, the paramedic asked if he could feel my tummy. I nodded thinking, *'You can't suck in fat, people!'* but tried anyway. I was obviously lucid enough to have a vain moment! It's like Nana always used to say, *'Always wear fresh underwear, because you never know if you'll need to go to hospital.'* That always seemed so ridiculous to me. If you are likely to be going to hospital, clean underwear is the least of your problems. Hell, if I'd known some cute ambo guy was going to be feeling up my stomach, I would have started doing stomach crunches six months ago! (There's that bloody hindsight again!)

Needless to say, I was in hospital for four days, and needed to have a six-inch cyst that decided to grow on my ovary, removed. You came to the hospital once to visit me. Zane and Dad came every day, along with my girlfriends, Aunty Leah, Aunty Nadine and Uncle Stuart. I was so lucky that Nana Lyn was able to come down, to help Dad look after me. She had twelve months sick leave up her sleeve, as she was considering retirement, and with her little body, exhausted from nearly thirty years running a kitchen full-time, owed it to herself to do so. You thought it was Christmas, as did I.

In the end, an unusual week for us, it really wasn't that big of a deal once all the pain was removed, and after my three weeks of recovery I was certain all would resume as positively as it had at the beginning of term.

That wasn't the case. But that was not our biggest problem either. After four weeks, we had not heard boo from Tide. He had stopped asking to come over and did not respond to any of our messages. His parents and I had always gotten along, and I also reached out to them. Silence! Not a polite response to anything and it was basically like Tide had dropped off the face of the planet. It broke your heart for months on end. With Noah moving to Queensland, your world became a lonely place for a teenage boy that needed the company of his mates.

*****

It was close to the end of term one and Sally invited us all to come along to a *Neighbours Day* celebration at Kareela Road. Sally volunteered at *Coffee on Kareela cafe* and I thought it would be a great idea to take Ireland, Zane, and you down to the little gathering. We got there and joined Sally at her table where she was selling potted plants and vegetables, and Emily was selling her handmade bags, jewellery, and key chains she had been making from loom bands. Ireland had a free sausage in bread before racing off to the park with Adam, where a Council worker was running games for any child that wanted to join in. I got Zane a sausage and shouted myself a cup of tea. You did not want to have anything, saying the smells were making you feel sick and within five minutes became very agitated. You pulled your hoody lower over your head and started swearing quietly under your breath, that this was all bullshit and you wanted to go home.

'*Okay, mate, can I just finish this cup of tea and we will go,*' I said in my calm, loving *I understand voice*. That didn't help, of course.

'*There's too many weirdos around here, Mum, I want to go now.*'

'*Hey, Jesse,*' Sally tried in her always kind, patient voice, '*do you want to pot-up a plant to take home, mate?*'

'No, I just want to bloody go home.' Your hands in your pockets, you were looking like a scowling teenage boy that was very unhappy. I could see that your anger was only growing and knew that was it.

'Do you want to go get Ireland for me please Zane?' He looked up at me, and I could see the disappointment on his face. He and Emily had always been the best of mates, and he was fiddling around with her loom bands and they were obviously conspiring in their happy way.

'Oh no, Mum, I don't want to go yet.'

I nodded. *'Sal, can you keep your eye on Zane and Moo while I zip Jess home?'*

'Of course,' She smiled. *'We'll have a cup of tea when you get back.'*

I hugged her, always grateful. *'Thank you,'* I whispered to her as I could hear you in the background— *'Hurry bloody up. I hate this stupid place.'*

You were angry on the way home and as soon as we stepped into the front door you walked by Dad, who was getting ready for a bike ride, and headed down to your room.

'What's happened?' He strapped on his helmet.

'Couldn't handle the people, the smells. Just wanted to come home.' I shrugged. *'I've got to get back, Sally has her two plus our two, and a stall to run.'*

'I'm going to swing by, I'll see you there,' Dad bent and kissed my cheek before wheeling his bike out the front door.

'Yep' I sighed, *'see you there.'* I went towards your room to say goodbye and see if you needed anything. *'Hey, mate, are you okay?'*

'Yeah.' I looked in at you, sitting in your chair with your head in your hands. It broke my heart. It was a sunny day outside. I wanted to see you laughing with friends, riding the bike Dad brought home for you three months ago that hadn't been used once. You'd quit Wing-Chun and didn't seem interested in much at all.

'What do you want to do with your day, love?' I tried to keep my voice normal, not show too much desperation that I could feel grow inside of me. *'If there's anything tell me, we'll do it.'*

'No, I just want to be here. Sorry, Mum, I love you.'

'You don't have to say sorry, mate. It's alright. I love you too.'

'Sorry. Sorry, Mum. I love you. I love you, Mum.'

'I know you do, mate. I love you too.'

After checking that you didn't want anything, I headed to the front door, hearing you call out, 'sorry' and, *'I love you,'* another ten times, repeating it over and over, as you often did after an emotional moment. I called out, *'I love you,'* as I locked the front door behind me and headed back to the *Neighbour Day* celebrations.

Dad had already arrived and was chatting to Sally and she had kindly poured me a tea. *'Are you alright?'* she asked peering over her glasses with that look that only Sally can give knowing, without me having to say a word, that all was not well. Hell, even a simple trip to our local area couldn't go smoothly. I just felt so bad for you. I could hear other kids laughing, and watched as teenagers walked off with each other, chatting away.

Sally handed me my cup and drew me closer to her. *'I don't know if you are interested, but there is a lady in the café, her name is Sandra, she's a counsellor and I have already spoken to her. She deals with anxiety. Just go in and have a chat to her if you need to.'*

I nodded and swallowed too much hot tea at once, burning my throat. I looked at your Dad who was entertaining Emily and Zane with a story. *'I'll just check on Moo,'* I said.

'No, I'll do that,' Dad smiled, *'Come on you two,'* he called to Emily and Zane, parking his bike near Sally, he led the kids off to the park and I placed my cup down near Sally's and walked into the café.

Sandra was alone having a cup of tea herself and I approached her with a smile and asked her if she had a minute to chat. She was warm, approachable and I felt I could talk to her till the cows came home. We made an appointment for me to see her the following week, alone first, so I could give her the rundown of your/our situation.

When that day came, I went prepared, with a list of everything I could think of that would benefit her, in helping you. I sat opposite her with my own open book and pen at the ready. I don't know if I terrified or impressed her, but needless to say, it was over an hour's worth of me reeling off as many events and issues as possible, whilst painting the picture of the *beautiful, sweet, confused, loving, kind-hearted, angry, lost, sad little thirteen-year-old I knew you to be.*

I didn't realise I, myself, had so many built up layers of rage within me, when I discussed family members letting me down where you were concerned. Feelings of betrayal ran deep and many issues I thought I'd left in the past were sitting on the seat beside me, as I let Sandra know how desperately I wished I could punch certain people in the face for the way they had treated you and spoken to you over the years. I tried to reassure her, I was not a violent person whatsoever, but just to imagine I could inflict some sort of pain on the people that had hurt you over, and over again, gave me a decent amount of cathartic joy.

She smiled and said professionally, *'Well, as long as you only imagine it!'*

She was lovely and very helpful, setting up a meeting to come to the house and start her sessions with you the following week. I left feeling grateful, hopeful, and emotionally exhausted. Dad met me in the driveway when I got out of the car. He instinctively knew I was going to be an emotional being and held me in his arms while I cried my heart out about so many of the things I had purged to Sandra.

Taking a deep breath and giving Dad a final squeeze, we went inside the house. Zane came up to me for a cuddle asking, *'Can that lady help Jesse feel happy again and get back to school?'*

I smiled down at him and kissed his handsome little face, *'I sure hope so.'*

****

That weekend we had to meet with Uncle Grant and his fiancée Nicole, in Frankston at Ferrari, to try on suits for their upcoming wedding. As they lived over in Preston, Nicole didn't want to stress you out by making you travel to the other side of the city to try on suits. She was such a caring, sensitive lady and genuinely cared for you and Zane. I don't know if her profession had anything to do with her strength of character but being a nurse at the *Royal Children's Hospital* for the past fifteen years, working in the palliative care unit speaks volumes in itself.

Although Uncle Grant had asked you and Zane to be his best men, he reassured you that you didn't have to get up and do anything on the day, just be by his side and enjoy the event along with the *eighty-odd* guests. You had always loved Uncle Grant and said to Dad and I you would try to be there for him.

The week before the wedding, Mr Reid gave us a ring, and scheduled in a home visit for a quick chat about where we were up to with your schooling. It was so nice to see him again, and we chatted with you over a cup of tea and homemade spring rolls. He voiced his concerns that you weren't back at school, after I had been to hospital, and said it sounded like separation issues, most likely due to the fact that you had been worried about seeing me get carted off in an ambulance. I tried to reassure him that wasn't the case whatsoever, that you were fine with me not being around. You were always okay when I zipped out to do shopping, catch up with the girls or even the occasional weekend I went away. It was so hard at times trying to explain to anyone, that your anxiety was what was stopping you going to school. Plain and simple! That was it! Not you, being worried about me. (Sometimes I wish you would worry about me, but that just wasn't your style. I could hit my finger with a hammer and carry on like a girl for a couple of seconds where Zane would show concern, and you would simply laugh. Not because you didn't love me or care, but that's just the way you handled certain situations where you weren't the best at communicating what you were feeling at the time).

After our chat, Mr Reid gave us the next date he would come in and set some maths and I thanked him so much for making the time to visit, which would be term two. He was the kind of teacher that truly gave a damn about the kids he had in his care, and although you didn't say too much to him when he was with us, you were happy and animated when he left. He did put you in good spirits.

*****

The afternoon before the wedding, Grammy had organised for us all to stay in the same function centre where the wedding was being held. It was so nice to have a family event to look forward to, and nothing said event more than a family wedding. Nicole stayed with her parents, and together with Uncle Grant and his stunning, tall blonde friend from England, Natalie, Grammy, and Poppy, we went out to a vegetarian restaurant for dinner. You were happy to have rice and broccoli, but when it came to the table, you instantly went rigid. You leaned across and whispered to me, *'The spoon looks dirty.'*

'Oh, mate, they wash them really well.' Kicking myself for not thinking ahead to bring a fork from home. *'Use your fingers, mate.'* I didn't really care what you used, just as long as you ate. It was after all, the night before the big day, and I needed you to keep your energy up. The photographer needed you ready and in his rooms by 8am for a couple of hours before the wedding started at 10am.

You ate nothing and thank the stars for good old McDonald's on the way to the function centre, as I don't think the muesli bars and apples I packed would have cut it.

The coming day was huge for Uncle Grant and soon to be Aunty Nicole. And it was huge for you too. I couldn't persuade you or Zane to have a fruit box or a muesli bar on your way out of our room as Uncle Grant collected you at 7.50am, and I was left alone hoping Dad would be able to get you to have a drink or a mouthful of food before the day really kicked off.

And what a day it was. Uncle Grant was the proudest man ever and Aunty Nicole was the sweetest bride. Standing up at the altar beside Dad and Zane, as the bride and groom pledged their undying love to each other, my eyes would constantly wander to the three men I loved more than anything else in the world. And one of them was going paler by each passing second as he stood in front of the eighty-odd guests, and the service continued.

My Mummy radar went up, and as Grammy and Poppy, along with Little Mama, were sitting in the front seat, I leant forward and whispered to Grammy, *'Jesse is going to pass out.'* She glanced over as did I, to see you reach back for the wall and lean against it, with Uncle John whispering behind me, *'He's going down'*

I believe Poppy got to you just in time and gently dragged you to sit between him and Grammy, as Grammy pushed your head down between your knees. I stroked your hair for a moment, from behind you, as Grammy instructed you to breathe deeply in through your nose, out through your mouth. As the newly married couple went to sign their wedding certificate, you regained some colour and drive and went back up beside your father and brother. I, along with many other family members was so proud of you that day. You had another hour's worth of photos after the ceremony and I was so glad when it was all over, to give you a hug away from everybody's eyes as we left for the bar to get you a drink. You drank down a coke as fast as I'd seen anyone drink something so fizzy. Driving home that night after such an eventful day, looking in the review mirror, you and Zane were asleep from exhaustion. For Grammy, watching her eldest son marry the love of his life that day must have filled her with tremendous love and pride. I felt the same way in that moment looking back at you both. You hadn't just survived the day, where you were the centre of attention along with the bridal party for hours on end. You had enjoyed the day with as much open enthusiasm as we had seen from you for a long time, and Dad and I could see your confidence bloom. You almost looked as proud of yourself as we were of you!

****

During the term one holidays you were content to have a quiet one, and the only person you really wanted to see was Tide. We rang, left messages, and in the end, you begged me to drive to his house, which we did. With no luck or response. I was frustrated at the lack of respect. I mean what's wrong with a simple text? Facebook message or phone call? My anger increased when I saw how deflated you became and even Zane told me he was worried about you feeling let down by your best mate. When term two began, we got into life's routine of getting things done, and dealing with your highs and lows was just another daily occurrence. I won't make excuses and say, due to your growing sadness, you were becoming a complete rude arsehole to me, but I certainly put it down to that. Sometimes the way you spoke to me made me want to rip my own head off. We were like an old married couple, spending too much time together, and we would speak to each other in a way that was probably too comfortable, with not enough respect either side.

Unfortunately, I became used to it, and if Dad heard you say, *'Get me a sandwich now,'* He'd certainly let you know what you could do with that sandwich. It was when Dad picked you up on your manners and the way you spoke to me, I would snap out of it and crack down on your attitude. There were some days I felt you absolutely hated my guts. And it killed me. And then the day came that I found the answer. It was not pleasant.

RISING HOPE

Sandra came for your first session, and she asked if you would like to be alone to talk with her or if you'd like me to sit with you. You wanted me to sit with you. She made you feel comfortable and asked you a few questions. You answered her questions quietly, eyes downcast, pale, nervously licking your lips. You almost seemed stunned as the session went along and I could see it draining you.

She touched on your trust issues and you told her you didn't trust anyone.

'Do you trust Mum and Dad?' she asked.

'I trust Dad, but not Mum or Sally.'

'Why is that, Jesse?'

'Because they said I didn't have to get out of the car when they took me to school that day, and they made me get out of the car.'

'Do you think they were just doing what they thought was best, and trying to help you get to school?'

'It wasn't what was best for me.'

I watched as you pulled your fingers under the table, watching Sandra carefully. Such polite, thoughtful answers.

'Do you think you can learn to trust Mum again, Jesse?'

'I don't think so. It's best not to trust anyone, that way you don't get hurt.'

My heart dropped, and I wanted to hug you and cry at the same time. I sat still, gripping my empty cup of tea.

'I understand what you mean, Jesse, but we have to be able to trust people in this world to survive, don't we?'

'No. I don't need anyone. I'm a one-man army.'

Sandra thanked you for talking to her and asked you if it would be alright if she came back next week for a chat. You said if she liked, looked at me and then slowly left the room after saying goodbye. She thought it was a good start and I had to agree. It was a start.

*****

Sandra's second session with you was productive in the sense it got you thinking about the family more, and how much we loved you. Sandra apologised to you as she pulled out a bunch of cards that had illustrated bears all over them. *'This is our family of bears, Jesse, and they can help you identify how you feel about members of your family'*

You sat and watched her quietly as she placed the pile of baby-looking bear cards down in front of you, not quite sure what to do with them.

'Just go through them, and if there's a bear in there that looks like Mum, Dad, Zane, or yourself, you can put them in a pile.'

You nodded and rechecked the first card, picked it up and put it to the side. The next card had a bear wearing a running outfit. You put that in the middle of the table. *'That's Dad.'*

'Very good. Dad likes to run?'

'No, but he exercises to stay fit,' you said reaching for the next pile and moving it over.

Sandra explained that we are all a bit like onions and have lots of layers, and you could pick as many bears as you thought would fit into each of our personalities. Zane's pile of bears consisted of a cheeky looking bear.

'Why did you pick this bear for Zane, Jesse?'

'Because he is an evil, annoying rat,' you said calmly. Oh, that made me so sad for Zane. All this time you hadn't been able to get to school, Zane worried for you. Asking if you'd had a happy day, when I went to pick him up from school. Putting up with you being nasty to him, due to your frustrations. You couldn't see past your own pain, what a gem of a brother you really had.

Dad's pile of bears was a musician, a runner, and a Daddy bear holding his cubs.

My pile of bears consisted of three bears. A very happy bear, an excited bear, and a sleeping bear.

'Why did you pick these bears for Mum, Jesse.' Sandra smiled. Yeah, they were a good pile of bears.

'Mum's usually always happy, and she gets excited about anything.'

Well, not entirely true but it's your opinion and that's what was counting right at this moment.

'What about the tired bear, Jesse?'

'Mum's always tired.'

'Why is that do you think?'

'Because of me,' you answered shortly.

Oh, that hurt to hear, and I deserved it! There had been times when you were yelling at me or being rude, not coping with things and taking it out on me and I would yell back, *'You are ageing me, Jesse, I am exhausted because of you!'* Fact! I was exhausted. But I shouldn't have blamed you openly, even if it was the truth at times.

Sandra removed the cards and you had a chat about trust again and the subject of Tide came up. It got pretty deep, and the depth of his betrayal in your eyes, in cutting you off so severely, came to the surface, revealing to me once more, how devastated you were by the loss of your friend.

Your answers to her questions were quick, quiet and I could see you become very tired towards the end of it. When Sandra left, you went to your room and closed the door. I began to tidy up the kitchen when I heard gut wrenching sobs that stopped me in my tracks. I hadn't heard you cry like that in such a long time. It was deep and to your core. I quietly walked down to your room, knocked once, and opened the door. You were lying on the bed, your arms around Koonie, crying uncontrollably. I sat beside you and rubbed your back.

'It's alright, love, it's alright.'

'Why does he hate me, Mum? What did I do? What did I do?' And your sobbing got deeper, reaching a new level of despair.

I leaned down and hugged your back as you pushed your face into Koonie's soft black fur. It said a lot about him as a cat as he stretched and purred loudly, almost matching your sobs.

'It's not you, mate. Tide obviously has his own issues. You were the best friend anyone would be so lucky to have, just you remember that.' What else could I say to a broken-hearted, desperately lonely thirteen year old?

I rubbed your back and let you cry it out. Once you stopped you lay there so quietly, I thought you had fallen asleep. As I tiptoed out of the room, you reached behind you and pulled the doona cover around you and Koonie, cocooning yourselves in a safe, private tent of warmth. You remained there for two hours.

*****

When Mr Reid came the following day, to work on some maths with you, you sat quietly, struggling on. It pained me to hear him ask you a simple maths question, and you struggle with the answer. And the thing was, on the simple questions, 4+4, 2x5, I knew you knew the correct answer, but you were so afraid of getting it wrong, (freeze response) you hesitated to answer the question, to the point that Mr. Reid repeated it, and patiently waited you out, for your memory bank to warm up. You had so many thoughts floating around in that mind of yours. Worrying thoughts, lonely thoughts, what if thoughts, and coping with all the information Sandra had been giving you, I knew you were as emotionally drained as I felt. He left more work and we as usual, looked forward to his next visit.

KELLY COOPER

Exactly one year and two weeks to the day your initial school refusal began, I received a phone call from McClelland College's Well-Being Officer, Kelly Cooper.

I answered the phone in my usual polite tone, *'Hello, Michelle speaking'*

'Hi Michelle, my name is Kelly Cooper, I'm McClelland's Well-Being Officer, and I'm ringing today to see what's going on with Jesse.'

Okay, so in my tired, depleted state, I heard the word *Officer*, silently shat myself, and immediately thought, we are being fined because we couldn't get our son to school. I was silent for a moment, then asked. *'What would you like to know?'*

'Well I am ringing you on behalf of McClelland, to offer Jesse some support, and see how he is going.' She had a very calm, kind voice.

'Oh, that is wonderful, thank you so much.' And I rambled on a little about how hard it had been on you, the year before, your trust issues, with me especially dragging you to Headspace, your retreating into yourself, becoming easy to anger and sadden. She asked quite a few questions and I answered as best I could, trying not to get too emotional. It was so nice to have someone to talk to that really wanted to help and seemed to understand a lot about anxiety in teenagers.

'It must be really hard,' she said kindly, *'I want you to know that we are not just here for Jesse, but for you also. This is family support, and I'd like to make an appointment for me to come for a visit next week.'* Her words gave me such relief, leaving me with the feeling of safety, of the chance to be heard. I was overwhelmed with gratitude, she was like an angel and I was very much looking forward to meeting her.

My voice broke when I thanked her so much for her call, and hanging up the phone, I actually cried my eyes out for a good hour. Couldn't believe it, just sat at my desk, and bawled like a baby. Yes, in the end my eyes were swollen red, but I have to say, knowing more help was on the way, it was therapeutic for me indeed to have a good old cry. I felt joy and relief in that moment, like I was no longer alone.

*****

When the day arrived for Kelly to come, your Dad decided it was important enough for him to stay home from work to meet her, and Sally who was having her morning cup of tea with me when Kelly arrived, stayed for the visit too. So, it was a warm little welcoming party for Kelly.

When I opened the front door, I immediately felt a sense of warmth radiate from her. Her smile was sweet, her eyes sincere and she had the most gorgeous acorn coloured hair that sat silkily around her pretty face. I don't know what it is about some of us women, but we appreciate good hair, and Kelly Cooper definitely had good hair. I liked her straight away. As did Dad and Sally. We sat around the dining table for a good hour giving her as many details about your journey to date, where I'd break down over some of the more difficult parts. She took notes, gave us some sound advice, and told us what an amazing job we were doing with you. She let me know especially she could understand how hard it had been for me, dealing with you being home for a year, with no real break, alongside trying to research and reach out to as many resources as I could to help you along the way.

At the end of our chat, she asked if she could meet you, which she did. You said hello to each other and she kindly asked you, if it would be alright, if she came back next week to have a chat and spend a little bit of time with you.

You agreed and when you walked back to your room, she smiled and said what a sweetheart you were. We thanked her, and I simply had to send her off with a hug. She was that amazing.

*****

Kelly's second visit the following week impressed me. The three of us sat on the couch to begin with, a cup of tea each, before Kelly asked what you'd like to do. You said you didn't know, and she asked you if you could show her your Xbox, so she could tell her seven-year-old son, she had done something *cool* at work today. Clever girl, knowing that would help relax you. And it did. She sat in your room with you, for over an hour watching you play, gently asking you questions about the game, about Tide, school, back to the game. She kept things flowing, simple and if she sensed you getting stressed, led you back to the game.

I really appreciated the way she conducted herself in your first meeting alone with you, she was completely down to earth and gave you real opportunities to slowly open-up. I wasn't even embarrassed about your broken window, still held together by duct tape! I was grateful for your large Minecraft poster that covered the four holes in your door that you had put there over time, in your fits of anger and rage. I was proud you had not lost your temper for two months now, and Dad was going to put a new door in for you this weekend. Of course, I eavesdropped a little, in our tiny house you eavesdrop when you don't want to! The fact that you spoke in sentences, not one-word responses, that you gave Mr Reid in your math sessions, or the short-clipped answers you gave Sandra, but complete, full sentences you gave on your own merit, I was so proud of you, and in awe of her. She could never understand the importance of the time and attention she was giving you, and how it was making you open up. I was beyond grateful.

Two weeks before you turned fourteen, I rang the Principal of McClelland College. I thought it was time I thanked him for the wonderful support and help given to us, by this amazing school.

Amadeo Ferra. (I had trouble pronouncing his name and thought of him as *Ferrero Rocher chocolate* for a time) He was a lovely, approachable guy, with so much passion for the school he commanded along with many dedicated people. After filling him in on your situation and letting him know how grateful we were to have Mr Reid and Kelly's help making you still feel a part of the school's community. I couldn't stress to him enough that, the thought of being cut off and left alone would have devastated me, for you. As much as you cringed and went pale at the word *school,* you still needed to belong to a group that housed friends, familiarity, and a future. He reassured me that he and the school would do whatever it took for you to come back to their fold, stating if it took a fortnight, to six months, to a year, they would be there for you. It had already been over a year by this stage, so I totally believed him.

After the last year, I knew I was not cut out to home school you to your maximum learning potential. One of us would have ended up, upstairs in Heaven with Aunt Dorothy and Nana Meek!

Amadeo thanked me for the call, as apparently, he didn't receive that many calls of thanks from parents, so was grateful to actually hear from one who was extremely grateful. It was a good phone call and I was happy that your name and journey was on his mind, even if only for the ten minutes we chatted.

*****

The week before your fourteenth birthday was explosively devastating. Every day you were argumentative and angry. Even if I agreed with you, you still argued with me thinking I was against you. Every day of the week. If I said to you, *'Hey, mate, let's get some of this maths done,'* using my most *fun* and encouraging voice, you'd tell me I was too stupid to help you do it and confused you anyway. Well, that was fine with me, and I had voiced to Kelly on the phone the week before, the maths work was adding too much negative pressure on our rocky relationship. You weren't in the headspace whatsoever, where you would just grab your maths book, sit down and slog away for an hour. (The time you started to do that made my heart swell with pride!)

During that week, you became so angry and down. You were simply not coping with *anything* and begged me to cancel both Sandra and Mr Reid.

Two days before your actual birthday, which was also a student free day for Zane, started off as a perfect day. I had some beats playing in the background, and all my paint gear lined up to redecorate one of the walls in the living area. I was on a roll, the sun was shining, Zane had spent the morning at Liam's, and Bec had just dropped him off. You had been invited to go and hang out also, but you had said no.

'Want to help me paint, mate?' I smiled at Zane, as he gave me a hug before heading off out to the backyard. *'Nah, I'm going to play on the trampoline for a bit, then watch a DVD.'*

'Okay, love, are you hungry?'

'No,' And off he went, calling to the cats on his way.

'Hey, Jesse, do you want to help me paint, mate?'

You came out of your room and strolled towards me. I noticed how tall you were, how beautiful you were in moments when your mouth was shut, and I could appreciate you for the little man you were becoming.

'What are you doing?' Of course, you asked the obvious, as I was standing there with paint pot and brush.

'I'm going to change this wall to white, get rid of the chocolate colour.'

'Why?' You didn't look impressed with the idea.

'Well, to open the room up a bit more, brighten it up, so it will give it that French-Provincial feel and match the furniture'

'That's dumb. You're going to make it look stupid and boring, making everything white. You should just leave it the way it is. Stop changing things.'

I dabbed some paint on my brush as I looked at you. I knew you hated change, and it amazed me that you changed your bedroom around every three months. You were frowning, hands in your pockets, as Zane ran inside, red-faced after a good work out on the trampoline.

'A change is as good as a holiday, Jesse, freshens everything up,' I said as I ran a white streak over the chocolate coloured wall.

'That's going to look good, Mum!' Zane slugged down some water, wiping some sweat of his brow.

'Thanks, mate. What DVD are you going to watch?' I soaked my brush back in the bucket, wiping off any excess so I wouldn't get drips. I wanted Dad to be proud of the job I was about to do. He never let me paint our walls as he was a perfectionist, but left this one job for me, as I think he was over me painting everything else white.

'Teen Wolf,' Zane replied as he walked off towards his room, referring to the *T.V* series.

'That's gay,' Jesse scoffed.

'That's enough, Jesse. Zane doesn't bag you sitting there playing Xbox or any movie you watch. Don't bag what he likes.'

'Stupid fat rat,' you persisted.

'Enough!' I said sharply as Zane yelled out.

'Shut up, you maggot!'

'Yeah, okay, Zane, Jesse, both of you stop it. I want us all to have a nice day for Christ's sake! Can we do that? Just have a nice, peaceful day. I'll paint; you guys do whatever you like. Just do it nicely! Please!'

As Zane had already gone into his room, I had no one else to look at bar you and said quietly, *'We just need one nice day.'* I was that desperate.

'You always blame me.'

'I am not blaming anyone, mate. I'm asking you both, to just be bloody nice! To get along, that's it! Simple.'

You walked off, thumping Zane's door as you walked past, mumbling something, which Zane responded to in a squeaky tone. I sighed, turning Pandora up and changed the station from Helen Jane Long to Nick Jonas and forced myself into the zone of *happy-happy, joy-joy,* and stroked away, enjoying seeing my walls become white. I was lucky to be able to enjoy that happy feeling, for twenty-odd minutes before my world tilted off balance yet again. The joys of motherhood.

I don't know what started it exactly, but I heard a *God almighty* scream from Zane and grunts from you, as you got into a physical punch on, both of you trying to give as good as you got. It was very rare you both slugged away at each other, so when you did, I did not cope well whatsoever. Looking back at my childhood, I remember trying to put Aunty Leah's head through our desk once, but that was only after she slammed the cotton tip into my ear as I was cleaning it! And as much as Dad had told me stories of him and Uncle Grant fighting as boys, I did not like seeing or hearing my two sons go at it, like they wanted to kill each other.

I turned the music down, after I dropped the brush into the paint pot, and headed down to your bedrooms, as you raced out of Zane's room, into yours, slamming the door.

'What's going on?' I asked in a concerned voice, as you started swearing from your room. I was on edge immediately as the swear word coming out of your mouth was one you had never used before, and hearing Dad tell your cousin on Xbox-Live a month ago, he didn't want to

hear that word ever again. (Starts with C ends in T- and I don't mean crappiest, creepiest, cheekiest, crankiest, crudest or casket! Although it's lucky none of us have ended up in the latter after all this!)

I pushed Zane's door open, and it saddened me to see him crying on his bed. *'What the hell is going on? Jesse knock off that bloody swearing!'* I yelled over my shoulder (setting a good example as always!) as I went to give Zane a cuddle. *'Mate, what is going on?'* Did I need to play the guessing game here? I rubbed his small back.

'Jesse came in here and asked me if I wanted to play Xbox and I said no coz I want to watch a DVD; it's my day off school and I want to relax!'

I ran my hand over his hair, sighing as I could hear you yelling out about Zane being a stupid fat rat.

'It's alright, mate, I understand.' I had explained to Zane so many times, that you got lonely and wanted Zane to play with you. I also understood that Zane needed his own space, especially as he went to school day in day out and supported you and tried so hard to understand your anxiety, even though it made his life difficult at times. When my little boy explained to me, crying for an hour straight one afternoon after you had called him names, to the point he could not take it anymore, about the darkness he could feel growing in his chest, set my alarm bells ringing.

'It's alright, mate,' I said again, hoping it would be.

'No, it's not, Mum, I'm sick of his SHIT!' My ten-year-old screamed at me, before bursting into tears of frustration once more.

'Pussy-Girl!' you yelled through your door, hearing your brother crying.

'SHUT UP!' Zane screamed again.

I could feel my blood begin to boil and got up from Zane's bed and walked to your door, banging on it firmly. *'Jesse, knock it off right now or I am going to ring Dad. I've just about HAD IT!'* I yelled. Hearing you scoff at your brother's tears had me seeing red. We all put up with so much trying to support your fears, your everyday worries. Your anxiety!! It was, at times, like living with an extra person in the house, and as much as I wanted to support, protect, love, and guide you to a happier place, I also had your brother to worry about.

'He told me to piss OFF,' you screamed. *'I just wanted to play Xbox with him!'* I could hear the desperation in your voice, and I got where both of you were coming from.

'It's his day off school, mate, he just wants to relax, maybe he'll want to play later.' I felt that sounded reasonable.

'Yeah,' Zane yelled out, *'Just coz you have every day off.'*

That, of course touched a personal cord with you, and you started yelling at him to *'shut his fat-rat trap.'*

'That's enough, Zane, that doesn't help, love.' I said gently, yet firmly, mentally begging you to stop as another insult spewed from his lips.

'Come on, Jesse! Enough.'

'You always take that maggot's SIDE!' you screamed through your door, and Zane screamed back that you were too stupid to understand anything.

You began screaming out that he was a stupid c, stupid c, over and over and over! It was making me want to rip my head off and roll it down the driveway so I wouldn't have to hear your explosive, angry and hurt words, which were worrying me to the degree, where I knew I had to get you to stop and calm down.

'Jesse, you need to stop it, stop IT NOW!' I went for firm and calm, not quite hysterical just yet. But, unfortunately, I could feel it building as you continued shuffling about, swearing, and screaming in your room.

You flung the door open, and every gift I'd given you the past few months, you angrily threw out in the hallway. A silver Buddha - I hoped you'd find peace in it, a Rhodonite gemstone – that promised to *assist* to reduce emotional imbalance and anxiety and promote serenity. That clearly was not working today. Followed by three candles, one of them, in a glass container that shattered everywhere; each one flung with a vicious, angry comment. I shouldn't have been overwhelmed with your reaction. But I was. Sadly so.

You were breathing heavily, and so was I. We looked at each other and you screamed at me to *'Piss off and go away from my room!'* Slamming the door again.

I stood, looking down at the shattered pieces, as you began to angrily sob, occasionally stopping to breathe, and continue swearing. I walked off to get the dust pan and shovel, as Zane came out of his room to see what had happened. *'He doesn't deserve that stuff, Mum.'* He said quietly, wiping his tears, away.

'Shush, it's alright. Don't come any closer, there's glass here.' I began sweeping it up and listened to you go into a fit of a rage because we were outside your door.

'Piss OFF, piss OFF!' you screamed over and over. I wondered briefly what the neighbours were thinking about this episode. Couldn't be helped!

'Please calm down Jesse, I'm cleaning up the glass you broke!'

You pulled your door open and looked at Zane and I. *'JUST PISS OFF!'* You screamed, eyes bulging, mouth set to beyond furiously angry!

I stood there looking at you and snapped. I could feel it inside, the overpowering urge to actually slap your face right off. You saw the look on my face, it wouldn't have been pretty as I stepped towards you, broom in hand and hissed, *'You need to shut THE FUCK UP RIGHT NOW BECAUSE I AM READY TO EXPLODE!'* (and the mother of the year award does not go to me!) Yes, it was so very wrong, but in that split second it felt so right letting my frustration, my anger, my fright burst out. All my reasoning had vanished. My kindness and good mothering instincts had completely left me. And although I knew I wasn't going to raise a hand to you, you did not.

You must have been scared for your safety, and lunged at me screaming, pushing me as hard as you could. I went flying backwards out of your room, fell over the exiled pile of shattered, unwanted gifts, and hit my head against the wall as I went down. There was complete silence for five seconds. I could not help the sobs that escaped me. I looked up at you, angry and sad. You slammed the door and I could hear the thump as you threw yourself on the floor, crying yourself.

I felt Zane's arms go around me, to help pull me up, he looked so sad.

'It's okay, mate.' I put my arms around him and led him from the hallway, closing the corridor door so you would not even hear us breathe, and get angry all over again. I left you for a long time, hoping you would come out to me when you felt you were able. After two hours, I quietly knocked on your door and gently pushed it open. You were wrapped up tightly in your green blanket, not moving an inch. I sat on the bed beside you and gathered you up in my arms, holding you like an infant, whispering, 'I'm so sorry, mate.'

That set you off, and your cries were inconsolable. You cried in my arms like I had not seen you cry before; it compared to the time you were overwhelmed, by the loss of your friendship with Tide.

You repeated over, and over, and over, as you sobbed, 'I'm sorry, I'm sorry, I'm sorry.'

I was in tears myself but hid it from you as I held you close, as I soothed, 'It's alright, mate, it's alright. We all say silly things when we're cross.' I squeezed my eyes shut as your wracking sobs tore at my guilt. How did we get here? Some days I asked myself that question a lot!

I opened my eyes to see Zane standing in the door way watching us. I opened my arm and he came towards us, and we had a group cuddle. I don't know how long we sat there. A long time. I think we were all in shock for the rest of the day, and quietly went about our individual activities, speaking to each other with the utmost cautionary respect.

Kelly came the following day, and we discussed our episode of shame. The embarrassment I felt, for my part, in the retelling of our tale, was my punishment for not handling things as I should have. She was very helpful and shed a sparkly bit of light, onto why you may have been stressed the past week. She believed that, as we were approaching your fourteenth birthday, you were probably, unconsciously struggling with the overwhelming, unwanted feelings of what I had put you through a year before, when you turned thirteen, taking you into Headspace without being honest. Making you feel trapped, uncomfortable and every other awful feeling you should not have been made to feel.

It made a lot of sense and increased my feelings of guilt. Let's put guilt right alongside mosquitos and hindsight please.

That guilt stayed with me, on top of the sadness I felt, when organising your fourteenth birthday. You were happy to go to the Frankston Foreshore with our group and I loved them for wanting to surround you on your birthday. Aunty Leah and Ireland came down also, which made you very happy.

As much as I wanted you to be able to have friends your own age around you, to laugh and be that teenage boy loving life and kicking goals, I was grateful to the friends we had, letting you know they supported you. I had reached out to Tide and his parents one last time, saying we would love it if they could join us. Of course, I heard nothing back. Thankfully, Noah did send you birthday greetings from Queensland, as he was always that sweet, considerate friend.

Sitting at the picnic table watching all you kids play a game of tag, Jacqui's fifteen-year-old daughter, Brooke, asked me how you were going.

'He's okay. He just gets a bit lonely, frustrated. He is missing Tide.' I pulled my jacket tighter around me as the chill of the late afternoon was setting in.

'I spoke to Tide last week about, Jesse,' Brooke said.

'Really?' I was hoping it was positive and nice. Teenagers, you never know what to expect.

'Yeah, he said why should he bother being Jesse's friend, if Jesse can't even bother coming to school for a day and be with him.'

I was, quite literally shocked by this ignorant statement.

'Oh, my god! Really? Does he not know a thing about what Jesse has been dealing with?'

Brooke shrugged, and her next comment proved he was not the only one in the dark, or ignorant. *'Well, can't Jesse just try to get to school one day. I mean, how hard can it be?'* She flipped her silky black hair over her shoulder, her eyebrows raised over her pretty, green eyes.

I tried to explain to her as much as I could in the brief five minutes we had, before Sally was yelling out, *'about time for a walk on the pier.'*

I was cold and tired. I'd had enough. Try indeed. Jesus Christ. The fact that some days you made yourself sick trying. It was so hard trying to explain to those that couldn't be bothered typing in a word themselves and doing a bit of research. If you cared, you'd look it up. I wasn't cross with Brooke, she had always had your and Zane's back. I was just sick and tired, of always feeling sick and tired by some people's ignorance. (Thank you, Anastacia!)

As we walked down the pier, you and Caitlyn walked ahead. My love for her increased in that moment. Your fear of the edge of the pier and falling off into the dark water had remained with you from toddlerhood till now. As Caitlyn knew this, she walked on the open side, leaving you fenced in between her and the rail. Seeing you walk with her, hearing her laughter as you said something witty or sarcastic, soothed my soul for a moment. Everyone was excited to discover the little seal, swimming around under the pier, his presence added to the magical feel, the day you turned fourteen.

I was determined this would be a great year for you. It had to be.

As the year went along, all our relationships grew. Your Dad did all he could, to allow you time to chat about anything at all that was on your mind, and both you and Zane worked harder on being civil to each other. I did everything I could to try to make everyone in my family feel loved, happy, understood, and safe. (We weren't always sitting around the campfire singing *Kumbaya*, but we were kicking goals in our own way).

Mr Reid came weekly, and you were seeing Sandra once a month. Kelly came when she could, as her schedule was overflowing. Things had a steady pace about them and you seemed to be settling into a quiet, calm, confident fourteen-year-old.

Having Mr Reid come over on such a steady basis, made our time together more comfortable and productive, and he became a member of our support family. I took joy in feeding him, wanting to give him something back, for all his time he spent with you. He wasn't just a teacher, but a man wanting to understand more about your anxiety. He would come with information he had collected at seminars, and conferences regarding Mental Health, and one day sat and read to us the information he had. Of course, everything he read was like a recital for my ears. But it was wonderful that he was trying to understand what you were dealing with and, it was good for you to hear too. Although you sat there, shell-shocked, as you had been in denial for quite a while that you did in fact have Anxiety. You preferred to call it *The Nothing.*

Mr Reid also mentioned the Connect programme at McClelland. It was for students that had a difficult time staying in mainstream school, due to a variety of issues— *loss of a parent, divorce, abuse, or a mental illness l*ike yours. It sounded interesting and it was good to have another option that you may be comfortable with down the track. You talked weekly about trying to get back to school, and with Kelly's suggestion, we started weekly drives past the school. The first time you did not speak once as our car left our driveway, as we made the short trip, to the front gate of McClelland College.

I really enjoyed the drive there, and I ached for the loss of your childhood; not being in school, laughing with your mates, learning, going on excursions. All the essential support school offered a growing teenager.

After the first week, we would stop the car for a few minutes, only if the school ground was clear of students. As the weeks rolled on, you slowly began to chat on the drive there, but always did your window up, and pull your hoody lower over your face as we approached the gate.

I asked you one day, *'Do you miss it, mate? Do you wish you were back in there?'*

You answered in true Jesse fashion, short and sweet, *'What do you think?'*

It was another day with Mr Reid where you sat at our dining table, going over some maths where he pulled out a timetable and gently suggested, we start planning to see if we could get you into one class a week, starting in two weeks.

I sat at my desk, typing, thinking, *'Good luck with that!'*

When Mr Reid left, we looked over the timetable and it looked pretty good. Starting time around 10am for one period. *'What do you think, mate?'*

You sat there, head bent over your work getting on with answering as many questions as you could, while it was all fresh in your head. *'Good. I'm really going to try, Mum.'*

'Of course you are love. Good job today.'

So, when the day came for you to get into that one period, you got up and had a quiet meltdown. I expected nothing less. I had to ring Mr Reid and let him know. He was patiently understanding. He was trying everything in his power to get you there. On his next visit, he jokingly brought along with him, a piece of rope, and told you he was going to tie you up and drag you to school. You thought that was funny. Steve Reid was in fact, a very funny guy, and often went into song here and there to get you in a relaxed mood or simply crack you up. Some of his comments would go over your head, but it gave me a very much, needed laugh, so I appreciated his efforts.

*****

FMC

Kelly had many connections in her job and kept her ear to the ground, searching for any other resource that may benefit you and our family, in helping you along your way. She came and had a chat to us about FMC – Family Mediation and Counselling Victoria. My first thought was wow, now we need family counselling. It took me fifteen seconds to get over my insecurities and not take this extra help given, personally, as my *failure* as a mother. I was in fact very thankful Kelly had suggested this service to us and put our family on the list.

And in the end, it was a beneficial arrangement. Dad and I went in for the first session and met with Stephen Brackenridge. He had worked in the field helping and supporting youths and their families for many years and had a passion about him I found endearing. We gave him as many details as we could regarding our situation and I had already written out a three-page spread from everything I could think of that would benefit him in helping you.

The headings were as listed, followed by a thick paragraph for each:

Separation anxiety in pre-school / Bullied for two and a half years at primary school / Counselling at 6 years of age due to like-panic attacks at bedtime / Started a new Primary School term three Grade Two / Bullied by cousin and friends / Very angry in Grade Six / Started missing one to two days of school a fortnight / Constant talk of death, dying / Always hated germs – Keeps room spotless / Quiet on trips to the point of almost being in a coma / Ruins family pictures-mostly of him and mum when he is angry / Won't use utensils in restaurants or eat at friends' houses / Believes the world is against him / Takes everything very personally / Attacked at milk bar, left alone by mate who was scared / Started Year Seven. Loved term one / Had scooter stolen from him term one holidays / School refusal started term two week two / Forced to go to Headspace - felt betrayed / Got tricked to go to school and forced to go into class against his will / Has moments of great sadness / Loss of confidence/ At times, a sense of deep loneliness.

I don't know what I may have missed, but I thought that would be a good start.

He glanced down at my notes, back at me and smiled. I would have loved to know what was going through his mind at that moment!

'Thanks,' he said before continuing on with many questions about Dad and I as individuals, and as a couple, our family's history, and any incidences in our own childhoods. The only thing I was willing to share there, was what a wonderful, hardworking mother I had in Nana Lyn, who worked full-time. Which left us in the care of our step-father, that perhaps, should not have been. Anything that may have happened in my childhood was going to stay there. They say *you spend half your adulthood getting over your childhood.* Mysteriously, that is true. It's not like you dwell on it, it's just there, lurking around from time to time in the background.

Dad was the same, mentioned how wonderful Grammy was, and briefly stated why his father was no longer in our lives. I have barely mentioned my step-father till now. He had caused irrevocable damage, and I didn't think talking about him or his issues, had a thing to do with helping you. (Mind you, I'm not the professional in this instant but, that's the way I feel). Our session was a little over an hour, and we thanked Stephen after we made a session time for him to come to the house and chat to you.

That was a day I was embarrassed for him to see your spider web window. (Need to get that fixed ASAP!)

You were a little nervous the day Stephen arrived, asking the usual questions before you had someone new come in; how long was he going to stay, what did he want exactly, and what were you expected to do? Once we explained to you that he was coming here to talk to you about anything you were concerned about in life. That you didn't have to say or do anything you weren't comfortable with, and he was generally coming here to listen, and help you think healthy, positive thoughts about yourself and your life. Those reasons were good enough for you and your session went well enough, that you felt comfortable to want to see him again. Your spirits were high when he left, and I noticed the more people we had to have come to our home the past two years, you seemed proud of yourself, and relieved at the same time when they left!

Stephen had also set up a session time for Zane at Karingal Heights, giving them the privacy to speak openly. As comfortable as Zane was with communicating easily with Dad and I, I felt this was such an important step for him to be able to lay his cards on the table and purge himself honestly about everything, and anything, and have a response that would give him the confidence to keep being and believing in himself, as a wonderful, loving, caring, and sensitive little being.

I kept my eyes on the time when I knew he would be in his session with Stephen, knowing it would be an emotional, challenging time for him. When I received the phone call from the lovely Pauline, who managed the school's office like Barack Obama had run his country; to say Zane was very emotional and a bit distraught after his session, and would I like to pick him up, I was there in a flash.

Once we were home and settled with a cup of tea, I sat down on my favourite chair, surprised when Zane crawled into my lap like a toddler and let it all out. *His frustrations, his fears, his overwhelming feelings of sadness at times when you took your own frustrations out on him.* It broke my heart. Zane was a strong little soldier in our war and talking so openly to Stephen allowed all the pressure to finally explode. Mostly all he was telling me, I had heard in the past. But for him to sit in my arms, and cry like a baby after discussing it with a stranger was all too much for Zane in that moment. I held him and reassured him what a wonderful son, and brother he was. I told him I was so proud of him. I was amazed at times that I had given birth to two such amazing individuals. I know I said at the beginning of our story that this wasn't about Zane. But it is. This story is about Zane, about Dad, about me and about you. We are a family that love unconditionally, hurt deeply, struggle with our failures and celebrate our wins, like millions of other families out there.

And we, all of us as individuals, have a voice in this story, your story, our story. Our family and friends, online support groups, and our support family. I am so grateful to so many people that have helped keep us afloat in times where the ocean seemed endless and our ship felt like it was sinking. Where would any of us be in this world without a little help from our friends?

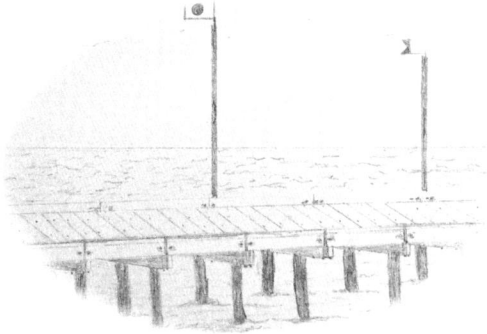

CRUNCH TIME

Mr Reid's aim was to try to get you into Head Start at the end of 2015, which was the beginning of Year Nine for 2016. The thought that you may have to repeat Year Eight, made you so unhappy and you felt the added pressure that if you couldn't make it in, you were going to be kept back. Mr Reid set up a timetable and reassured you that you could make it in, for a class or two in the coming fortnight. His faith in you and the heavens above were that great. Although you were desperate to make that happen, unfortunately it was another hurdle you could not overcome.

Once we realised we needed another option, Mr Reid chatted to you and I about the Connect program at McClelland and set up a meeting with the Connect teachers after school so you could meet them.

After the school day was done, we picked Zane up and headed off to McClelland. You seemed pretty calm, although quiet. Having Zane with you and knowing Caitlyn was going to meet you at the front gate, gave you a bit of added security, and we walked into the smaller building to meet the two Connect teachers and see what our options were.

You remembered Miss Harry, who had taught you Year Seven maths the first term you attended, and she remembered you. The other lady seemed very warm, giving, and there was a certain spark to her personality. Carol McNair. (Nan to you and any other that were lucky enough to be surrounded with her no-nonsense - I'm here to help you and I've been around too long to put up with any bullshit - attitude!)

It was clear they were both passionate and enthusiastic about their roles in providing education and care for the students that didn't have it as easy as others or had similar issues like yours. We were given a package of information as the two ladies asked you a few questions and tried to get you to open up in a comfortable way, where they weren't crowding or overloading you. Mr Reid of course was there to support you and be the familiar face, occasionally cracking the odd joke which I always appreciated. (*Laughter does in fact make the world go around again, once it has fallen off its axle*).

I took in the entire scene: the caring staff encouraging you and giving you as much positive, informative information as you could handle – and the more information I was gathering I felt at peace and such a sense of relief. This could be it!

CONNECT is a re-engagement program for students that don't cope well in mainstream. Some students either wag or simply do not come to school and Connect offers those students a small class environment where they can have one on one time with a teacher and also have art therapy available to them, which is brilliant for traumatised and anxious kids.

The Outreach and Connect teachers, put in so much effort to build up the students' confidence, and I had seen that time and time again with the way Mr Reid had interacted with you over the past eighteen months. Carol continued explaining about the opportunities Connect gave their students, including the mentoring program and community-based programs that helped the students develop their social and communicative skills, as a lot of them don't have the capacity to verbalise their feelings. Carol also mentioned they were not shy in offering any child a hug if they needed it, along with breakfast and boundaries. I was beginning to feel that the Connect program was a perfect fit for you. Glancing around the room I noticed it was not overcrowded with school stuff but just enough posters, books and school work here and there to make it look the part. A quick look at you, and I noticed the signs of how nervous and unsure you were, but you were acting your way through any discomfort beautifully, nodding in the appropriate places when you were spoken to and even smiling here and there, thanks to Mr Reid. I was loving the feel of the rooms and believed that these teachers went above and beyond in their roles to help their students and I could see you in the future, being a part of this little community, feeling you belonged and could grow confidently as a student. I was excited and overwhelmed for you. -*Was this it? Our chance for you to slide into this comfy little space?* It was my deepest wish for you, for it to be so.

Both Miss Harry and Nan said to you, it would be awesome if you could come into a class, even for five minutes before the end of the year so you could meet the other kids and start your Year Nine work with them. You nodded, as you had been, and we thanked them graciously when it was time to leave.

Getting into the car and driving off, Zane commented on how nice the ladies seemed and he thought the classroom and subjects were cool.

'What do you think Jess?'

'I think it will be good,' you replied.

That was good enough for me, as it was for your Dad when we told him all about it. He read over the information and said it sounded like you would fit into the program beautifully.

****

Mr Reid came the following day to see if we could get you into the Connect class the next day for second period. I thought that would be a great idea especially as the year was coming to an end and the Connect classes finished a week before mainstream, so it didn't leave us with too much time. He asked you a lot of questions to see what your thoughts and feelings were, to which you replied, *'I don't know,'* to most of them. You were quiet and nervous, and he could feel it and let you know, he would still be around the Connect rooms, and you would still see plenty of him. He wanted to relax you a bit and make you laugh so he began singing Michael Jackson's —*I'll be there to love and comfort you.* Man he cracked me up. You dropped your head smiling, trying to hide. In the end, you sounded pretty happy with the schedule Mr Reid had set, and as I was placing our tea cups in the sink I was thinking, *My god, this is really going to happen!* (Yes, I could still delude myself with hope even at this stage).

Saying goodbye to Mr Reid, I closed the front door calling out happily, *'That was so cool, Jesse. I think Connect is going to be the perfect fit for you, how do you feel about it all?'*

I turned to you smiling and was sad to see the angry look on your face as you spat out, *'How do you think I feel. NO ONE GIVES A FUCK HOW HARD IT IS! YOU JUST DON'T KNOW HOW HARD IT IS!'* Your tone indicated everything you were feeling; an overwhelming fear and panic which resulted in pure anger and frustration.

I stood there nodding. I totally got it. Although it saddened me for you, and what you must have been feeling inside, your screaming and cursing no longer upset or shocked me. It was the pure tell-tale signs that you were feeling trapped, lost, and desperate. It must have been so exhausting for you.

I rang Mr Reid and let him know how you reacted once he had left, and you probably wouldn't be able to make it in for that scheduled period. He handled me cancelling you once again, with a supportive attitude.

As the year drew to a close, we had at least three to four home visits a week in between life and focusing on the other individuals in the household. Stephen, Steve, and Kelly, along with the new Psychologist from FMC, Greg. By the time Greg was coming on board, Kelly was leaving us for another position. I knew she would fill it as enthusiastically as she had done with us, giving us the support and advice we needed to help us move forward as a positive family unit. I personally was sad to see her go as I had loved the *Mummy moments* we had shared over a hot chocolate or a cup of tea, laughing and close to tears at times with how much we loved our children, discussing openly that there was absolutely nothing we would not do for our children to make them happy. *(Of course, I don't mean spoiling them rotten and letting them get away with murder!)*

When Greg came for his first visit to get to know us a little, you would not come out of your room and refused to meet him, so tired of all the faces this year had brought with it, and Greg totally understood and appreciated the fact that, you at least called out *hello* through the wall. I understood how drained you were towards the end. I was too, and as much as I was so appreciative of all the help we were getting to help you with your anxiety, sometimes, it got so draining retelling parts of your story. It made me relive many painful, sad, and regrettable incidents all over again. Greg and I had a great first session and covered some good ground in preparing a plan to support you not only getting back to school for 2016, but in coping with any situation that may cause avoidance and severe discomfort.

As the week was coming to an end, and the Connect classes closed down for Christmas, we had a home visit from Carol. It was a stinking hot summer's day, and I wished I'd offered some cold fruit instead of my homemade fudge I delighted in stuffing Mr Reid with. Carol sat down at our kitchen table comfortably and chatted to you and I about all the fun you would have with the other kids next year, along with the activities she had in mind to do, plus it would be a good idea for me to take you to Cube 37 in Frankston over the holidays, where some of the students had their art displayed. It was lovely that she seemed genuinely excited to have you join the Connect program with her next year. I was hoping you felt her enthusiasm as much as I had. Having her sit in our home, I felt a connection with her and liked her survival spirit immediately. She was a kindred spirit, another soul that had been on this earth after life itself had taken its toll, yet she still had the passion, energy, and drive to do so much more for others, showering them in her endless source of light.

We never took for granted, the individuals that supported us all on this quest to help you. Because they gave Dad and I the strength to believe in ourselves as parents that loved you deeply, that wanted nothing but the very best for you, to have you believe in yourself again. And that's the common denominator in all of this. All these wonderful individuals that were so very perfect in the positions they held, wanted you to be all you could be. To end 2015 with their support and the prospect of what they would do for you the following year, gave me so much relief and I looked forward to your Year Nine schooling with joy.

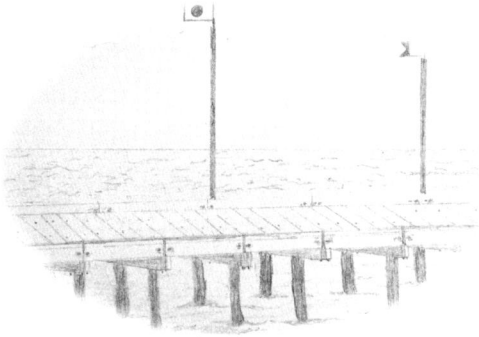

2015 - CHRISTMAS

For the past six months, you had constantly asked me if we could have Christmas at home this year, and could Nana Lyn, Grammy, Poppy, Uncle Grant, Aunty Nicole, and Ireland come!

Well, it worked out well that we had Ireland stay with us for two weeks right up until Christmas Eve, as Aunty Leah had gone overseas to Amsterdam. So, we celebrated Christmas Day, with Ireland, on Christmas Eve, and were blessed enough that everyone else on your wish list, also wanted to come down and spend the holiday celebration with us. Nana Lyn arrived a few days earlier, so we could spoil her and enjoy her vibrant company as always.

Three nights before Christmas Eve, Ireland, Zane, and you were having some entertaining conversations with Nana Lyn about life and things in general. Nana constantly had you all enthralled with, her very blunt, straight to the point answers to your many questions. *Did you believe in God and if so, where did God come from? Who really made the world? Where do you go when you die? Do you want to be buried or set on fire when you're dead? What did you want to be when you grew up? What was it like being a kid a hundred years ago?* Questions Nanas' enjoy, being surrounded by their grandchildren looking up at them with so much love in their eyes, taking their word as gospel! Nana Lyn loved it, and creating harmless mischief in her answers, most other Nanas would not give. She not only had you all in stitches of laughter but knew how to make each-and-every one of you feel like everything was going to be alright at the end of the day, no matter what.

The fire crackled away on this chilly December night as the hour grew late, and Zane and Ireland went inside for a DVD. You decided to stay outside and talk to Nana, always enjoying her company and any chance to have some much appreciated one on one time, to chat to her. And this particular chat, went on for three and a half hours. You talked non-stop. I think it amazed Nana as much as it amazed me. We had been trying to get you to talk to everyone and anyone all year.

On Nana's last trip ten months prior, after my operation, you had barely said boo to her, which never bothered her. She always had the approach that, if you needed her, you knew where she was.

And there you sat, outside with the fire roaring, telling Nana your life story as you saw it. And there I sat in the bathroom, backside balanced on the pointy edge of the bath, for almost four hours, listening to every word you had to say, enraptured in what you thought and felt, as so many events in your life had helped bring you to where you were today.

I felt relieved, excited, and sad the more you spoke, about how you felt at kinder. To life before Zane, and after he came along. Even though you knew we loved you, you still felt we loved Zane more. That we always took his side. (I already knew that's how you felt. It still hurt to hear you say it).

Talking about your first primary school, feeling sad and scared. Loving your new primary school once you made friends. You felt shy, you told her. You loved your Grade Four teacher, saying she was one of the best you ever had, you felt she really listened to what you had to say, and made you feel important. She was the one who really got you reading confidently. (It's amazing what a brilliant teacher can do for one child, let alone hundreds. It's those teachers that really make a difference).

You said in Grades Five and Six you felt happy, had some great friends, and looked forward to high school. When you started high school, you enjoyed it, and were excited about the class structure and making new friends.

Of course, you covered how you felt about bullies, the milk bar incidents, and throughout your in-depth conversation, Nana asked a lot of questions, which was so good for her, to really understand where you were coming from, and what you had been through. It was good for you, as her questions forced you to think about the answers and I got so much information. Mind-blowing, heart -warming, numbing information. I could never thank my Mum enough, for being the most sensational Nana to my sons. She certainly was your biggest fan.

One question Nana asked you had me frozen to the spot though, and it left my heart in my throat.

'And how do you think you got this anxiety, Jesse? What do you think started it?'

'I don't know,' you answered her. *'Just life.'*

Life! There you have it. Out of the mouth of a fourteen-year-old. Just life.

It was a fabulous Christmas, and we were all secretly thrilled that you had had such a great talk with Nana. It was such a relief for Nana, Dad, and I that you opened-up so completely and communicated how you had been feeling. It would have been so therapeutic for you.

Grammy and Poppy spoilt everyone as usual and broke the news that they were taking us on a fourteen day cruise to New Zealand in November 2016. I feel the need, to constantly say thank you to Grammy. She was the queen for making the dream of family holidays, become reality.

Although I had a little bit of worry about how you would go, being away from home for that amount of time, I was too excited to be overly concerned, and with eleven months in-between now and then, there was plenty of time to prepare you. I also had to get over my own fear of being on a ginormous cruise ship, in the middle of the ocean, and block all thoughts of the *Titanic* out!

I felt drained at the end of 2015. But it had been a great year. We had taken many steps beside you, and you had come such a long way. As a fourteen-year-old, fighting so many of your own demons. There were many times I wish I could have merged into your thoughts to understand exactly what you were thinking and help turn your dark thoughts towards the light. Being loved by you gave me the strength to go on, whilst loving you deeply gave me the courage to find the answers and seek help wherever I could.

Every day we are alive, is a new day and the opportunity to do what we can for those we love. For those we have yet to meet. Grammy put up the synopsis for Thirteen, on the Anxiety group we are a part of online. I was overwhelmed with the reaction from so many people reaching out. Many saying, *'Your story sounds like our story. Have you been in my home? It sounds like you are describing my family!'* And I responded, *'I am telling your story, and my story, this is for us all!'*

2016 – CONNECT

The week before school began, I asked you to try on your uniform. You said you had and it still fit you. I took your word for it. The next day I got a phone call from Carol, (Nan) asking how you went over the holidays, and how you were feeling about coming into school. We chatted for a few minutes, and she told me what day I could bring you to school, and we would start with ten minutes in the car park. I was feeling confident that you could do that.

And you did it. Tuesday, Wednesday, and Thursday, for the first few weeks. You didn't put your shoes on. That meant we couldn't get you out of the car. Smart boy! You were a little panicked the first day we drove into the visitors' car park and pulled your hoody down low. Nan came over and told you how proud she was of you. She *truly* understood how nervous you were, and she jumped in the back seat, so we could remain inconspicuous, to any students wandering here or there between classes. We chatted for a good twenty minutes and she made you laugh a few times, with her forthright commentary and opinions of her classrooms activities, before giving us a hug goodbye before we left.

It finally felt so easy! We did it! We got you into the car, and into the school carpark!

The following week after we left Nan, we took off to the Karingal Hub, as you wanted to spend your birthday money from the year before, on The Walking Dead box set. As we walked towards Sanity, I was pointing out the cute little kittens at the pet shop, when a man blocked our path grinning from ear to ear. Mr Steve Reid. We were both so happy to see him, and I immediately went to give him a big hug hello. It was like seeing an old friend again. He went to shake your hand, as he was telling you how proud he was of you getting into school as often as you were. You ignored his hand and went in to give him a hug also. That's what you thought of Mr Reid!

I was on Cloud Nine those first few weeks. I was simply so proud of you pushing yourself, getting up and organised to get into the car and see Nan. You were kicking goals!

On a Wednesday, the Connect students were off to join the mainstream students in an awesome new program called, The McClelland Academy Program, or MAP, which had started when you began Year Seven. That left the Connect rooms empty of students from 12pm onwards. Although Nan had a plan to get you into at least one class before the end of term, we started off by seeing if we could get you out of the car and into the Connect building when the other kids weren't about, hoping that would make you more comfortable.

It was a step I was nervous about. I knew it had to happen, wanted it to so desperately, but I'll admit I became anxious about your reaction when we had to push forward and change what you were comfortable with. That's something all mums face, with kids with anxiety. Our kids become comfortable and feel safe with a routine then, because of reality, we have to change it on them, and then we are the bad guys. The fact that I was getting you into the car three times a week and to the school to chat with Nan, was a huge success for us as it was. But, we couldn't just sit in the school's car park for the rest of the year now, could we?

I was watching the time closely on the first Wednesday that we were going to see if we could get you out of the car. As I thought Nan was going to meet us in the carpark, I felt a bit of relief knowing I wouldn't have to try to get you out of the car on my own, until five minutes before we left the house, Nan gave me a phone call asking us to meet her inside the classroom. *'Sure thing!'* I had replied happily. She would have not guessed I was about to vomit up my heart! I hung up the phone, preparing myself how to tell you, this was the day you were expected to do more than sit in the car, in the visitors' car park.

I walked down to your room, knocked, and said quietly, *'Hey, mate, you know how it's a bit hot outside today, I think we should go into the classroom so poor Nan doesn't have to come out to the car. What do you think?'*

You sat in your chair doing up your shoe laces and froze. I knew instantly you were about to pop off your rocker, so I quickly said without a beat, *'Actually, don't worry about it, we'll just drive in and I will race your school work into her and say hello, okay?'*

'Okay.' You stood and pulled your hoody on.

'Grab your work and let's go, mate.' On the drive to school, I was thinking of calming, supportive ways I could get you out of the car. We pulled into the parking lot. There was not a soul around. Our car was parked in front of a few Australian native plants, facing towards the Connect building.

I got out of the car and asked you to pass me your work. You undid your seat belt and handed me the paper work you had finished.

I thought to myself, *Just press him gently,* and said, *'Hey, mate, do you know what. I reckon you can do this. You have made amazing steps so far, imagine how fantastic you will feel if you get in and say hi to Nan for five seconds. I really think you can do it, mate. What do you think?'*

You shrugged and said quietly, *'I don't know.'*

I smiled. *'I reckon you can do it, come on, mate, we'll sneak through the garden, no one is around and we'll race in. Won't Dad be so proud when we tell him, Jess?'*

Your hand moved to the door handle, my heart was in my throat and I kept thinking over and over, *we're nearly there, we're nearly there.* I had the keys in my hand ready to press the lock down as soon as you shut the door. And as you got out I locked it down fast, and quickly moved around to the front of the car, whispering, *'Let's go, mate.'*

And off we went like a couple of bandits, moving stealth-like towards the entrance of the Connect classrooms. I couldn't help the giggle that escaped me. Ridiculous to some I'm sure, but in that moment, you and I were winning the Australia Open, the AFL Grand Final, the Olympics and yes, you get my point. The moment for you, was that huge!

'I'm so proud of you, mate!' I said, giving you a quick hug as we walked into the building. I wanted to laugh my head off with joy, Jesus, we were out of the car! Walking around the corner, who was the first person we saw? Mr Steve Reid. I'm sure he was as proud of you, as I was in that moment, and I know Nan was over the moon to see you, trying to contain her happiness for us both in front of you.

It was a sensational fifteen or so minutes and Nan took us into the art room to show you some of the cooler stuff that some of the students had been creating. You were quiet, but responsive and I was thrilled to see you, my fourteen-year-old boy in a classroom, the first time in close to two years! Hugging Nan goodbye, she squeezed me and gave me a wink when your back was turned. She knew. She just knew.

You wanted McDonalds, I would have given you the world. I dropped you home where you wanted to be, along with your reward feast, and went to Sally's with the biggest smile on my face and burst into happy tears as I said to her, *'He made it in! He made it in!'* And we hugged it out, laughing celebrating with one of her famously brewed pots of tea. So, so proud of you.

Dad and I told you every five seconds for the next two days, non-stop, how proud we were of you. It was a moment, a feeling we wanted you to hold onto. Yes, we were proud of you all the time, but we knew how much harder it was for you, when you pushed yourself and made that extra effort to break through those uncomfortable situations.

And throughout terms one and two, you got into the routine of going in to see Nan every Wednesday anywhere from ten, up to thirty-five minutes. She was so good with you, talking about your future, your hobbies, sports, school work and she let you know what a great effort you had been making, so far, this year, getting in to see her weekly. She understood what it meant to you, and how much of a success it had been in your journey.

Her experience and expertise were finessed to the point, if she felt she was pushing you further than you could go at the time, she would pull back ever so slightly so she wouldn't lose you completely.

Halfway through term two, we needed to get you in for more than one day visiting with Nan, and she asked you if you thought you could try to do at least five minutes in the classroom with the other kids on a Tuesday. You said that you would try, and we left that day, two days before you turned fifteen with a plan to get you in the following Tuesday, followed by your normal visit on the Wednesday.

For your fifteenth, we had offered paint ball and asked for your suggestions on how you would like to celebrate your birthday, but you chose to surround yourself with our friends and family at home. It was a great gathering, despite the Melbourne showers, but with the fire raging and our wonderful group of party goers, you had a sensational celebration. There was proof in how far you had come the past couple of years, with managing your anxiety, when you removed yourself from everybody and went either for a quick walk or into your room when it all became a bit too much.

The beauty of all those that loved you, were now used to you becoming overwhelmed in social gatherings, even at home, and allowed you the space you needed to get your thoughts together and re-join your friends in your own time.

It was the Monday after you had turned fifteen, and I was asking you if you were all set to go in for your five minutes the following day.

What occurred after I asked that question, shocked me with the fact, that yes, I was so happy for you, with how far you had come in the past two years, whilst feeling nothing had changed at the same time. It was like you were in Year Seven all over again and your fear, frustrations and stress revealed themselves in such a ball of chaos. I know how emotionally drained I felt when we had one of those days, where you couldn't articulate exactly what was going on upstairs in your mind, and it would all rush to the surface in a swell of pure anger. If it exhausted me, I can't imagine how drained you must have felt.

You went into a complete rage that went on and off again for over four hours. Swearing, throwing things in your room, yelling, and then storming out to the lounge area to give me your opinion on life and things in general.

I tried the, *let's sit down and chat approach* and said, *'Calm down, we'll have a cup of tea and talk about whatever you need to get off your chest.'* That did not work.

Walking into a different room worked for a few minutes, but eventually I needed to come out and get on with things. If I looked at you the wrong way or said anything in what I thought might lighten your load, you began swearing at me.

'You never listen! Fuck school, it doesn't matter if it's five minutes or five hours, you don't get it! Piss off you dickhead-sob! You're useless! You don't give a shit!' The words, I could handle, as you hissed at me in your rage, with your deep, fifteen-year-old voice, although they tore my heart to pieces. I was numb to the meaning of them, as I knew you were pushed to your limits in those moments. What I struggled with, as a little niggle of fear began to grow, when *my outraged,*

frightened fifteen-year-old, yelled in my face, advancing in anger, was when you pushed me. That physical touch of pure anger.

You had gotten so tall, so strong and it shocked me for a split second that you were so outraged you didn't seem to care that you could potentially hurt me. It had been a year ago, two days before you turned fourteen, that you had pushed me so angrily.

I locked myself in Dad's and my room for quite some time, before you decided to vacate the lounge and head back to your room. When things were silent, I crept back out and went into the kitchen to put the kettle on for a much-needed cup of tea, feeling the added pressure, that no doubt I would have to text Carol, to let her know I would not be able to get you in for five minutes the following day. Although she supported you in all your efforts, she too must have felt frustrated in those moments where we couldn't help you step as far forward as we knew you could go, if you just believed in yourself and let the fear slip away. Easy for us, as adults to think like that.

When the battle finally ended, and all calmed, you were apologetic and tried to explain that you felt I didn't understand how hard it was for you. That you did want to get in for more days, that you wished you could. Of course, I reassured you that both Dad and I understood where you were coming from and yes, we knew how hard it was for you, day-in, day-out because we too, lived with the predator that could at times create such debilitating situations for our entire family.

You were so exhausted at the end of the day and unfortunately the next day wasn't any better, so sadly you missed the Tuesday and your normal Wednesday session with Nan.

I spoke to you, to see if at this stage, you were willing to talk to your psychologist, Greg, whom I had met with at the end of last year. That conversation set you off on a decline, where you tucked yourself in your room and would not speak or interact with anyone for the remainder of the day. When you were open enough to speak about seeing Greg, you asked me to help straighten your bed whist we chatted, and I noticed the past few days after you lost control you became increasingly pedantic with your room, making sure that your quilt cover was precisely tucked around your bed, with not a single crease in view, and everything else was in its place. You felt you couldn't control what was happening around you, but you could control how orderly you kept your room.

You explained to me, that the thought of walking into and sitting down in a class after you hadn't done so for quite some time, made you feel like there was a hot fog spreading in your head, and fire balls in your belly making you want to pass out to escape the pain.

'I'm fifteen now, Mum, and I know I'm not going to die. Sometimes it just feels like I will. Like I have no control over what is happening to me. I hate this feeling.'

'I know, mate. I know. But things are going to get easier love, and we are here with you every step that you need us to be. We love you and we are so proud of you. It's not always going to be like this.'

****

As individuals, we all cope with life's hurdles differently and what appears a simple street crossing with clear lights and signals for some, can be a highway to hell for others.

And that's the way of the world, isn't it?

I think for all of us parents, not just those of us with a child who is living with anxiety; it can be so exhausting watching our children struggle constantly with feelings of loneliness, confusion, confliction, doubting themselves time-and-time again, as they fail to see the light, at the seemingly endless tunnel when darkness clouds their confidence and self-worth.

Families represent a team of individuals, each with their strengths and weaknesses that help that unit survive and strengthen each other.

For Dad and me, it has always been so important to us, that you really believe we support you with each and every single step you make, big or small, now and in the future, and although you have your days where you feel you are not a part of our unit, we would not survive without you in it. You are that amazingly unique and special.

I felt it was time to make another quick call to our principal Amadeo, and once again, thank him for the school's support so far, this year. I could not express my gratitude enough, especially where Mr Reid and Nan were concerned. Yes, they may have been simply doing their jobs, but it was more than that to us. On the occasions they made you laugh, they became rock stars in my eyes.

And with such a wonderful support network, along with our family and friends, you constantly push yourself.

Being open and discussing your anxiety with people who knew I was writing *'Thirteen'*, made me feel so grateful to those that opened their own hearts with me, as they shared their individual, painful journeys.

Talking with Zane's Vice Principal, we connected as two mums who both knew the battle of supporting our children who suffer, at times, so cruelly with the silent predator. Chatting with this sophisticated lady, who did so much for the students at Karingal Heights, made me feel so humbled that she would share some of her past grief and heartache. So many of us out there, supporting each other, communicating, and sharing the often-heavy burden, of living with someone who suffers from anxiety. Sometimes it takes the simple words of, *'I totally understand where you are coming from and what you have been going through,'* lightens the load to the point of, I can carry on.

Two years to the day your school refusal began, and how very far you have come. That night, you asked for a haircut, and popped on your school spray jacket and allowed me to take your photo to send to Amadeo to put on Compass. Your first student photo for High School. It was a real moment for me as the last time I had taken a photo of you in the bright purple top, was your first day of Year Seven, back in 2014. The laughing boy with a cheeky glint in his eye, looking forward to his new adventure, not knowing what was coming.

The remainder of the year, was full of so many ups and downs, and it constantly amazes me that human beings have such strength at times, to simply keep on going.

Terms two and three, you did keep getting in to see Nan, with the occasional cancelling of days. We encouraged you every step of the way, but I could feel as we went along, you really couldn't push yourself any further than what you were.

Unfortunately, the week Zane was turning twelve, was filled with such tragedy, that as animal lovers, we struggled with our sadness and loss for days on end. Our beautiful, grey fur baby, Tardwell, passed away after a major operation. I sat with him, throughout the night, unable to sleep, watching his eyes fill with a knowledge, that this was his end.

It's heart-breaking not being able to do anything for a loved one who is in pain. I am one of those humans that constantly chat away to my animals, like they get every, single thing that comes out of my mouth! I explained to Tardy how special he was, how much we loved him and how sorry I was that he was in pain. I don't know if he was, but those beautiful deep green eyes looked heavy and sad. I felt beyond useless in those hours, patting his luxurious fur, trying to give myself as much comfort, as I was him.

We woke Zane early, to tell him we were taking Tardy back to the vet. He, of course, was beside himself. And after letting you know the night before, that things didn't look too promising for Tardy, Dad had wrapped his arms around the blanket you had rolled yourself up in and hugged you whilst you cried softly. It's another kind of torture; for a parent, unable to take away their child's pain and grief. We didn't want to wake you, so left Zane in front of the cartoons with Koonie, as we carried Tardy out to the car.

Karingal Veterinary Hospital staff, were amazingly sympathetic and extremely supportive with their advice that the best thing for our Tardy, was to have him put to sleep. Those that have made this decision for a beloved pet in pain, know how truly heart-breaking it is. Carrying his heavy, grey body back out to our car, crying like a baby, I never thought I'd ever feel such desolate pain. *(I was, once again, oh, so very wrong.)*

I guess some may see the coming scene as comical, putting all grief aside.

We got home, with Tardy, and placed him on a soft blanket on the kitchen table, arranging him in a sleeping position. I mean, we couldn't bury him, as you hadn't had a chance to pat him goodbye. Zane was beside himself, and that broke my heart a little more. The day outside was perfect for this moment. Grey clouds full of gentle rain. We lit a candle, and I dashed out to pick fresh lavender to pop in a pretty jam jar beside his soft, furry body. Dad, Zane, and I sat around the table, quietly crying, patting him, and talking about what an amazing cat he had been. Koonie had walked in through the cat flap, out of the rain, and had perched up on his cat tree, seemingly oblivious to our pain. But he was feeling it too. He had been beside Tardy earlier, as we packed him into his cat carrier.

I rang Nana Lyn to share our sad news. She was upset herself, as only the month before we had travelled down to Glenormiston to bury her fur baby, *Stinky*. Sally and Jacqui came by, full of tears and hugs. It's a beautiful thing when you have the type of friends who can sit around, with cups of tea, and say farewell to a creature of importance, without batting an eyelid, to the fact, that a corpse is laying on the dining table, like a banquet. As we sat there, talking and stroking, we all began to realise that Tardy was becoming quite firm. Hard. Cold. I freaked out, thinking how that may affect you! So, we began heating up the water bottles to lay him on, and gently put one on Tardy's body, that was rapidly becoming uncomfortably rigid. I did not want you to pat him when he felt so hard, cold, dead. At least this way we could keep him warm and soft for when you got up. I began to plot, that no matter the cost, I would get him stuffed for you, to be able to sit at the end of your bed!

Throughout the entire morning, throughout our tears, we were all so worried about how his death would affect you. We all were certain you would become angry and devastated, in your grief, that you may put a hole in the wall. We really had no idea how you would handle it.

You surprised us all. You were sad, of course. But you were calm, quiet. Maybe too quiet.

But we all handle things differently. You wanted me to call the taxidermist, so you could have Tardy always. After a phone call to a Taxidermist in Langwarrin, the cost was affordable for sure. $800 to have Tardy around, was a price I was willing to pay. I would do anything that would make his passing, easier on you.

'How long has it been since puss passed?' Was the first question the sympathetic taxidermist asked me.

'Seven hours.' I responded sadly.

'And has puss been kept cold, in a fridge or freezer since?' He asked hopefully.

'Oh, god no,' I responded. *'We've kept him warm on the dining table with hot water bottles, we didn't want him going hard!'*

'Oh, that's not good, love. That's not good at all. His fur will probably drop out if that's the case.'

His advice in the end. Bury Puss.

So, we all stood out in the rain, and buried our magnificent, majestic cat. Death sucks.

Not being able to sleep the night before, as I had sat with Tardy, I was exhausted and looked forward to hugging my pillow. Unfortunately, another little soul was suffering along with us, and for the following two nights in a row, poor Koonie walked the hallways, crying out for the brother he had known since they shared their mother's womb. It broke all our hearts. The next day, after researching *cat adoption* agencies, Jacqui and I headed down the coast into Mount Martha and adopted a gorgeous little British Shorthair. She had been given the name, 'Maggie-T', as she was a voluptuous little creature. Maybe two to four years old, had had a kitten and had been from one home after another. Apparently, she did not like to be held.

You were beyond ecstatic that our new cat, Nala, spent the next two weeks in your room as she settled into her new home. Koonie and she got to know each other through a barrier we made, thanks to the advice of Jackson Galaxy and his helpful, entertaining show, *'Cat from Hell'*. After a few days of hissing and doing general cat-antics, the two became very good friends, and Nala settled right in.

Nana Lyn came down, and we all celebrated Zane's twelfth birthday, dancing to whatever beats you kids selected, through to Abba. It was in fact one of the best birthdays we had had in years, which says a lot, as they always seemed to be brilliant. What I did not know, was that night, when all were preoccupied with party movement, Nana decided to share a glass of her wine with you. Fifteen years of age! Luckily you thought it was disgusting. Looking back, I'm so grateful you had the opportunity to have a beverage with your Nana. (Although I strongly disagree with underage drinking!)

September came along, with a scheduled meeting at the school, to see what else they could do for you. As we had been unable to get you to feel confident within yourself to attend a class, along with the other students throughout the year, it was time to look at what your next step would be for your future education. I know you felt you were so far behind the other kids your age, as it was, and the thought of having to read or write in front of anyone made you feel like a failure. If I was going to the shops, you'd approach me, asking me if I could write a list of things you wanted. I'd say, if you write it out, I'll get anything you'd like. Even writing in front of me, your own mother, made you uncomfortable.

Dad finished work early, so he could attend the meeting with me, and although you were invited along, we could not persuade you to come with us. You were frightened you were going to get kicked-out of McClelland and no matter what we said, we could not convince you that everything was going to be all right. You carried the extra burden, feeling guilty that you had let Carol down, by not being able to attend a class. As always, putting more pressure on your tired, beautiful mind, to the point that you would rage, or despair.

In the end, it was more than all right. It was a new beacon of light that our ship needed to head towards, to help you, for your future development in many areas. Mr Reid shared with us, his insight regarding Oakwood School, and why he thought it would benefit you.

Of course, at the start, as I listened to Mr Reid list all the qualities Oakwood had, I was internally having a conversation in my head as to how I would present this information to you, and, thinking about how you may react. But, as Mr Reid continued giving us as much information as he could, in the allocated meeting time, my nervous system began to relax, and after Dad and I had a day or two to process the information given, we felt so sure that this was the right direction for you.

Mr Reid and Carol had decided it was best for them to share the news with you, that this opportunity would be beneficial for you. The following week they came for a visit and started off by chatting to you about the progress you had made the last couple of years. Mr. Reid asked you to write down three things you'd like to do in the future. You wrote your short list, and Mr. Reid moved in for a look, hesitating before pointing to one of the words and asking you, *'What's this one Jesse?'* It was spelt *Raper*.

'I'd like to be a Rapper,' You replied.

'You might like to add another 'R' to that word mate.' He said, chuckling.

After you pencilled in the much appreciated *R*, Mr. Reid and Nan began to fill you in about Oakwood School, and asked if it was something you'd like to have a go at. You agreed easily, after all, two people you had grown fond of, that weren't related to you, made any proposition sound good to your ears. Mr Reid got out his computer and filled in an expression of interest form online, then and there. Done. Next step.

*****

The September holidays were a welcome break, and we decide to venture off to Nana Lyn's. We took Emily away with us, and it was a week of complete rejuvenation. We all pitched in and painted Nana's outdoor furniture. I created a pretty garden where Nana sat, doing crossword puzzles, and reading her copious amounts of books, when she had her days off.

You chopped the largest stack of wood, with poor Nana looking on, having a heart attack that you would put the axe through your leg. I simply told her to stop looking. You were at your absolute happiest when you were doing something useful and physical for Nana. You were proud of your bulging biceps, and the fact that you had shot up another few inches as the year rolled on, and now towered over Nana.

You, Emily, and Zane scooted for hours, speeding down the hill of Trufood Road, while I filled Nana in on the latest developments of your schooling future. Although we talked almost every day on the phone, to sit and have uninterrupted conversations where we could look at each other and share our deepest concerns regarding you and all your battles. How proud we were of each, and every one of your accomplishments, and how far you had come the past couple of years. It was beyond therapeutic for me, and for Nana also, as she expressed, the more she understood your anxiety, and what you battled daily, she felt empowered to help you. An amazing Nana to say the least.

CAITLYN

For a parent, having the support of loved ones, be it family or friends, during a difficult time, is essential to surviving the experience and getting through the ordeal in one solid piece. Or at least mostly solid! For a young person, that is magnified tenfold. Caitlyn had always been a big supporter of you in general, but when it was made clear to her, by Sally, how severe your anxiety had become, throughout Years 7, 8 and 9, she was most concerned, and became interested in any way she could, to help you.

Her attitude and self-confidence blew me away at times, with her level-headed direction and maturity for a girl her age, and I believed Caitlyn was simply born to rule her world. As a student, she was every teacher's dream. To list a few of her awards and achievements: In Grade Six, she was School Captain and received the Dunkley Shield award. She entered high school with confidence and excitement, and was in the Elite Performance Program, was also a part of the Student Leadership Council as a Year Seven Leader, competed in the Da Vinci Decathlon, was first in Year Seven and Eight category of the Japanese Speech Contest and was Year Seven Dux for Music, P.E, and Year Seven Overall Dux. And if you think you are overwhelmed or exhausted by her amazing accomplishments thus far, wait, there's more!

In Year Eight she carried on with her brilliant leadership skills and was on the Student Leadership Council, was the first recipient to receive the Collin Bowes Memorial Shield and received the All-Round Athlete Award. In Year Nine, she came second in the Japanese Speech Contest, for year 9 and 10's, and made it to the school's athletics, regional competition for triple jump and long jump, and qualified for the State Relay competition in Little Athletics. In Year Ten, Caitlyn qualified at State level for triple, and long jump in Little Athletics, with an exciting trip to Japan to look forward to. Throughout those years, Caitlyn also attended Youth Group, and volunteered at Coffee on Kareela and as a waitress for special events at her church, such as Mother's Day High Tea, or singing, playing the flute and narrating the Christmas pageant.

Caitlyn was not only tall, blonde, and beautiful, but her happy heart, was full of love, compassion, and adventure. When an invasive wave of anxiety and depression hit Caitlyn, during Year Nine, it rocked Sally and her family's world altogether.

Caitlyn is, in your words, '*One of the most caring people I know, for a kid our age.*' That statement is correct and does not just apply to one of Sally and Rob's daughters, but two. Knowing Emily from the age of eighteen months, to a teenager has been a privilege, and with Zane being six months old when they first met, along with growing up together, they become each other's best friend. Her strengths: she is loyal to a fault and has more integrity than some adults I know. Emily has always been caring and thoughtful to the point of worrying about so many other people around her. And with her worry, came the burden of anxiety, at such a young age. So, although this was not Sally's first rodeo with the silent predator, it was, once again, a different monster that was attacking her eldest daughter.

It was so hard, seeing my good friend, who had supported me and our family through thick and thin, suffer with such worry for her daughter. Sitting over a pot of tea one day, Sally explained what had been happening to Caitlyn, how her depression and anxiety often left Caitlyn unable to move when she felt overwhelmed. With no thought of how to do anything but sob her heart out.

My own heart was full of empathy and sympathy, as I listened to Sally talk about how she was feeling. Another mother, heart-broken with disbelief that this was happening again, to another one of her babies. Feeling fearful, along with a lack of control and helplessness, of being unable stop her daughter from feeling so desolate. She summed it up perfectly when she said, *'The list of my feelings about Caitlyn's experience with anxiety is endless, how can it not be? As mothers, we want all things for our children and when they face obstacles as severe as anxiety or depression, there is no protecting them. We can't help them in any way, other than trying to understand their fears and acknowledge them as being real.'*

I could not agree more.

When Caitlyn and I had a chance to speak about how she had been feeling, she confessed to me, that she was shocked with the fact that she had anxiety. *'I can't believe I, of all people, have anxiety!'* And, I can appreciate why she would say this. Being such a positive, outgoing, confident girl from the get go, she assumed she would be immune to something like anxiety or depression. As we have come to understand, anxiety, like cancer, has no prejudice, it does not discriminate. It's the stigma associated with depression and anxiety, where *people* discriminate, through ignorance, be it being misinformed or lack of knowledge. For Caitlyn, it was more misinformation combined with the self-stigma, along the lines of – *'I can't believe I have anxiety. I'm confident, strong, and talented. I should be able to snap out of it.'*

For all those out there that have, like my family and I, been impacted by the stigma and discrimination associated with anxiety or depression, please check out the Beyond Blue information paper: Stigma and discrimination associated with depression and anxiety. Beyondblue.org.au – Very informative and helpful.

NEW ZEALAND

September rolled into October, and along with Thomas moving in with us, we were all starting to get very excited about our cruise in November, to New Zealand. Those of you who have planned a major trip, with a child with anxiety, it can be one of two things: An absolute nightmare, or an amazing experience in which they relish.

The entire experience for me, was beyond amazing– exhilarating; and the break I was so looking forward to. To not have to cook or clean up after a meal for two weeks! I'll say no more! The cruise ship itself was breathtaking; the Emerald Princess wasn't your average party ship. Refined, elegant, luxurious without being pretentious. Too much fun, despite the Tasman Sea being an absolute nightmare to cross and return on, leaving many a paler shade of green.

To visit the Land of the Great White Cloud, was a momentous experience in my life, and I will remember it fondly always. Our first sight of land, the majestic Milford Sound, blew me away and brought tears of absolute joy to my eyes. To see snow peaking the breathtakingly vast mountains, dolphins swimming beside the ocean liner and the general overall feeling of being overseas, along with the joy of having my children have the opportunity, to have such a wonderful trip with all our family. Epic.

To experience the South and North Island for days on end, with fresh eyes and adventure in my heart was everything and more than I could have asked for, and to set foot in *Hobbiton*, was everything Zane and I had dreamt of since the day Grammy told us we were going.

So, although the entire family had an absolute ball and were energized every moment of the fourteen-day trip, you, my poor little darling, were not so delighted during this adventure.

Although our house may be small, you still had the privacy and space of your room. Our cabin was tiny, yet cosy, with a large oval window with views that made us smile as soon as we rolled out of bed in the morning. And although we didn't spend a great deal of time there, it was home for fourteen days, and crowded enough for you in the first five, before you became used to being in such close quarters with your other three family members.

The days were busy when we were onshore, wanting to see as much of the stunning countryside as we could, we made the most of the hours on land, and although you loved the fact that you were in Jacqui's country, you were uncomfortable with the process it took getting off, and back onto the ship, along with all the queuing, the hundreds of people standing around, waiting for buses, or boats, going through customs, and everything in-between.

You didn't complain outright, but you were uncomfortable. We all expected it and rolled with however you handled yourself on the day. In the first few days, you did not come up to the dining areas to eat. You didn't like the smells or the lines of constantly hungry people. Zane and I would serve up a tray of bread rolls with butter, or jelly, peanut butter cookies and any other morsel we thought you might enjoy and bring it to our room for you.

After a few days, you did come out to the dining areas, but not once in the days on board, would you enter the food area to explore all the delicious options. Grammy was a love, and along with Dad and I, she got you different morsels to try, along with some of your favourites, so you didn't starve. At least you were now joining us in the dining rooms, so we did have a few meals together with Grammy and Poppy, Uncle Grant, and Aunty Nicole.

One of the best things, once you and Zane got to know your way around the ginormous vessel, was the nights you would go and meet Poppy and Grammy for a show, followed by supper and a hot chocolate, before calling it a night. After a busy day, Dad and I enjoyed seeing you freshen yourself up, making sure you looked your best, spraying your body spray everywhere and doing your hair before you left our cabin with Zane. It was such a feat for you.

On the down side, for the entire trip, you were abusive to me, when discomfort hit. And as often as that was, that you'd pop off like a frog in a sock, let's just say I was delighted by the sheer size of the Emerald Princess, because at times I simply needed to escape your hostility and hide. It stung me to my core, how cruel you were to me at times. Even understanding why you snapped at, and insulted me, in the crunch time of your absolute panic and discomfort, it still hurt and blew me away. I mean, I considered myself to be a pretty cool mum, and it amazed me that you could make a dent in my self-confidence with a backhand comment or two!

When our trip ended, and it was time to depart the docks, we got on the bus that would take us to Sydney airport, before flying out to Melbourne. What blew me away, after treating me like an irritating insect for fourteen days straight, was that you chose the seat next to me on the bus. You sat, put your arms around me and hugged me in public, followed by, *'I love you, Mum.'*

I simply hugged you back, knowing you were that relieved, we were on our way home, and heading back to your comfort zone.

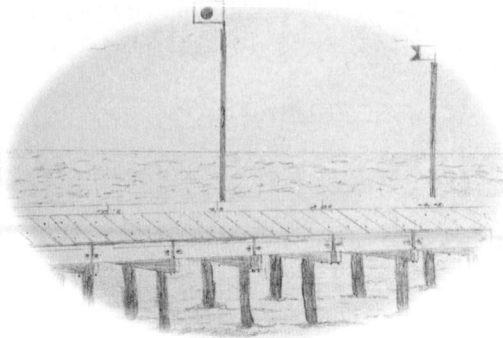

THOMAS

Eighteen-year-old Thomas, had matured into a nice lad, and had developed a cheerier disposition towards life, which Dad and I understood was not always easy for him. With a touch of anger-management issues and depression, we were here to support him in any way we could. When Thomas reached out to us and asked if he could crash with us for a week or two, Dad and I agreed we could certainly help him out. After explaining to you and Zane that Thomas needed us, and a roof over his head for a little while, then asking you both if that was okay with you, you went straight to your room, with the spare mattress making sure a bed was made up comfortably, along with your side table, loaded with snacks. That's the kind individual you were. You wanted Thomas to feel loved and welcome, to have a safe, warm bed to sleep in whilst he was between homes.

A week or two, was in fact three and a half months, and in that first month we saw such a big change in you, your energy levels and attitude. You really enjoyed having Thomas with us. It's amazing what several years break, can do for cousins. The last time you had spent any length of time together was Ireland's birthday party, where you had had the can of coke launched at your head, along with unpleasant, verbal abuse. In the years gone by, dealing with your anxiety and life in general, you had learned so much about yourself, your family, both immediate and distant. Dealt with supporters and non-believers of your struggles. You'd grown taller, proud of yourself, your home, and your family.

Thomas himself had been through many ups and downs and was relieved and grateful to be in our safe-haven. As I said earlier, life and its experiences, both negative and positive, shape us all. Having Thomas live with us, gave me the opportunity to bond with my nephew again, after so many years not spending quality time together. We had plenty of laughs, in between Thomas's difficult moments, and I learned that an eighteen-year-old can effectively rake the backyard, whilst texting non-stop, and amazingly, not trip over his pants that are hanging half-way down his backside! Pure skill.

Every day, after Zane finished school, the three of you took off to the park, and spent a good hour or so playing basketball. It was so nice to see the three of you get along, have a laugh and chill-out together. There was a day, Thomas and Zane returned home without you, saying that you had left the park to come home ages ago. Which you had briefly, going to your room, and leaving again. Dad and I had presumed it was to go back to the park. Zane had said no, you hadn't been there for at least thirty minutes. Dad was concerned enough to jump on his bike and pedal off to see if he could find you.

When he returned minutes later, a smile on his face, I felt such relief. Where had you been? You had taken yourself off to the milk bar, you and Noah had visited a year before. All by yourself, not a single care in the world. Thomas didn't really know what the fuss was about, until we explained to him that you and Noah, had been assaulted by a group

of nit-wits, and in three years, had only gone there once with Noah, and on this day, on your own. He said it made him feel sad he hadn't been there for you all these years, to help protect you and simply be the big cousin you needed. And in the months that Thomas lived with us, he tried to understand your anxiety, but did become frustrated at times when he simply did not get it. One of those moments, was for Zane's Grade Six graduation night.

Despite all the emotions, of my baby leaving the primary school years behind, I was so excited for Zane to start his high school journey, with just a touch of sadness in the very back of my mind that you would not be there, at school with him.

In the last five minutes as we were getting ready to get into the cars to head off to the McClelland PAC, you decided you might not come. I expected it. I knew how to handle it, and went about doing so, as Thomas went out the front of the house, and verbally expressed how shit it was, that you wouldn't even make the effort to get to your own brother's graduation.

Luckily, you were inside the house, and did not hear him, which would have made the situation worse. So, whilst gently encouraging you that all would be well at Zane's graduation, and explain to Thomas that it wasn't like you didn't want to go, you just felt you couldn't, I kept myself centred, calm and present to all the situations at hand. When you just walked out the front door and got into Grammy and Poppy's car, I felt like fist pumping the air a million times over. We could all sit back together, as a unit and enjoy the hour or so that was Zane's Grade Six graduation. Another end of an era, in the life of a family, with school aged children.

2016-EVERYTHING CHANGES

Nana Lyn came down the following week, and we had a graduation party for Zane, along with Sally, Jacqui, Bec and all their tribes. We had a brilliant afternoon, celebrating another big year, and looked forward to Christmas in the next five days.

Nana was so relaxed, laughing her head off with the girls, commenting that this was the most fun she had had since she was last down for Zane's twelfth birthday. You danced with Nana once darkness fell over our backyard, firelight flickering here and there, and looking at you, holding Nana so gently made my heart smile. She looked so tiny and fragile, beside your growing frame, and as always, you treated her with such love and respect.

When Nana passed away, six days later, Boxing Day morning, in our home, while you were sleeping, it broke me more than I ever thought possible. Broke my soul to pieces. And the thought, that I would

have to wake you with such devastating news. I have no words. Zane, Ireland and Thomas, Dad and Aunty Leah were grieving in the lounge area, whilst waiting for the ambulance to take Nana to the Frankston hospital, where we would soon follow. As broken as I was, I found the strength to go into your room where you slept soundly, and stroked your hair until you woke, and gently whispered the news in your ear.

Your weary eyes said all of your heart-break, and I did not breathe for fear I would choke on the sob that wanted to escape. I knew if I gave into the overwhelming grief that was building, I would never stop. When I rose from your side and turned to head off to the hospital, Sally stood there, wearing a look of utter sadness. She had lost her beautiful mother five years prior, and since that time, Nana had been like a second mum to her. When I put my arms around her, I felt a calmness that frightened me. Surely, I should have been screaming the roof down or pulling out my hair like a normal person! There must have been some-thing wrong with me for sure.

And in the days that followed, two things became clear to me. *Kids can be so durable, and grief sucks more than I ever understood.*

I hadn't slept for forty-eight hours, and whilst all slept around me, I got to organising the packing for our trip home to Glenormiston. Nana, being the most organised woman in the world, had planned and payed all costs up front, years earlier, for her funeral to be in Terang.

I decided to tidy up Nana's suitcase. It gave me a sense of peace, touching her things. Folding her clothes, smelling them, seeing her tiny little slippers. Her hair brush, favourite necklace. Her perfume. A life-time of memories in every scent. The sense of peace lasted less than two minutes, as I held her singlet to my face, and breathed her scent in deeply. I lost the plot in a very big way. I started screaming at the top of my lungs, over, and over again, to the point of no return. And the fact was, the first scream that escaped my lips stunned and shocked me si-lent for two and a half seconds. But then, I can't tell you how good it felt, so I simply kept right on screaming; passionately, heart-brokenly, sadly, and possibly a hint of demented, screaming until I was hoarse.

Man, I am so surprised I didn't scream my head completely off! I punched my thighs till I could no longer feel them, that too felt great at the beginning. (Sore for a few days after.) Then the crying kicked in, and I cried till my face looked like a bowl of raspberry jellies. And through it all, all my explosive, emotional, grieving commotion, the entire household of boys simply slept!

When Thomas, Zane, and you all got up hours later, I asked you all, *'Did you hear anything?'* I left it at that, not wanting to explain what I had been up to.

In which you all replied, *'No.'*

I was grateful. I certainly didn't want you all to be more upset than you all already were.

Who did hear me? A knock at the front door that afternoon, brought our lovely neighbour, Sharolyn over, asking Dad, *'How's Michelle doing?'*

I think after hearing my inconsolable screaming session, she knew exactly how I was doing! I was more grateful than mortified for her concern, and treasured the fact, that she and her husband Eddie, had been wonderful neighbours to us, for over seventeen years, and had probably heard bits and pieces of our lives play out over that time. The good, the bad and the oh, so very ugly!

Time. Time heals all wounds.

As broken as we all were, grieving Nana, we began to heal together, with our family, our friends, and Nana's friends and co-workers. We bid Nana farewell with a beautiful service, and my heart swelled with pride, watching you, Zane, Thomas, and Dad be Nana's pallbearers. She was such a big, important part of so many people's lives. The most amazing mother. An incredible Nana. A unique, magical individual. We will miss her forever.

Dad and I worried deeply about how you would handle Nana not being around. You started writing, constantly hunched over your little book, pencil in hand, scribbling away any chance you got, at any hour. You didn't want to share what you were writing at this stage, and that was fine by me. You were finding a way to grieve and heal, and have Nana beside you. I was relieved in the moments that we would talk about her, and you would say how much you missed her. At least you felt you could say that, to communicate those feelings was big for you, and when you said it, in that sad, deep voice, I'd smile, put my arms around you and tell you how much Nana loved you. I wanted to take away any sadness you felt, but you feeling it was your love and loss for Nana. A woman that had been there for you, one hundred percent, your entire life.

As the beginning of the school year approached I was concerned for both you, starting Oakwood and Zane, starting Year Seven, hoping you would cope with these big changes after such a tragic loss. It had only been a handful of weeks, and I was still learning to breathe and function as a human being, whilst carrying so much pain. I had published Dark Angel twelve days before Nana passed, and sadly, I was too numb afterwards to focus on marketing her and giving her the attention she deserved. How could you both possibly focus on such big, new steps forward, when I couldn't remember what I was meant to be doing from one minute to the next? Sitting on the loo, ten minutes would pass as I'd stare blankly into space thinking of my Mum. Missing her beyond words, and I'd think, *S'pose I should get up now,* although there were days I didn't see the point. Or, I'd walk into a room, and wonder why I walked into it in the first place. Putting the kettle in the fridge after I'd filled it, and absently munching on the dry cat biscuits one afternoon as I patted Koonie. (Grief. It does strange things to us all!)

Yet, you both seemed *outwardly* fine, and getting on with the school holidays and spending time with friends certainly helped your grieving process go gently and smoothly. But I was nervously curious how things would go when the reality of a school routine started back. When the day finally came that you both had to take that next step in starting your new school journeys, my own grief was eased, as you both settled, seemingly comfortable, into your new routines.

2017 - OAKWOOD SCHOOL

Zane looked as handsome and adorable in his McClelland College uniform, as you did on your first day three years ago. He was nervous, along with the 100 or so other Year Seven students, and hung close to his group of friends, as Dad and I bid him goodbye for his first day of high school. I didn't cry. I had to keep it together as we had to get back home and get you ready to head into Frankston for your first weekly meeting at Oakwood School. The brochure in the office outlined in detail what Oakwood was all about. Very impressive to say the least:

'OAKWOOD'S PROGRAM: The aim of Oakwood School is to engage students with a personalised learning plan that focuses on the development of literacy, numeracy, social development, art, and physical education.

Oakwood School provides:

A positive, quiet learning environment.

Small classes and individual learning support.

Case management based on the learning and behavioural needs of the young person.

Partnership with agencies to provide holistic support and services as required.

*Oakwood School believes that all students should be able to thrive in mainstream schools, however they know that for a small percentage of students, this is not always possible.

*Oakwood School provides learning opportunities for students aged 10 to 18 years of age who have disengaged from school, or where a mainstream school learning environment is seen to be inappropriate to meet their needs.

*Students seeking enrolment at Oakwood School are generally:

*Not currently enrolled in school.

*Not attending and at significant risk of disengaging from school.

*Demonstrates patterns of chronic disengagement with little likelihood of maintaining a connection to a learning program in school, or successfully transitioning to employment.

In essence, the character for Oakwood School is to bring teachers and learning opportunities back to vulnerable young people who might be connected to a range of mental health, or child protection and youth workers, but have been disconnected from school and teachers.'

We could not have asked for a better fit for you, at this stage if we tried, and once again felt so blessed for the people and services available that helped make your journey living with anxiety, smoother. Anything positive I have said about McClelland College, Oakwood was that times a thousand.

The principal and staff at Oakwood School were amazingly experienced, and helped you transition throughout terms one and two, as your induction process continued. Your classroom teacher, Paul, was brilliant with you, and sitting in the office area, waiting to pick you up one day, hearing your laughter flow throughout the small area, filled my soul with such content.

There were days you'd get snappy at me as I waited for you to shower, get dressed, and head out to drive you to your new school. You'd grumble about your hair not looking good, or you needed a new jumper, or simply complain about something relevant to you, that obviously helped your nervous system cope. I'd simply take a deep breath and let you quietly mumble out all the frustrations that helped you work through your fear and unease of your situation. Once there, and after you'd completed your session, you were so proud of yourself, and chatted happily as we headed home again.

Of course, it wasn't all smooth sailing. After almost three years not being in a structured school routine, there were days I could not get you into see Paul, and I'd have to make the phone call to Oakwood's administration lady, Dawn. Professional, supportive, and understanding Dawn always knew the right thing to say to a mother with a teenager who had been on this emotional, exhausting journey. Another brilliant individual, placed in the perfect role to assist those in need.

I understood how hard it was for you at times, feeling exposed and vulnerable when you had to answer maths questions, or do spelling. You knew you were behind and that in itself, made some days getting into class, harder for you. The circle is in fact, always vicious.

One young man, dealing with the burden that so many suffer. Some days, seemingly effortlessly. Others, most definitely not.

There were a few people I had chatted to, on the online support group - Children with Anxiety/Anxiety Disorders - that approached me with the question, *'Do you just have the one child that is experiencing anxiety?'*

And for a long time, I'd answer, *'Yes, just the one.'*

They'd respond, *'You're lucky, I've got two,'* or *'What I wouldn't do for just one, I've got three.'* They are the super heroes conquering the world as far as I'm concerned.

My answer was rapidly changing in 2017.

As much as Zane was a confident, mature boy, and always had been no matter his age, we had our eyes open and were on the look-out for any little signs that may disrupt his smooth flow through life. A touch of separation anxiety developed in his last two years of primary school, along with on-going night-terrors. One night I had turned the light on, after hearing him yelling out numbers, to find him sitting up in bed, using his finger to write out maths problems on the wall. Other nights, waking to him crying in his sleep, thrashing about, yelling out. I'd gently wake him with cuddles, reassuring him everything was alright, and soothe him with soft, tender words until he fell back to sleep. What amazed me each morning, was that Zane had no recollection of what occurred the night before.

When I needed to do any shopping, when school was out, Zane was more than happy to come with me, and would loop his arm through mine as we headed into the Karingal Hub. But as we approached the shopping centre's sliding doors, he would ask me not to speak to him whilst we were shopping, and explained he didn't want anyone hearing us, or looking at us. As mature as I knew he was, to be able to explain and express himself, I had little alarm bells going off in my head. Remembering the days when we would go shopping, and you would get grumpy with me if I simply asked you if you wanted to make a pizza for tea or what yogurt you wanted. You would snap at me, and quietly ask me to shut-up. Constantly terrified that someone would look at us or notice you.

Zane had, in the past, enjoyed sleepovers, and hanging out at his mate's place after school, but that all slowly came to an end. That wasn't an issue for us, being a household with friends and family popping in and out, you both had plenty of opportunities to be healthily social, but what was becoming a struggle for Zane, was his worrying thoughts, continued night terrors, and slowly-building anxiety to the new structure of high school, the pressures of the demanding work load, along with the joyous antics of school-yard bullies. Put that on top of supporting his older brother for the past few years, seeing his mother cope and not cope, worry that Dad works too hard, and being a twelve-year-old boy, still mourning his beloved cat, and the loss of his Nana. Seriously, how much can a little human bear?

As much as we would never want to put any pressure on you and Zane; try to protect you both from any worries we have as adults, such as worrying about the mortgage, bills, or any adult problems, that's just not reality. Sometimes, kids hear conversations adults have with each other, phone calls to family or friends discussing things and life in general. It just happens. So, although we wouldn't want to burden you, sadly to say, like most families, we probably, unintentionally, have. Sharing is caring, right? No.

The first two weeks Zane was handling his big change quite well, but the little cracks in his shield were beginning to show. When I saw my little boy walk into the lounge one morning, after showering and dressing, sitting on the couch, pale face hiding as he held his head in his hands, my heart sank a little lower, as I sat beside him and rubbed his back, I asked him, '*What's up, love?*'

His hands shook as he attempted to do his school shoelaces up and his voice quivered as he answered, '*I feel like I'm going to be sick.*'

He certainly looked like he was going to be. I waited for him to finish his task of tying up his shoes and his eyes met mine when he finished. I pushed his long, blonde hair off his forehead, which felt clammy. I could see his chin wobble a little, as he was forcing himself not to get upset.

'*What's wrong, mate?*'

He started crying, burying his face in his hands, '*I just feel sick and my stomach really hurts.*'

I stopped breathing, as the past came and slapped me hard in the face and told myself to get a grip. '*Well, what do you want to do, love, do you want to stay home, or do you want to go into school for an hour and see if it passes?*' I at least wanted to give him an option, as memories of me not handling your initial anxiety, reared its regrettable head.

Zane stood and walked over to his bag, wiping his eyes as he went. Taking a deep breath, he said, *'I'll push through, Mum. Come on, I don't want to be late.'*

'Are you sure?' I did not like the feeling that was creeping into the pit of my belly.

'Yes, can we please just go?'

I worried the moment I dropped Zane off, till the moment I received a call from the school's office that morning to come and collect him. After signing him out of the office and getting him set up on the couch at home, I stroked his hair asking if he was okay. He simply curled into a ball and closed his eyes, reaching out a hand for me to hold.

It wasn't our first morning like that, where he insisted on going to school, and not too long after, whether it was an hour, or three, I would receive a call from the lovely, efficient administration ladies at the office, to come and collect him, as he was not feeling well.

There were afternoons I would pick him up from school, and he would get into the car and not speak a word. We'd get home and he would quietly unpack his school bag, laying out his homework on the kitchen table, sit over it, head in hands and become completely despondent. On two occasions, he sat like that, for two hours. Not communicating in anyway, just sobbing quietly. I never thought I would see a child of mine, be so stressed over school work, three weeks into the school year, and I wondered *how many other hundreds of overwhelmed, little souls, starting Year Seven, were coming home the same way, making themselves sick with worry.* And for Zane, only weeks after the death of his Nana. Then, there were the weekends where Zane wanted no talk of school. He said he felt stressed when the *'S'* word was mentioned and wanted to forget about it for a day or two, and just relax and enjoy his free time. Fair enough, I could relate to that, but come Sunday night when I asked Zane if he needed his sports uniform for Monday, he would look at me with such a serious expression and say in a bewildered tone, *'It's Sunday Mum, I told you not to mention school on the weekend!'* Needless to say, I left his school and sport uniform for him to organise after that.

Halfway through term one, when Zane woke after another night of stressing about not doing good enough, or feeling like he couldn't cope with the work, or any incidents with *unsavoury* characters I was greeted by, a pale, sad face, and I simply told that pale, sad face, to go back to bed, and rang the absence line. That afternoon, Zane and I ended up having a conversation, where I asked him if he thought it was a good time to reach out to our family counsellor Stephen, from FMC, so he could have a chat to him about everything he was dealing with. He responded, *'Yes, only if you come with me, Mum.'* Easy. Done.

I know, for me personally, when Zane got to the point, of not being able to get into school for three weeks in a row, I was feeling a little bit frazzled myself. What sort of mother was I that I couldn't get my sons to school regularly? I'd think to myself, *'Please no, not again.'* I was so desolate that I couldn't ring Nana Lyn and say, *'Can you believe this, Mum? How the hell have I failed my poor kids?'* And then, not be able to hear her ever-valuable response. It didn't take me too long to get over myself, probably thirty seconds, and in these times I would turn to Dad with his practical common sense approach and reasoning acting as the positive poison that prevailed over my growing weeds of self-doubt and feelings of failure. We all may have gone down this road before, but the path is different, and not all trees weather the storm the same way. Your anxiety was very different from Zane's.

It's interesting, dealing with a child, suffering from anxiety, the second time around. I certainly wouldn't say I'm an expert, but with your anxiety I felt in control with being able to help and support you, in managing your anxiety, and Dad and I encouraged you both to open-up and discuss your worries, and to reassure you, we would always be here for you.

But, with Zane, I felt it was a whole new ball game, and I didn't understand the rules yet. Some of them maybe, but not the important ones, and it did kind of scare me a little. For me to even gently, mention school, and gauge where he was at, where he saw himself in a week or two, with the possibility of getting into a class, would have his eyes fill with tears that would not fall, a dark look upon his face, and he would not speak, sometimes up to six hours. It was the big freeze, even with the slight, gentle mention of school. The night after Zane's parent-teacher interviews, Zane had increasing abdominal pain, which resulted in a trip to the doctors, two nights after, a call to Nurse-on-Call, and a trip to Frankston hospital at 10.30pm. Throughout the night, Zane was respectfully poked and prodded, and then taken to the Monash hospital at 8am. After many hours of similar treatment, uncomfortable fondling of Zane's body parts, along with an ultra sound, finally appendicitis was ruled out, and sixteen hours later, we were sent back home.

Having a chat to Stephen that week and filling him in on what had been going on, he nodded wisely and simply said, *'Anxiety pains.'*

Picking you up from Oakwood one afternoon, four weeks into Zane not being at school, you turned to me and said, *'Zane needs to get back soon, Mum. The longer he stays away, the harder it will be for him to go back. Just speaking from my experience.'*

How far you had come. And how correct you were. We were approaching the end of term two holidays, and had spent six days in Glenormiston with Aunty Pam, Cousin Hannah, Emily, and the

Taylor clan, along with Jacqui and her girls. Nana Lyn's yard needed a lot of attention, as her gardens were large, and weeds grew outrageously fast in Glenormiston's luscious, volcanic soil. Dad and you came down for two nights, and it was the first time you had been back to Glenormiston, since Nana's goodbye service. It was, in fact, the first time, you had left the house in six months, apart from getting to school once a week. I know I was looking forward to term three, where you would be going into school, three days a week, and being in a larger class of more than just you and your teacher, I was hopeful you would click with at least one other student, that may lead you to a bit more of a social life, outside of our close friends.

Although your disposition was a lot happier, and you were certainly more confident in life, being your mother, I did so desperately want you to have friends your own age, where you could laugh, be silly, let your hair and guard down and simply be a sixteen-year-old boy, without a worry in the world. I was grateful that Noah and you continued being great mates, despite the fact he was in Queensland. Of course, there were also your Xbox Live friends, and in this day and age, it was a comfort to hear you laughing, and strategizing with C-balls and other on-line mates. I don't know if there were too many deep and meaningful conversations between you all, but it was still communication with kids with the same interest as you. It was something.

Then I think of Zane as term three approaches and I try to calm the flutter of disturbed, uncertain butterflies that want to keep me awake into the early hours of the morning. Seeing his little face cloud over in darkness when the 'S' word was mentioned. Seeing him briefly upset, when I let him know Stephen had resigned, and would no longer be a support person to him. Watching him look slightly terrified after mentioning that I had contacted Headspace. His little mind was evidently crowded with a whirlwind of thoughts, and I doubted my ability in helping my little boy.

I pulled out the many fact sheets I had, along with scrolling to my iPad screen, where I had saved many search engines to the home screen. *'Right-O,'* I thought to myself. *'Let's refresh and read up on recognising the symptoms of anxiety, and how best to take action!'* A great, easy site to take in information: *parents.au.reachout.com*

I read on, nodding to myself, feeling slightly empowered that most of what I was reading, still sat fresh at the front of my mind. As I continued reading, I felt those butterflies beat their wings slowly, determinedly. I read a few lines that pointed to Zane.

Types of anxiety disorders: Generalised anxiety disorder. Anxiety or worry that isn't about one specific thing but can be about many everyday situations.

314 · MICHELLE WEITERING

And that was what Zane was worrying about: What book or folder to take to the correct class. Making it to the correct class and building on time. Worrying about going to the toilet at high school, and dealing with the bigger kids when he got there. Stressing out about a toilet routine at home, so he wouldn't have to go to the toilet at school. Not eating or drinking, so he wouldn't have to go the toilet at school.

Social Anxiety. Fear of being in public situations where people might judge you.

Zane had been called gay numerous amounts of time in Term one, by a girl his age. Commenting, *'He was too cute not to be gay,'* and *'He always looked lonely, so he must be gay.'* Always in front of a group of kids. Sure, some could take that as a compliment, but not a twelve-year-old boy trying to figure it all out, and deal with a new routine.

Separation anxiety disorder: Extreme fear of being separated from a loved one or home.

Yep. Tick, tick, tick. And then reading on to see a number of factors that have been shown to increase the likelihood of someone experiencing an anxiety disorder: Personality factors, such as your child being highly sensitive, an ongoing stressful event, or trauma such as grief. Tick. Next.

As I read on, I admitted, I had to tick a few of those boxes for myself. After all, the loss of my mother, my best friend only months ago, still blankets me in a world of pain. And that's normal, as Aunty Louise says, *Nana deserves every tear I shed.* Happy or sad. And I knew, on top of my grief for Nana, was my worry and concern for my boys' present and future situation. Deciding a future plan, regarding Nana's property, possibly saying goodbye to the childhood home I'd lived in since I was twelve, and life in general, was gently beating me up. But, as an adult, I knew what I had to do to help myself, and I was open to it. Meditation, being mindful, trying to get a decent night sleep, diet, and exercise. It's great in theory for sure. Like Grammy says quite simply: *'With problems that cause us stress or anxiety, do the following. If you can recognise that they are totally out of your hands, then: 1-*

Stop blaming yourself. 2- Find the positive. 3-Set them aside till they are either in your hands, or solvable!' Great advice.

In the last week of the holidays, Sally and I took you all to Gravity Zone and you had an absolute ball. The joy to see you happy with the people you felt the most comfortable with, made me smile from ear to ear. After your hour of non-stop bouncing, we took Hungry Jacks back to Sally's, as it was our last chance to spend time with her and the kids, before the Taylor clan took off to Canberra for three weeks.

Seeing you and Zane sit at Sally's kitchen table together with Caitlyn, Emily, and Adam, brought a flash back from when you were in four-year-old kinder, and you, Zane, Caitlyn, and Emily, were tiny little beings, sitting around the kids' table, stuffing your faces happily with ice-cream, playing with Mr Potato Head; carefree and innocent, thankfully oblivious to the coming darkness.

And here we all were, so many years later and you had all come such a long way in your own rights. How fast did the time go? Caitlyn had made such progress with fighting her demons, and we were not only happy for her, but so proud. Of course, she would have ongoing days, like you, where situations would arise, and she would have to breathe deeply and be kind to herself, be brave. But to see her really smile again, after months of battling, was like the clouds had parted, and the sunshine could fall on us all once more. That's how I felt, when I saw you all really let go and laugh, smile, tease each other. Kids being kids, without the heavy burden such as anxiety or depression. Like life wasn't tricky enough for a person, let alone growing teenagers!

Watching you all sit around, gas-bagging was therapy for my soul. Sally smiled and said, *'It makes me so happy to have both you boys here together. It's been forever since you've come for a visit, Jesse.'*

'I know,' You said as you finished off your last nugget. *'I've been busy.'*

Emily laughed. *'Yeah sure, Jesse, really busy!'*

316 · MICHELLE WEITERING

You nodded as you looked over at Sally who asked you a question for the second time, as the voices in the kitchen were a rowdy noise of happiness and chatter about the school holidays.

I stood at the kitchen bench, cup of tea in hand, listening. It was impossible to get a word in, so I didn't bother and happily let the conversation flow non-stop around me, as Sally asked again. *'Hey, Jesse, have you read any of Thirteen yet?''*

I laughed, shaking my head. *'I ask him every day when I'm writing, to come and read some of it, but he says, 'I'm too busy!'*

Caitlyn laughed too. Usually if I asked you for any help or needed you to do a quick something when she was visiting, you would always yell out *BUSY* in a chirpy voice!

You usually did what was asked, but in your own Jesse time. Which could have been ten minutes after I had asked you, or three hours.

'Are you going to read any of it, Jess?' Sally tousled your hair, waiting.

And you responded as only you could; leaning against the chair, your arm stretched over the back of it, bringing your frozen grape up to your lips with a kind of grin, you said in your dry tone, *'I don't need to read it, I've lived it.'*

It was such a brilliant statement, and as simple as that for you. You had lived it. You are still living it. Every single day. And like Caitlyn, you have grown and taken the steps you have needed to, to deal with your anxiety. You informed Grammy, on a recent visit, that you felt your anxiety was, *'Fading away.'*

So beautifully put, Jesse Weitering, you amazing boy.

And here we are, neither at the beginning, the middle, nor the end of our journey. Proud doesn't even cut it, when I look at my boys. For one of our sons:

Jesse. He feels he is winning the battle, conquering life, smiling, feeling strong and confident. He is excited about his future, writing his songs, putting all those feelings into deep, heartfelt lyrics. He deserves to be after every emotional hurdle he has overcome; still overcoming, with such strength and determination, pushing himself to his limits. He is a champion.

Zane. Our little man who has just turned thirteen, and it's like the clock has sprung backwards, and here we go again. I don't know what lies ahead for my boy with his big, beautiful, sensitive heart. I know he is overwhelmed with life at the moment, it's hard not to be at times, even for those without the added burden of a mental illness. There's no time to be exhausted. But I admit, I am. And that's okay, as well as being only human, I am also, a more positive, stronger mother today, than I was three years ago. I am more aware, more able to help and guide our boys, along with my beautiful Jade, with Nana looking down on us all. Our theme song for now: *'Fight for you,'* by Morgan Page.

I'm getting ready for the next step in Zane's journey, and fingers crossed our Headspace experience, along with Zane's, Futures In Mind appointments, will go smoother than Jesse's did! Live and learn, mea culpa, and all that jazz.

Like so many other families, loving, and living with their kids with anxiety or depression, we are doing all that we can, with love in our hearts, and determination, that in the end, everything will be alright. It has to be. Life's too short, and no matter how hard some days are to roll, strut, or fall out of bed, we have to keep on, keeping on, so let's do it with conviction!

This book, of course, was never intended to be a self-help book. When I first started writing, *Thirteen* and Underwater, I was on a mission to simply share our journey, and Jesse's story. We felt so shell-shocked in the beginning, so alone, and in the first few weeks, lived in a daze of disbelief. When I re-read the journals I had written about our young Jesse, to see if they could help shed any light on our situation, I was overwhelmed at what I hadn't seen, as little indicators at the time.

Finding the online groups, with such strong, positive support and understanding, was like finding a loaf of bread in the freezer, that saved you from getting dressed (the dreaded bra!) and head out to the super-market on a Saturday morning. Reading their stories and realising so many struggled, I felt so alone and judged and it made me think: can I make one person feel they are doing an amazing job of caring for their loved ones? *Can I share, that no parent is perfect even with good intentions? Can I make one person nod their head, chuckle, and say, 'Yes, I am actually coping quite well with my situation.'*

If I can make just one family be a little kinder to themselves, cut themselves some slack and not beat themselves up for every little mistake, or maybe know who and which service to reach out to for help, then my work here is done.

Warmly, with love in my heart to you and your family. Michelle.

A NEW ME

Life was once a misery.
The world was dark, I couldn't see.
Through the flow of tears from my eyes.
It felt never-ending.
Thought I was trapped in sadness.
I had no-one, was at my lowest.
The hope I had was out of reach.
But all that's ending, it's ending.
'Cos I was someone I didn't know, unfamiliar to me.
Now I feel I've got somewhere to go, it's a new me.
I now realise who I am, who I'm meant to be
Hope is here, I understand
It's a new me
It's a new me!

Caitlyn Jane Taylor 15 years of age.

Crá

Like the quiet beat of a drum it begins, thrumming softly, steadily, strongly I am here. I am here the journey of light, of love, of life. It beats. It beats! Surely this is where it all begins, the tales of pure magic, of Blessings

I will Cherish that light lovingly, eternally with all that I am Surrender my life, my soul for yours All that I am, because of you at the beginning, oh so easy at the beginning. Love Laughter Joy...it flows, so steadily it flows Mother of the year award is mine, always mine...tightly, proudly held in hand. I won't let it go. Surely I won't let it go? Years tumbling, turning, but clearly, suddenly, sadly, not enough,...never enough

Constant questions, judgement, I feel my heart break! Now, a crippling dullness, doubt, a fading light Always searching for the answer that will bring you peace, happiness I pray. I pray Hearing your questions, cries for help like a never ending beat of the drum in a haunting melody...in my veins...throbbing...on and on... Brave face for the outside world, but I am still just one. Only one.

Reaching for answers, solutions slipping away as I am constantly running up the hill, the never-ending hill Once so young, positive and full of life Why? So easily does the flutter of doubt creep in...a nibbling parasite the soul crusher, to steal my dreams? My heart? My small spirits light? Crushingly Conflicting, how much more can I take? Feeling alone. Two sided Faces...Judging. I need to Nourish your soul...whilst keeping mine Alive

A frowning barrage, what are you doing? Thinking? It's clearly not enough You are a mother? You are not made of the right stuff! Can't they see my exhaustion, my constant quest for the love of my son, my mind a flood of poisonous doubts drowning the real me. It's all too much. So much pressure, I know I'm punishing myself...draining, fading, I can't disappear I made you a promise...I'll always be right here.   MW

RESOURCES

ONLINE GROUPS:

- Children with Anxiety/Anxiety Disorders. Facebook
- Support Group for Parents living with children with Anxiety and Depression. Facebook

Helpful Online Sites:

- ReachOut.com   parents.au.reachout.com
- AnxietyBC   anxietybc.com
- beyondblue. Depression. Anxiety
- www.beyondblue.org.au 1300224636
- Mental Health Australia   maustralia.org   Contact us/Need Help
- Headspace National Youth Mental Health Foundation Ltd
- https://www.headspace.org.au
- Mindful Apps:
- Smiling Mind: Mindfulness Meditation
- https://smilingmind.com
- Headspace: Guided Meditation

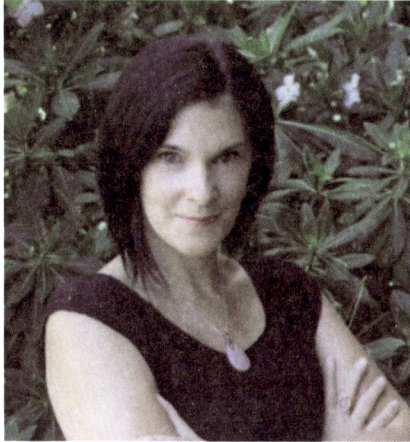

ABOUT THE AUTHOR

Michelle Weitering, better known by her pen name as Mickey Martin, resides in the Frankston area of Victoria, Australia, with her treasured husband and sons. She writes about love, life and the world we live in today, because of it and to escape it.

Her writing is raw, emotional, compelling and can at times be confronting. She writes from the heart with the main purpose to be purely entertaining and reflect the best aspects of life. Friendship and laughter, love and loyalty, always mixed with a bit of grit and darkness. No-one wants boring, right?

Mickey has previously published The Given and Dark Angel, Books One and Two of The Given trilogy and is currently rewriting The Given. The trilogy will be released in a box set, in the not too distant future, finishing with Book Three, The Guardian.

In between re-writing The Given, finishing The Guardian and plotting future writing projects, Mickey put all on hold, to write the challenging and personal journey about her son's battle with the silent predator that is mental illness, in her new book, Thirteen and Underwater. Launching May 2019. It is her wish to share her family's journey, dealing with the increasingly prevalent disease, Anxiety, that wreaks havoc on millions of individuals every single day. Thirteeen and Underwater is told with brutal honesty and humour. No matter how difficult some days are, and you feel you are failing as a parent, there is always a silver lining to every dark cloud.

Wanting to put her beloved area, the Mornington Peninsula on the map, Mickey is currently conjuring up a twisted paranormal romance possibly titled Sins of Sorrento or Sinners Shadows. (Sorry, no mention of Werewolves or Vampires will be in this novel!)

A second book in this series will be based in her beloved childhood hometown, Glenormiston South, where she will bring an eerie, paranormal theme to the historical and once thriving Glenormiston Agricultural College. Dedicated to her beloved mother, Lynette Martin, who resided at the back of the college for over 35 years.

To escape the busyness of the world, Mickey spends time in her garden, giving back to Mother-Earth, enjoying plunging her hands into rich, composted soil creating gardens for humans and animals alike to relax in.

Mickey is a member of the PWC – Peninsula Writers Club, and loves being surrounded by her enthused fellow writers.